Distributed Databases, Cooperative Processing, and Networking

Distributed Databases, Cooperative Processing, and Networking

Shaku Atre

McGraw-Hill, Inc.

New York St. Louis San Francisco Auckland Bogotá Caracas Lisbon London Madrid Mexico City Milan Montreal New Delhi Paris San Juan São Paulo Singapore Sydney Tokyo Toronto

DISTRIBUTED DATABASES, COOPERATIVE PROCESSING, & NETWORKING
International Editions 1993

1 2 3 4 5 6 7 8 9 0 JJP UPE 9 8 7 6 5 4 3

Acquisitions Editor: Gerald T. Papke
Book Editor: Sally Anne Glover
Director of Production: Katherine G. Brown
Book Design: Jaclyn J. Boone TPR4

Library of Congress Cataloging-in-Publication Data

Atre, S., 1940-
Distributed databases, cooperative processing, and networking / by Shaku Atre.
p. cm.
Includes index.
1.Distributed data bases. 2. Computer networks. I. Title.
QA76.9.D3A92 1991
005.75'8-dc20

ISBN 0-07-157673-8

91-23401
CIP

When ordering this title, use ISBN 0-07-112579-5

Printed in Singapore

About the author

Shaku Atre is an internationally renowned expert and lecturer on database and end-user computing. As a speaker, she has the reputation of using a "common sense" approach, providing fresh insights, and being able to explain complex things in simple terms. These qualities are also evident in her writing.

Ms. Atre is president of Atre, Inc., a leading consulting, software development, training and publishing company specializing in database disciplines, based in Rye, New York. Before heading her present company, Ms. Atre was a partner with Atre/Computer Assistance, a division of Coopers & Lybrand. During the fourteen years previous to that, Ms. Atre held a variety of management and staff positions at IBM, including faculty member of the prestigious Systems Research Institute.

Besides writing articles for and being quoted extensively in computer trade periodicals, Ms. Atre has written several books; among them is the classic *Data Base: Structured Techniques for Design, Performance and Management* (2nd edition, 1988), published by John Wiley & Sons. This award-winning book has been adopted as a textbook in over sixty major colleges and universities worldwide, including Harvard and MIT. It has been selected by book clubs and translated into Spanish and Russian. She also has written an authoritative book, *Data Base Management Systems for the Eighties*, covering major mainframe-based database management systems. Another book authored by Ms. Atre is the unique *Information Center: Strategies and Case Studies*, published by Atre International Consultants, Inc. This book has also been very well received by the industry.

Shaku Atre holds a master's degree in statistics and has done research in applied mathematics at the University of Heidelberg, Germany.

To my mother.

Contents

Part IV
Evaluation and selection of DDBMS software

Acknowledgments

The success of my previous three books—*Data Base: Structured Techniques for Design, Performance and Management*; *Data Base Management Systems for the Eighties*; and *Information Center: Strategies and Case Studies*—encouraged me to write another practical book on distributed database technology. But any work of this type needs the help of various people.

My special thanks go to my assistant Nancy Carafa for having to read my almost illegible handwriting and for word processing numerous iterations. Her organizational talent and diligence have kept this project on schedule. Bill Chattin deserves thanks for providing help, with his liberal arts background, in editing the manuscript in various stages.

My editor, Jerry Papke, with whom I have worked since my first book, gets a big thank you. Devon Manelski, a college student and our part-time summer assistant, is much appreciated for successfully making it through word processing this book in its first stages. Steve Polilli is appreciated for reading parts of the manuscript. I would also like to thank Bill Inmon and Bob Holland for their constructive reviews. Lara, my house-help, receives a thank you for providing me with an uninterrupted supply of tea while my writing gobbled up hours at a time.

Thanks also go to the publishers and editors of my articles, from which I have drawn some material for this book. My thanks go to Igor Zuyer, Kurt Proegler, Daniel Keller, and Joe Roden for material for chapter 10.

I also want to show my gratitude to my mother, to whom this book is dedicated, who encouraged me to do whatever I wanted to do.

My special thanks go to my children, Tushar and Nisha, as well as my husband, Prabhu, for showing a tremendous amount of understanding for my professional endeavors.

Introduction

It appears, looking at newspaper advertisements, that the medicine for all the ills of data processing is a distributed database management system (DDBMS). Almost every computer magazine, when opened, drops a card for some free seminar promising enlightenment on the distributed database architecture.

A true distributed DBMS should have a two-phase commit capability, an extensive recovery mechanism, a sophisticated locking functionality, horizontal and vertical fragmentation features, and many more capabilities. And in order to support all these features, a DDBMS needs an active, integrated, global data dictionary/directory. (In this book, we will cover all of these features in understandable text with supporting examples and diagrams.)

How are we going to implement a distributed database environment if we haven't mastered the telecommunications network at all levels? How are we going to manage a distributed database environment if we haven't mastered the centralized version of a database? What type of organizational structure with data administration and database administration is needed in order to make the distributed database environment an acceptable and welcome solution to the problem of scattered data? How will we pinpoint the failure when it occurs, and how will we recover from it? What type of data dictionary/directory capabilities are needed to support "intelligence" to provide the "single-system image," which is the main theme of a distributed database? And when we say distributed database, do we mean distribution of data, or of functions, or of resources, or of responsibilities—or maybe of guilt? This book provides answers to all of these questions.

The book's main objective is to address the needs of database analysts, designers, database administrators, and application development managers. The book provides step-by-step methods for implementing networks and efficiently organizing and managing distributed database systems and cooperative processing.

Topics covered in this book are as follows:

- Defining a distributed database (DDB) environment.
- Defining a cooperative processing environment.
- Describing the pros and cons of the distributed database and cooperative processing environments.
- Creating awareness of political and management issues.
- Setting up a matrix of features of a distributed database.
- Describing mainframe-micro connection capabilities.
- Discussing departmental computing and its role in a distributed database environment.
- Explaining client/server computing.
- Discussing potential applications of a distributed database.
- Showing networking configurations and connectivity requirements of distributed databases.
- Describing features needed to implement networking capabilities in order to make distributed databases and cooperative processing successful.
- Answering a number of questions that may come up in a distributed database environment.
- Providing a glossary of terms to clarify any confusion created in the industry.

These objectives are explained with the help of a number of concepts. Concepts handled in each chapter are explained in short in the beginning and then explored in more detail throughout the chapter. The repetition is intentional. It enables the reader to browse through the concepts and either read further for details in the same chapter, or move on to the next chapter.

Sometimes people use different terms to mean the same thing and the same term for different things. Client/server computing, cooperative processing, and distributed computing are three such terms often used interchangeably.

Client/server computing splits the processing of an application between a front-end portion on a PC or workstation, which processes local data manipulation and maintains a user interface, and a back-end portion on a server, which handles numerically intensive processing and a sizable database to be used by multiple clients.

With the proliferation of microcomputers and workstations, application development and processing could, and should, be done on an optimal hardware platform. This is *cooperative processing.*

Cooperative processing should have the capability of spreading data or a given application across several computer systems. Cooperative processing makes optimum use of all systems on a network, and makes data available to a user connected to the network.

The material of this book is organized into six main parts. The parts are: distributed databases, cooperative processing, networking, evaluation and selection of DDBMS software, an appendix with questions and answers, and a glossary. The first four parts consist of several chapters.

Part I covers distributed databases. Chapter 1 introduces the reader to various terms and concepts covered in the book. Chapter 2 covers potential environments, support requirements, and optimization issues for a distributed database. Chapter 3 covers the distributed database management matrix, with different criteria for evaluating a product. A person should be aware of these criteria when evaluating a DDBMS and when designing, implementing, and using a database under a distributed database management system (DDBMS).

Performance is one of the major issues in the database environment. One of the trickiest features to be implemented with the distributed database management system environment is data synchronization for integrity purposes. Maybe we don't need one-hundred percent synchronization and, as a result, integrity of data. Some data has to be accurate up to the minute or even up to the second. Some data may be updated at longer intervals.

Chapter 4 covers forces moving users to a distributed database environment. It also covers some of the implementation issues, the benefits as well as the pitfalls, of a distributed database. Finally, Chapter 5 reviews IBM's distributed database direction (DRDA: Distributed Relational Data Access).

Part II covers cooperative processing. Chapter 6 explains the concepts and terminology of cooperative processing. It also looks at cooperative processing strategies.

Chapter 7 focuses on the downsizing issues of cooperative processing implementation. It also analyzes the organizational impact of downsizing and gives tips for success in downsizing.

Part III covers networking issues. Chapter 8 analyzes the connectivity and networking criteria and provides an overview of various types of networks. Chapter 9 goes into the details of implementing client/server architecture, with its benefits and pitfalls.

Part IV includes how to evaluate and select DDBMS software, with Chapter 10 covering specific questions to ask when choosing DDBMS software. This chapter was developed over the years in my consulting assignments at various organizations, in particular, Chemical Abtracts Service, a Division of the American Chemical Services, Database Management Systems Project, in Columbus, Ohio.

The glossary is extremely important because the data processing motto has been for many decades, and continues to be, if you can't dazzle them with your brilliance, confuse them with terminology. Adding to the confusion is the fact that many people use terms, thinking they know what they're talking about, but they don't really understand the very terms or concepts they're using. In the glossary, the terms that are used in distributed databases, cooperative processing, and networking are fully explained. The glossary also covers related terms for these three fields, from hardware, systems software (e.g., operating systems), subsystems software (e.g., database management systems, DBMSs), applications software, and associated areas. As far as hardware is concerned; I'm not just referring to mainframes; I'm referring to mainframes, mid-range machines (also known as minicomputers), workstations, and microcomputers or PCs. Distributed computing allows an application to run on more than one system: a PC, a minicomputer, or a mainframe.

This book looks at all aspects of distribution. Throughout, the book takes into account all the technical and managerial intricacies of distributed database environments, offering a realistic look at both the potential benefits and pitfalls of distributed databases.

Part I

Distributed databases

1

Overview

A distributed database does not necessarily require cooperative processing (see FIG. 1-1). A *distributed database* is a collection of autonomously processing storage sites, possibly at some distance from each other, connected with a data communications network. *Cooperative processing* is the ability to distribute resources (programs, files and databases) across the network. Cooperative processing is a subset of a distributed database environment, which in turn is a subset of connectivity and networking. Since cooperative processing represents computing on an optimum platform, it needs data available on all platforms. A *platform* consists of hardware, systems software (also known as the operating system), applications software and supporting utility software. Cooperative processing is just one form of a distributed database environment, and no form of a distributed database environment can function unless platforms are interconnected via some mode of networking.

In most organizations, data has been stored in various formats, in various storage media, and with various computers; some information has been stored redundantly and some has been stored only once. Information is created, retrieved, updated and deleted using various access mechanisms. In these organizations, distribution of data has already occurred and will continue to occur in the future.

A distributed database management system (DDBMS) should provide access to the distributed data. A *DDBMS* is a database system in which the physical data is distributed across different machines, but the system presents a single database image to the user. Technically, it's extremely difficult to provide a single database image, and no vendor has a complete solution. A DDBMS is a full-function database management system that provides end-users and application programmers access to a distributed database as if it were stored at the local site.

In a distributed database environment, the computer used for developing the applications is invariably also used for running these applications. On the

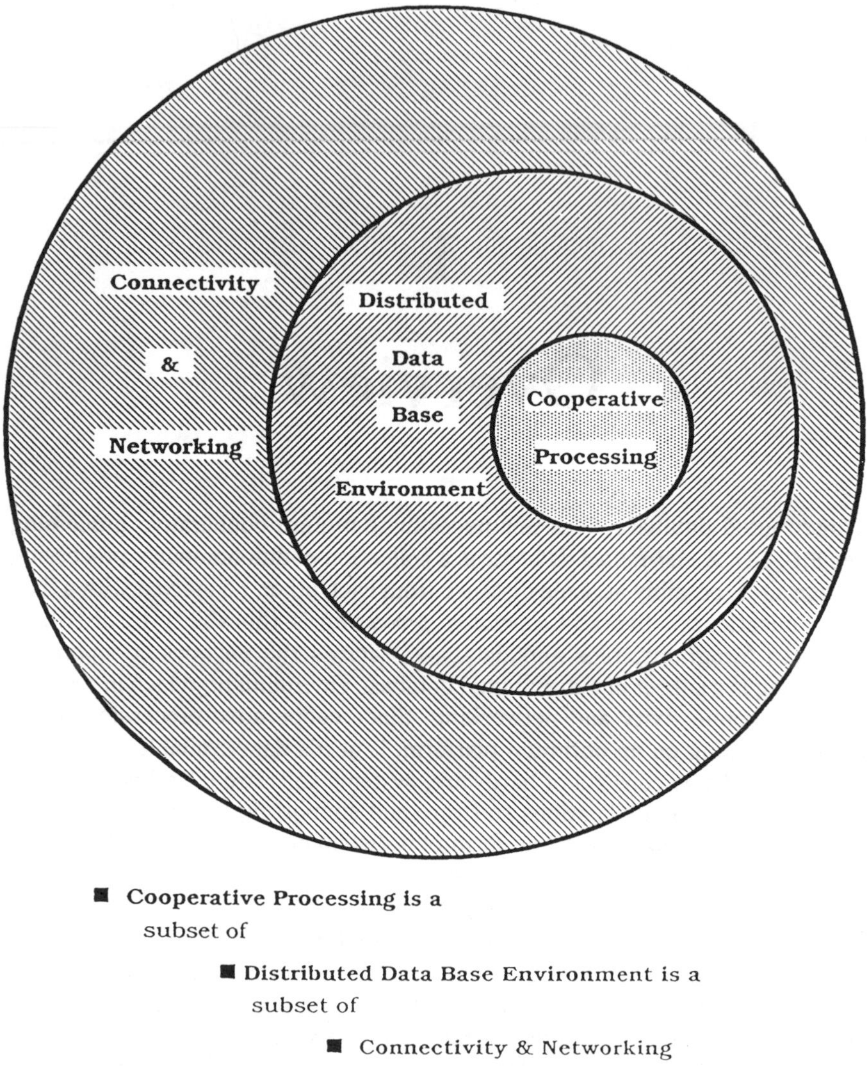

Fig. 1-1. Cooperative processing is a subset of a distributed database environment, which is a subset of connectivity and networking.

other hand, cooperative processing assumes that we want to develop our applications on an optimal platform and run these finished applications on an optimal platform. The best development platform is not necessarily the best platform for execution. Cooperative processing, similar to the distributed database environment, should allow transparent access across any platform so that users don't have to know if the resource is local or remote.

When we refer to cooperative processing, we are not concerned just with new development; we are also referring to existing application systems. When we maintain applications, we are not only removing the so-called "bugs," but we are also enhancing the system with new functionality or changing some of its existing functionality. Maintenance is not necessarily always correction of errors. We enhance the system and, at the same time, with newly introduced code and changes made to the logic, there is a good chance we may introduce new errors. The decision that needs to be made is: should enhancement of functions be done on the platform where our existing system is running, or should it be developed on some other platform? Should the new system then be ported, or should it be kept on the existing platform? That is cooperative processing. Cooperative processing needs to have data available on the platform where we are developing and running the system. That is a distributed database. And that's the reason for saying cooperative processing is a subset of a distributed database environment.

Cooperative processing assumes that we have a distributed database environment. A distributed database environment does not necessarily select the optimal platform for execution. We already have distributed data in many places. We are not necessarily going to create distributed data; we already have it. Just look at the millions of microcomputers installed where, on many of the hard disks of those computers, the same data is duplicated. A disk drive is like a garage; the bigger the garage you build, the more junk you collect.

A cost analysis needs to be done to determine whether it's better to reclaim the space that is not effectively used, or cheaper to buy more disk space. In many cases, it's more cost effective to buy more disk space than to spend time evaluating data and deleting data. Besides, when something is deleted today, someone will surely come looking for it tomorrow. Thus, in most organizations today, data is already distributed. People just don't know where it is; and if they know where it is, they don't necessarily know how to access it. With a distributed database environment, we are trying to get a handle on data. In order to implement a distributed database environment, computer resources have to be connected. Connections between computers can be established with networking. And that's the reason for saying that a distributed database environment is a subset of connectivity and networking.

Let's evaluate what a hardware platform is in the context of cooperative processing (see FIG. 1-2). The major hardware platforms are mainframes, minicomputers, workstations and microcomputers. I like to refer to these as three and one-half platforms. The growth of mainframes and minicomputers is expected to be much slower in the next ten years. The major growth is expected to be with workstations and microcomputers. Though the distinction is blurring, *workstations* are the more powerful single-user desktop systems, often from vendors such as Sun or Hewlett-Packard. *Microcomputers* are the personal computers popularized by IBM and Apple.

The mainframe seems to be destined for the role of a "giant" file server or a "giant" database server. We will discuss this issue in Chapter 9 when discussing client/server architecture. Mainframes are going to continue to run the already developed batch and interactive applications.

- **Mainframes**
  - Mainframe as a "Giant" File Server
  - Batch, Interactive
- **Minicomputers**
  - Will they become "Extinct"?
  - Which major players will survive?
  - Batch, Interactive
- **Workstations & Microcomputers**
  - Online
  - RISC vs. CISC vs. MISC*
    - Which RISC? •• Which CISC? •• Which MISC?
  - Standalone or Networked?

*RISC: Reduced Instruction Set Computing
CISC: Complex Instruction Set Computing
MISC: Minimum Instruction Set Computing

Fig. 1-2. Hardware platforms.

It could easily be predicted that minicomputers, sometimes also known as departmental computers, will not have the growth of the past unless they have some special niche carved out. Although the growth rate of minicomputers is expected to be very small, the installed base of minicomputers is also going to continue to run the already developed batch and interactive applications.

Other major hardware platforms for cooperative processing are the workstation and the microcomputer. What are the major differences between, on the one hand, workstations such as those from Sun Microsystems, HP/Apollo, Silicon Graphics, DEC and IBM's RS/6000, and on the other hand, microcomputers, including IBM PC compatibles and Apple's Macintosh? Three major differences that are disappearing quickly are that workstations have:

- More storage and more power than microcomputers.
- Better graphics capabilities.
- Better networking capabilities compared to microcomputers.

Software is where we are going to see major growth over the next few years. That means a corporation's chief information officer (CIO) has to put aside about a fifteen percent budget increase year after year for software licensing. The increase will impact all platform categories. One of the major obstacles in cooperative processing and distributed databases is going to be getting a handle on different types of software products, which are mostly incompatible and have overlapping functionality.

As far as cooperative processing is concerned, new skills need to be learned. If an application is to be developed on a workstation or a microcomputer, and it's to be ported to a mainframe, the question is whether this all will be done by the same person who has expertise in using mainframe software, or someone else with a different set of skills. It will probably not be the person trained in mainframe CICS (Customer Information Control System, an online software subsystem from IBM), because the CICS person doesn't think too highly of microcomputer-based application development. The problem is cultural in nature. Many mainframe-based professionals are still "character-based" people. Character-based processing is more dominant in a mainframe environment as compared to the graphics in a workstation or microcomputer environment. Before microcomputer screens were available with fancy graphics, reports were printed in letters and numbers. Even when a graphic representation was needed, the crude picture was composed of characters. On the other hand, microcomputers and some minicomputers produce letters, numbers and graphics from a matrix of small dots.

Mainframe-oriented staff are still in control of many data processing functions, and they resist change. Furthermore, they often have systems in place that effectively control attempts to change the status quo.

Job Control Language (JCL) is a mainframe bastion where outsiders are effectively excluded. Just try to submit a JCL stream where a left or right parenthesis is forgotten. It dooms you to another wait of at least several hours.

If there are so many barriers, why move to a distributed database (DDB) environment? Do we need to? And if so, why? If not, why not? Who distributes data and what are the benefits of the DDB environment for an organization? It's important to consider mapping an organization to the DDB environment. As we all know, technology is much easier to handle than politics. Technology doesn't talk back to us. In any organization, implementation of a distributed database environment will create some political problems that are not necessarily present in a centralized database environment. Various locations will need to be networked, and most of these sites previously had autonomy.

Computer architectures

Mainframes and most minicomputers are based on CISC (Complex Instruction Set Computing) architecture, whereas most workstations are based on RISC (Reduced Instruction Set Computing). The latest entry seems to be MISC (Minimum Instruction Set Computing). Some new workstations will be using the MISC technology in the future.

CISC, RISC, MISC (See FIG. 1-2.) Eventually, RISC is going to take more market share from CISC. It will be a triumph of Reduced Instruction Set Computing over Complex Instruction Set Computing. You might ask, why didn't we have RISC to begin with? Why do we have to go through the complexity first to come down to the reduced instruction set's simplicity? In order to implement RISC, it's necessary to have substantial real memory. When real memory was expensive, CISC was implemented. So it's not like someone intentionally went through CISC and then arrived at RISC. The main question now is, which RISC? Sun Microsystems, Motorola, IBM Corporation and MIPS are some of the contenders that manufacture RISC processors, just to mention a few. Another development is MISC (Minimum Instruction Set Computing). Another question is, would the workstations, whatever their architecture, be standalone or networked? It's estimated that in the near future fifty percent of the workstations or microcomputers will still be standalone and the other fifty percent will be networked.

Cooperative processing doesn't usually employ all types of platforms at the same time. Only two platforms are used at the same time in a majority of installations, the two platforms being either mainframe with microcomputers, or clustered minicomputers with microcomputers. However, if the file server is considered a middle platform, then there are three platforms that are used concurrently. The file server, in most instances, is a high-powered microcomputer or a workstation, but it could even be a low-end minicomputer.

As time progresses, a number of applications will be developed for microcomputers that will be nodes of a local area network (LAN). A *node* is, technically, a point in the network at which data is switched. A node in a network consists of a computer processing facility such as an operating system for executing user processes, and a DBMS, if present. A powerful workstation will be the file server. A file server is a computer that maintains a set of files in client/server architecture. In a distributed database environment, as well as with cooperative processing, connectivity and networking are the two major issues to be dealt with.

Mainframe-micro connection

It's imperative to establish mainframe-micro connection, not only for end-user computing, but also for application development. A majority of microcomputers are employed by end-users. But the term end-user has its connotations. Does it mean it's the end of the user or that the user ends there? Sometimes users feel that way.

While considering mainframe-micro connections, the sense of ownership possessed by the end-user needs to be emphasized. If these end-users were asked to put all of "their" computers on the network, these computers will go "underground" or into the closet. The main reason for the success of these microcomputers has been that the end-users can turn them on, and they can turn them off, whenever they want to. They no longer have to wait two or three hours to get one line of text on the screen, which has sometimes been the case when connected to mainframes.

End-users have been very creative in purchasing microcomputers. In one company, a purchase order was submitted for two hundred "giant calculators." The purchase order had no problem getting approval because the microcomputers were called calculators. Some companies purchase microcomputers in pieces. They just buy the keyboard, the screen, and the mother board, and then they assemble it. Up to a certain dollar amount, there is no need to go beyond the end-user's department for approval. For smooth approval, the purchase order is kept below that limit. Many times these charges for the equipment are buried in travel and expenses!

Distributed databases and networking

There can't be a distributed database environment or cooperative processing unless a network is in place. A computer network consists of a collection of circuits, data switching elements, and computing systems. The switching devices in the network are called *communication processors*. A network provides a configuration for computer systems and communication facilities within which data can be stored and accessed and DBMSs can operate. The ultimate sophistication of the network is dependent on the types of applications to be run. The type of network will also be determined by the type of environment. Various types of networks include local area networks (LANs), metropolitan area networks (MANs), and wide area networks (WANs). Local area network software controls the traffic on networks of personal computers or network operating systems within an office, building or locality. A LAN allows users to exchange and share data, and use the same peripherals such as printers or databases. A metropolitan area network spans the metropolitan geographical area, whereas a wide area network covers global areas. Besides the types of networks, it's necessary to determine the types of protocols to be used.

Connectivity is a logical concept that is implemented physically with the help of networking. It could almost be said that the network will be the computer during the upcoming years. The two most popular LAN technologies are Ethernet and Token Ring. We will take a look at the pluses and minuses of each in Chapter 8. IBM's Systems Network Architecture (SNA), with VTAM (Virtual Teleprocessing Access Method) and SDLC (Synchronized Data Link Control), forms a major contender in the WAN market. SNA is IBM's data communications architecture defining levels of protocols for communications between terminals and applications, and between programs. Discussion of networking leads us to client/server architecture.

Client/server architecture

Client/server architecture is a frequently used term in networking. We have had client/server architecture all along, because we have had clients and we have had servers. A *client* is someone or something that is requesting to get something done, and a *server* is someone or something that accomplishes the task. A server is a program that responds to a request from another site through a Server Requester Programming Interface (SRPI). A server should be looked upon in contrast to a requester or client. The concept is no different than many forms of teleprocessing long in existence, although client/server architecture strives for a greater range of capabilities.

How is client/server architecture implemented? In many installations a client/server almost appears as a "dressed up" LAN. Client/server architecture and its implementations must mature, especially in terms of the robustness required for production environments. A major challenge will be connecting disparate hardware implementations that are used as clients and as servers. A committee called Remote Data Base Access (RDBA) group is trying to come up with guidelines for connecting disparate distributed systems.

At any given time, there are a number of vendors with products of various capabilities. It's quite common for some vendors to form partnerships with other vendors whose products have capabilities that their own products don't have. The partnerships try to provide solutions to business problems. Because the alliances formed often conflict with existing alliances, choosing partners has become a game of musical chairs. A needed capability in the distributed database environment is remote microcomputer access to mainframe data. One of the languages used in providing remote access to data is Structured Query Language (SQL). IBM's relational DBMS offering for the MVS operating system is DB2, and SQL/DS is for VM/CMS and VSE operating systems. DB2 and SQL/DS both use SQL as a programming language.

SQL is the IBM and ANSI standard for access to relational databases. SQL is relational data language using English-like, key-word oriented facilities for data definition, query, data manipulation and data control.

SQL is a nonprocedural (or rather, less-procedural, as compared to COBOL or FORTRAN) set-oriented language for the relational data model. SQL can be used within application programs or interactively to define relational data, access relational data, and control access to relational database resources.

Many other products, such as DBMSs and tools from Oracle, Sybase, Ingres, and Informix, also use SQL. SQL is a quasi-standard in relational environments as far as a language is concerned. In the eighties, almost every product became relational. If you believe the marketing literature, every product now supports client/server architecture; every product has an SQL interface, and every product will soon be object oriented!

Cooperative processing is a subset of the distributed database environment which, in turn, is a subset of connectivity and networking. In order to be effective in computing in upcoming years, an organization needs networking expertise. This means that an organization has to add the new function of networking with someone responsible for it. As mentioned earlier, connectivity is the logical concept, and networking physically implements that logical concept by connecting various hardware platforms.

A file server, which maintains a set of files in client/server architecture, doesn't imply only a LAN. An organization could have a mainframe as a "giant" file server. But since various types of machinery are connected, there is going to be some disparity in speed. Mainframes have been running at a much faster speed than the transmission media have currently been able to. That means a person has to be made responsible for balancing the work load. A mainframe could work as a "giant" file server, and it will still continue doing its batch and interactive processing. COBOL programs are still here to stay, and some new development will even be done in COBOL for batch and interactive processing, though not to the extent of that done during the past. There will still be new development to maintain existing applications.

Two-phase commit

One important capability of a distributed database environment that needs to be explored at this point is *two-phase commit*. Two-phase commit is a protocol that is used to ensure uniform transaction commit or abort between two or more participants (transaction managers and database management systems). The protocol consists of two phases: the first, to reach a common decision, and the second, to implement this decision. One participant is defined as the coordinator, who manages the execution of the two-phase commit protocol. During a commit, the coordinator makes the commit or abort decision and coordinates the two-phase commit process.

Quite frequently, the term used to refer to a synchronization process is "two-phase commit." In concept, it's nothing more than making sure, before an update or delete is performed, that every node where replicated data is to be updated or deleted is going to be available for the operation. In the first phase, the system takes a "roll call" to find out if every node is ready to accept the update or delete. Every affected node should send back the "okay" signal. The database records that need to be updated or deleted are locked. The granularity of the level of locking will depend on the DDBMS product used.

In the second phase, a commit is performed. Now, someone will say, if two phases are better than one, then why aren't three phases better than two? It's a very logical question. But, at the same time we have to consider the law of probability. If in the first phase every node is fine, and in the second phase a commit is not issued, then the longer it takes, the higher the probability that something may go wrong. That's the reason why three phases are not necessarily better than two. Again, a two-phase commit is not necessarily one-hundred percent failsafe, even if in the first phase you get an "O.K." from every node. When a commit is issued during the second phase, something may still go wrong, but the probability is smaller than in the successful first phase. That's why backup, recovery and rollback are the major features of the distributed database environment.

In order to evaluate candidate applications for a DDB environment, it's recommended that an inventory of existing application systems is taken.

Inventory of existing application systems

In the production environment, checks will still be printed with the mainframe, at least for many years to come. Interactive processing for the existing application base will be done with the help of a mainframe. We have already invested a substantial amount of money in these applications. Conversion will last many more years. After conversion, an organization will be at a status quo with where it was before, and it will have lost many years in between. Because of prior investment and the huge amount of time required for conversion, most organizations are not converting existing applications. A few functions that need to be totally changed are the ones that are converted to different platforms.

In order to achieve the highest benefits of conversion, systems that are less than five years old need not be converted. Development of systems implemented during the past five years probably started three years or so before the date of installation. As a result, five-year-old systems are, in reality, about eight years old. When a mainframe-based application system is implemented, we get a system that is already three years old on its first day on the market.

There are also some systems that never officially went into production but are still in the test phase. The application system might be printing checks, but it's still in test mode because proper documentation was not done and proper procedures were not followed to accept the system as a production system. One of the guidelines for determining which application systems should be converted and which should not, is as follows: If a system is less than five years old, don't touch it. In ones between five and ten years old, some smaller sections should be changed. The ones that are older than ten years are the ones you want to look at for conversion, because in reality they could be fifteen years old. This means you have to spend some time taking inventory of everything that you have today (see FIG. 1-3, representing various criteria that need to be considered for taking an inventory). Taking an inventory of applications is a part of the planning function. The inventory has to be done under a deadline, because many times the planning stage is never finished. By the time planning is done, everything has changed, so the planners have to start all over again. Often, the planning function is given to people who have retired on the job but have not yet told the company!

When taking stock of existing applications systems, the mid-range computers can't be forgotten. There are a number of installations with departmental computers, also referred to as minicomputers or mid-range machines. The main question today is, will they become extinct? Minicomputers that have found a special niche, such as manufacturing, the medical field, or with some specialized application, will survive. But standalone minicomputers will be replaced by workstations or by powerful microcomputers. They may also be replaced by low-end mainframes. A minicomputer has become a sandwich with mainframes above and workstations or microcomputers below. Besides, minicomputer is no longer an "in" word, and that's the reason why, nowadays, most minicomputer vendors are selling their products as servers.

**	Name of Application System (Prioritize)	Name of Application System (Prioritize)	Name of Application System (Prioritize)
What Function does it Support? (A/P, G/L, Payroll, A/R, Inventory Control) *			
How old is the Application System? (Development Started, Production Installation)			
Which Department(s) does the System Serve? (Accounting, Payroll, Human Resources)			
Indicate any Interdependencies for the System (A/P must finish before G/L can run)			
Is this System considered Production (scheduled), Demand Processing (Ad-hoc), Decision Support?			
Response time Requirements & Frequency of Usage (Batch Processing 24 hr. turnaround, 2 second response time, End of month cycle)			
Which Hardware is Used? Give exact description. (IBM 4381 Model 21, DEC VAX 8800)			
Which Systems Software Used? (MVS/XA, VM/XA, VMS, UNIX, MVS/ESA, VM/ESA)			
Which Sybsystem Software Used? (IMS, DB2, CA:IDMS, CA:DATACOM, Oracle, Ingres, SQL/DS, ADABAS, SUPRA)			
Which Teleprocessing Monitor Used? (CICS, CA:IDMS/DC, IMS/DC, SHADOW, TASKMASTER)			

* A/P: Accounts Payable
G/L: General Ledger
A/R: Accounts Receivable

** (Items listed in parenthesis in this column are only some of the examples)

Fig. 1-3. Inventory of existing application systems and outlook for future development: a matrix.

	Name of Application System (Prioritize)	Name of Application System (Prioritize)	Name of Application System (Prioritize)
Which Programming Language Used? (COBOL, RPG, NATURAL, PL/I, IDEAL, MANTIS)			
Which Report Generator or 4GL Used? (FOCUS, RAMIS, NOMAD, QMF)			
Which Data Dictionary/Directory System Used? (DATAMANAGER, IDD, CA:UCC-10, PREDICT, IMS DB/DC Dictionary)			
Which Microcomputers are Used? Are they used in conjunction with the Mainframe or Minicomputers or Workstations?			
Is either Mainframe to Micro or Departmental to Micro Down-loading/Uploading established? How? Which Tools?			
Name Overlapping (redundant) Data with Other Systems. (Customer, Order Entry, Accounting)			
Is the Data stored separately for the System?			
Are the End-Users' needs being satisfied well? Are there any deficiencies?			
Are there any Management concerns?			
Were there any enhancements done to the System? When? How long did they take? How many work months were used?			
Any plans for redoing the System? Any CASE tools planned for usage? Methodologies?			
Name some Subject Data Bases that can be used by other Applications.			

Fig. 1-3. Continued.

	Name of Application System (Prioritize)	Name of Application System (Prioritize)	Name of Application System (Prioritize)
DASD requirements (e.g. 350 cyl - 3380)			
What major classes of Data are used by the System? (Customer, Claim, Accounting)			

Fig. 1-3. Continued.

Various types of software

Systems software is the operating system, or Systems Control Program (SCP). (See FIG. 1-4.) IBM has a whole set of systems software for various hardware platforms. IBM came up with SAA to tie together this patchwork quilt of software. In the DEC environment, future development of VMS is an issue. But there is an installed base of thousands of VMS systems. One of these days, we may possibly see some of IBM's operating systems, as well as DEC's VMS, running under Unix. IBM's version of Unix, AIX, could possibly be an alternative or augmentation to SAA implementation.

- Systems Application
  - Application Development Tools (Ease of Use)
  - Programming Languages
  - Vertical
  - Ease of Conversion
- Office Automation
- Data Base Management Systems
  - End-User
  - DP Professionals
- 3rd Party Software
- Online Transaction Processing (OLTP)
- MAPS
  - Manufacturing Automated Processing System
- UNIX Positioning
- Communications
  - Local Area Network (LAN)
  - Metropolitan Area Network (MAN)
  - Wide Area Network (WAN)
    - Single Vendor Network
    - Multi-Vendor Network
  - Connectivity
    - Homogeneous
    - Heterogeneous

Fig. 1-4. Software.

AIX is IBM's modification of Unix for the RS/6000, PS/2 and System/370—the AIX family definition. Basically, it's an enhanced version of AT&T's Unix V. AIX is the version of Unix which is used, together with Carnegie Mellon's "MACH," as the basis of Open Software Foundation's (OSF) Unix. DEC's VMS operating system may have to coexist with Ultrix (DEC's version of Unix) or with AT&T's Unix. The U.S. government has established Unix as a major criterion in the bidding process for government jobs. That's one of the reasons for IBM to get involved in AIX development.

Ease of use will be looked at in the nineties to determine which programming language will be used. Ease of use affects all areas of a distributed database environment as well as that of cooperative processing. Ease of conversion is another consideration regarding application software, because conversion is like changing a tire on a moving car. It's something that not too many people can do easily.

Networking software

Various types of communications software provide either single-vendor networking or multivendor networking. Connectivity for homogeneous as well as heterogeneous environments will be of paramount importance. Attention needs to be paid also to areas outside of North America when it comes to communications. Europe is home to many of the world's largest corporations, and it's pretty far ahead in networking in spite of the different countries, languages and government regulations involved. To further complicate matters, most telephone systems are run by government agencies. There should be common protocols to communicate throughout the world.

Open Systems Interconnect (OSI) is an area of interest for the entire world. Fiberoptics is another important aspect to be looked at. Japan has put aside billions of dollars for fiberoptic installations.

Office automation is not only word processing. That's merely a part of it. Electronic mail needs to be used very carefully. Some people have reported that when they had just regular mail, they took two hours a day to take care of it. Now, with electronic mail, it takes three hours a day. That's definitely not a productivity increase. Anybody can now put a few letters together, sign on to an electronic mail system, and send a message to a number of people with one key stroke. This means that in electronic mail, the distribution list has to be scrutinized so that everyone doesn't get anything and everything. Many people feel very uncomfortable not looking at everything that's in their "in box." Office automation, with electronic mail, is a part of an organization's distributed database environment.

We are also moving more and more into Online Transaction Processing (OLTP), and that's going to be one of the major applications in the distributed database environment. Manufacturing is another major user of the distributed database environment, and Unix is going to be one of the major contenders there.

Information-processing architecture

Case study Consider an international insurance company providing the following types of insurances: life, medical, casualty and loss, and automobile. (We are going to have a very simplistic view of the organization's business for the sake of making concepts understandable. In reality, the insurance industry has become extremely complicated.) Policies are written for policy holders by insurance brokers. Premiums are paid by the policy holders. Claims are submitted. The insurance company has to determine what claims are to be paid and the amount of time for payments, as well as who the recipients are.

The insurance company is a national organization. Business is conducted nationally. Policy holders, insurance brokers and, also, computer systems handling information processing are scattered internationally. (See FIG. 1-5.)

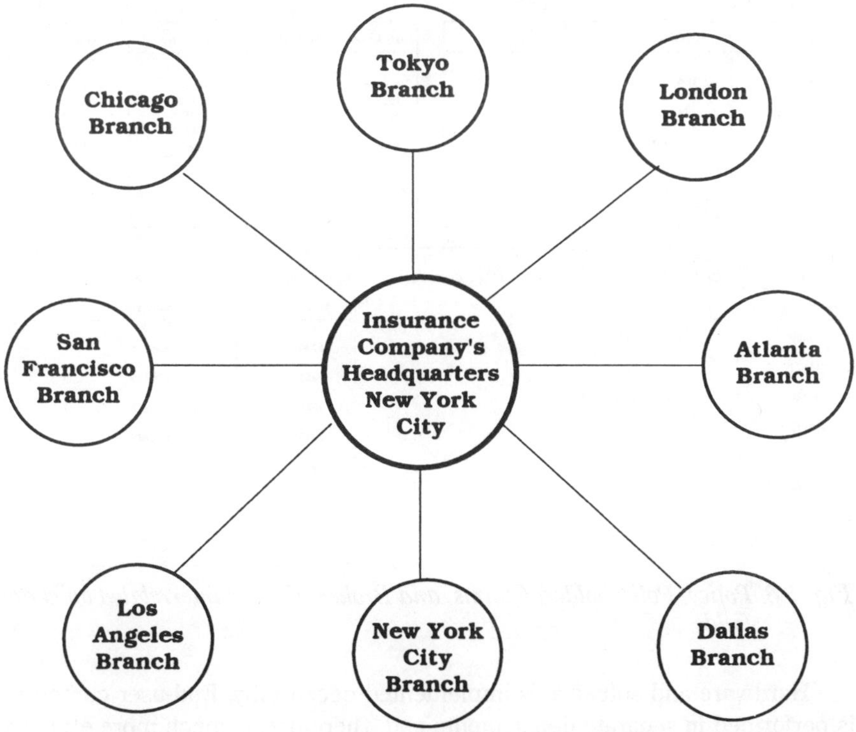

Fig. 1-5. The International Insurance Company doing business across continents. Computing is centralized, as well as decentralized.

Any successful business has the following functions:

- Planning
- Marketing
- Sales

- Revenue production
- Accounting
- Research and development

Some of these functions (or business architecture) are performed centrally, and some are performed decentrally. Some of the data collected is stored centrally. Some of the centrally located data is stored at various branches. Data architecture, representing policy holders' data, premium data, claims data and payment data, is also centralized as well as decentralized (see FIG. 1-6). Part of the network architecture is implemented at the central location, the headquarters, and a part is implemented decentrally. (See FIG. 1-7.)

Policy File

Policy-No.	Policy-Type	Policyholder Last-Name
245867	Life	Smith
856745	Auto	Carroll
643489	Life	Finneran
468912	Home	Simon
679435	Medical	Karel
346515	Medical	Carroll
. . .	. . .	. . .

Policyholder File

First-Name	Last-Name	Policy-No.	Rep-No.
Thomas	Finneran	643489	2345
Joan	Carroll	856745	6748
Ann	Karel	679435	1367
Susan	Simon	468912	4589
Joan	Carroll	346512	6748
. . .	. . .	. . .	. . .

Claims File

Policy-No.	Claim-Date
643489	January 15, 1992
346512	March 30, 1992
856745	February 18, 1992
468912	April 11, 1992
643489	March 5, 1992
245867	February 8, 1992
. . .	. . .

Broker File

Rep-No.	Policy-No.
6748	856745
1367	679435
4589	468912
2345	643489
6748	346512
. . .	. . .

Fig. 1-6. Policy, Policyholder, Claims, and Broker files are interrelated on certain fields.

Hardware and software is implemented decentrally. End-user computing is performed in separate departments and, therefore, is much more effective. End-users don't have to wait long hours to receive the required information for decision making. Most of the data required by insurance brokers for Atlanta and vicinity policy holders is available in Atlanta, just as Chicago data is available in Chicago. New applications are designed such that the local needs are satisfied locally. A major problem remains with the already developed mainframe-based applications that are mostly centrally developed.

Our example of an international insurance company works as a number of companies in different locations when it comes to running the business, but it

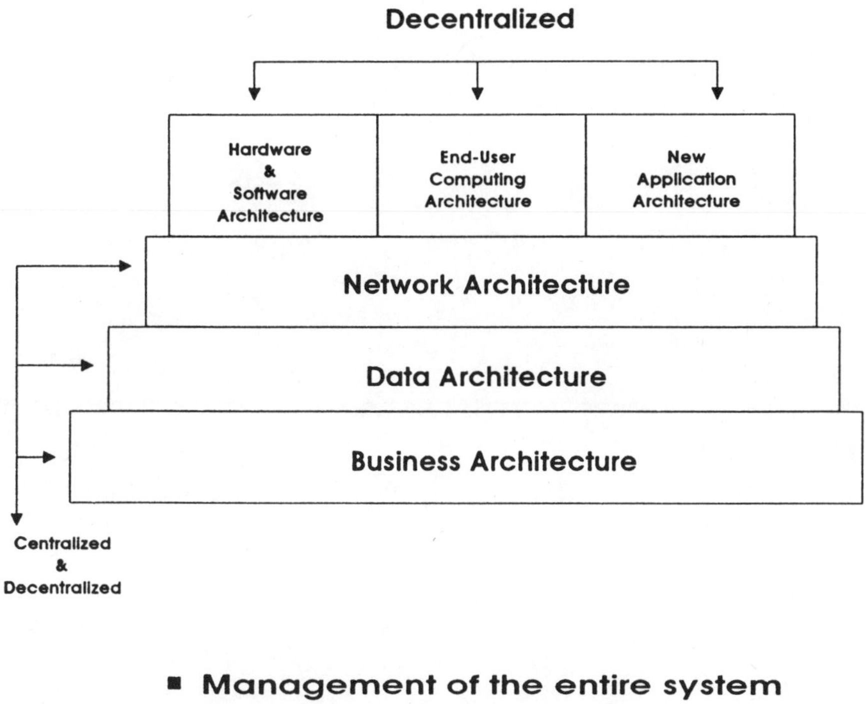

Fig. 1-7. Information processing architecture.

functions as one large company when it comes to pooling resources for research, development, planning and marketing.

Only if an organization can function efficiently as a centralized and a decentralized company, depending on the needs of the clients, does it make sense to implement a distributed database management system.

2

Distributed databases

Just what is a *distributed database environment*, anyway? It's a database (see FIG. 2-1) that has data elements under control of multiple, independently operating nodes linked by a communications medium. A *node* is defined as one or more CPUs (central processing units) that share main storage under the control of a single operating system.

The International Insurance Company may have independent operating nodes in New York City, Chicago, San Francisco, Los Angeles, Dallas, Atlanta, London and Tokyo. All nodes may be linked by communications media. Data may be distributed at these nodes. The distribution may possibly be done in two different ways. One could be a functional distribution (see FIG. 2-2). From a business perspective, for local decision making, it might be advisable to share all data about all types of policies (i.e., functions) at the nodes (see FIG. 2-3). That means all data about all policies underwritten for the policy holders living in the vicinity of San Francisco should be shared on San Francisco's node and, respectively, other nodes should be treated similarly. Implementing a "buddy" system might also be considered so that all San Francisco data is shared in Los Angeles, and vice versa. If one node goes down, at least for a certain timeframe, the other node could "pitch in" with the data that's temporarily not available. We will discuss the synchronization problems that the buddy system may introduce.

An operating system itself could have multiuser capability, multitasking capability, or both. A multiuser capability implies multitasking, but multitasking doesn't necessarily imply a multiuser environment. OS/2 is a multitasking environment, but it is not a multiuser environment, whereas Unix is a multiuser and, as a result, a multitasking operating system.

Multiuser capability means multiple users can run applications at the same time. The operating system keeps track of who is running what. It also makes

Distributed

Data Base:

- A *Data Base* which has data elements under control of multiple, independently operating *'Nodes'* linked by a *communications medium.*

- A *Node* is defined as one or more CPU's with shared main storage, under the control of a single operating system.

- A *'Communications Medium'* includes, but is not limited to, channel-to-channel connection, shared DASD and teleprocessing equipment.

Fig. 2-1. Distributed database.

Node	Information about Types of Policies stored
New York City	Auto & Medical
Chicago	Medical & Life
San Francisco	Home
.	.
.	.
.	.

Fig. 2-2. Functional distribution of the data stored at various locations.

Node	Information about Types of Policies stored
New York City	All policies held by clients living in the vicinity of New York City.
Chicago	All policies held by clients living in the vicinity of Chicago.
San Francisco	All policies held by clients living in the vicinity of San Francisco.
⋮	⋮

Fig. 2-3. Geographical distribution of the data stored at various locations of The International Insurance Company.

sure that resources, such as the central processing unit and disk storage, are shared by the users. It also makes sure that data is not mixed up when it's provided to the various users. Unix is an excellent example of a multiuser operating system. One user can run a spreadsheet, another a database management system, and yet another can run desktop publishing.

Multitasking capability means that one user can run multiple "tasks" on the same node. Since the node consists of only one processor it will run only one task at a time. But it will give the impression of running all tasks at the same time. One task may be a spreadsheet, one task may be a database management system, yet another can be desktop publishing. OS/2 is an example of a multitasking operating system. Ramifications of multiuser systems and multitasking are in backup, recovery and performance. Backup and recovery in multiuser systems are more complicated than in multitasking.

A node could be a microcomputer, a workstation, a minicomputer, a mainframe, or anything that has one or more processors. A node must have *intelligence*. Intelligence means it has a processor and memory for storage. With this definition, dumb terminals don't qualify as nodes.

A person can work with a "dumb" terminal only when it's connected to a processor or a node. Once it's disconnected from a processor or a node, it doesn't have processing capability. It's almost like an electrical appliance. As long as the appliance receives electrical power from a socket, we can use it. Once it's disconnected, it becomes "lifeless" unless it runs on batteries.

The potential environments for a Distributed Data Base are with:

- Heterogeneous Hardware
- Heterogeneous Systems Software
- Heterogeneous Application Software
- Heterogeneous Organizational Setup

Fig. 2-4. Potential environments for a distributed database.

Potential environments

When we refer to a distributed database environment, we refer to different ways (see FIG. 2-4) of representing data: on heterogeneous hardware platforms, under different operating systems, under the control of possibly different database management systems, as well as different application software. It's also possible that the organizational setup is heterogeneous, resulting in a naturally decentralized processing environment.

As stated earlier, a distributed database is a collection of autonomously processing storage sites, possibly at some distance from each other, connected with a data communications network (see FIG. 2-5). A data communications network is a collection of transmission facilities, network processors, and so on, that provides for data movement among terminals and information processors. Voice transmission lines (e.g., conventional analog telephone lines) are not necessarily fast enough for transmitting data. Digital and fiberoptic-based networks are faster and much more reliable. It will be some time before all

Distributed Data Base

- A collection of **AUTONOMOUS** sites with reasonable storage capacity
- Sites connected via
  DATA COMMUNICATIONS NETWORK
- Data Access should be:
  TRANSPARENT to data location
  SYNCHRONIZED to preserve data base integrity
- Data may be: (any combination of)
  DISTRIBUTED some data at one site, other data at another site
  PARTITIONED logically related data (i.e., a table) could be physically split between several sites
  REPLICATED multiple copies of data maintained at several sites
- Control is distributed
  CONTINUED OPERATION despite site and communications failures

Fig. 2-5. Distributed database.

transmission lines are digital and then fiberoptic-based. A vast majority of communications lines are still made from copper and use analog transmission.

Processing at widely scattered sites could be slow, depending on the propagation delay and queuing. Queuing is a major inhibitor in the distributed database environment and should be carefully considered. That means the DDBMS vendors have to take into consideration queuing as a major variable in their optimization algorithms. In the distributed database environment, not only one distributed database algorithm needs to be taken care of, but multiple distributed algorithms running at distributed sites also have to be considered.

Data access should be transparent and synchronized. *Transparency* means that when the users are accessing the data, they don't need to know where the data is stored, in what format it's stored, and how it's to be accessed. They should be able to simply ask for it, without having to deal with any representation details. A person making a telephone call from New York City to San Francisco doesn't have to deal with the mechanics of the way the phone call is routed. One time, the call may go from New York City to San Francisco via Dallas. At another time, it may go from New York City to San Francisco via Chicago.

In a distributed database environment, some data is going to be replicated for various reasons. One of the major reasons is providing better performance when data can be accessed locally, instead of having to transfer the data from various locations. Another reason for storing some of the same data at multiple locations could be availability of the same data at multiple nodes if some of the nodes storing that data are not functioning (in computerese, they are "down"). Replicated data minimizes the dependency on one and only one node. But the other side of the coin is that when the replicated data is to be updated, it poses a major problem for synchronization.

In the case of The International Insurance Company, the data from San Francisco could be stored in Los Angeles, and vice versa, by implementing the "buddy" system. When updates are done at one node, how are the same updates done to the other node instantly? Guidelines have to be established to determine which replicated data needs updates and at what intervals. Data could be distributed, which means some data could be stored at one site and other data could be stored at another site. Data could be partitioned. *Partitioning* means logically related data could be physically split between several sites. It could also be replicated. Multiple copies could be stored in many places. Even if a DDBMS provides support for all these capabilities, databases must be designed based on the needs of the business. Partitioning and replication capabilities should be used only if the business needs dictate it. These features shouldn't be used just because they are there.

A distributed database first has to support business architecture, data architecture and network architecture. If organizational control is distributed, it's possible to provide continued operations in spite of failure of some sites and of some communication connections.

In replication, exact copies of a database are spun off for local use. These copies are sometimes called "snapshots." A *snapshot* is a named, derived table that is stored for read-only data access. Creating a snapshot is similar to executing an SQL query. The definition of the snapshot and the time of its creation are stored in the system catalog. The snapshot is "refreshed," or recreated, according to the interval specified in the snapshot's definition.

Partitioning, sometimes called fragmentation, refers to the practice of partitioning or separating data relations (tables) on the basis of relevant informational content. *Horizontal partitioning* allows a personal database to be partitioned among managers so that each manager only receives the data referring to the employees under his or her supervision. *Vertical partitioning* allows users to have a logical view of the database for their area of responsibility, such as marketing or financial data.

Considering behavior patterns, we know that people would keep the information they need as close to them (and as far from others) as possible. Such islands of information are very useful when viewed from an individual's perspective, but they are enormously redundant from a corporate perspective. One of the main missions of the distributed database environment is to strike the balance between not storing the same data redundantly at various nodes and, at the same time, also providing adequate performance to satisfy individuals. It's feasible to store data redundantly and in "split-up" tables. But the view provided, which is called the *logical view*, and the impression created has to be of unity for the enterprise at large.

Data became distributed during the course of normal business practice. As more people became involved in the process, the data environment continued on its way toward maximum distribution. "Distributed" concepts are nothing new, and have in fact been around since corporations began using different computers, no matter what size, capacity and capability, to serve different divisions or corporate functions. Before implementation of distributed databases, synchronization was typically done manually. When we speak of a distributed database environment, we are implying that synchronization of most data will be done automatically by software.

Not all the technical difficulties associated with implementing distributed databases have to do with the products themselves. The evolutionary process in which applications are developed throughout an organization may hamper a distributed approach. One example is "antirelational" data embedded in numerical databases. Numbers for many organizations are not just numbers but can also designate unique categories of information. Consequently, the data has different meanings in different geographical locations or divisions within the same company.

Furthermore, certain types of organizations are structurally unsuitable for a distributed database environment. Some businesses have centralized control, which would not mix with this approach. On the other hand, an industry more receptive to the distributed database approach is the insurance industry with a number of scattered insurance agents.

Major themes

The major theme of the move to distributed databases is a single-system image (see FIG. 2-6). This is the goal that must be achieved so that users of data don't have to know where the data is stored, how it's accessed, and what its format is. It's almost like the telephone system. When a call is made from New York to San Francisco, that call may go through Dallas, because that's the best traffic route for that time. It may go through Chicago on another call, but the people talking on the line never think about the mechanics of routing, nor do they need to think about it. A switching mechanism will do whatever is needed. It's transparent to the caller, who just wants to speak with the person in San Francisco without any delay.

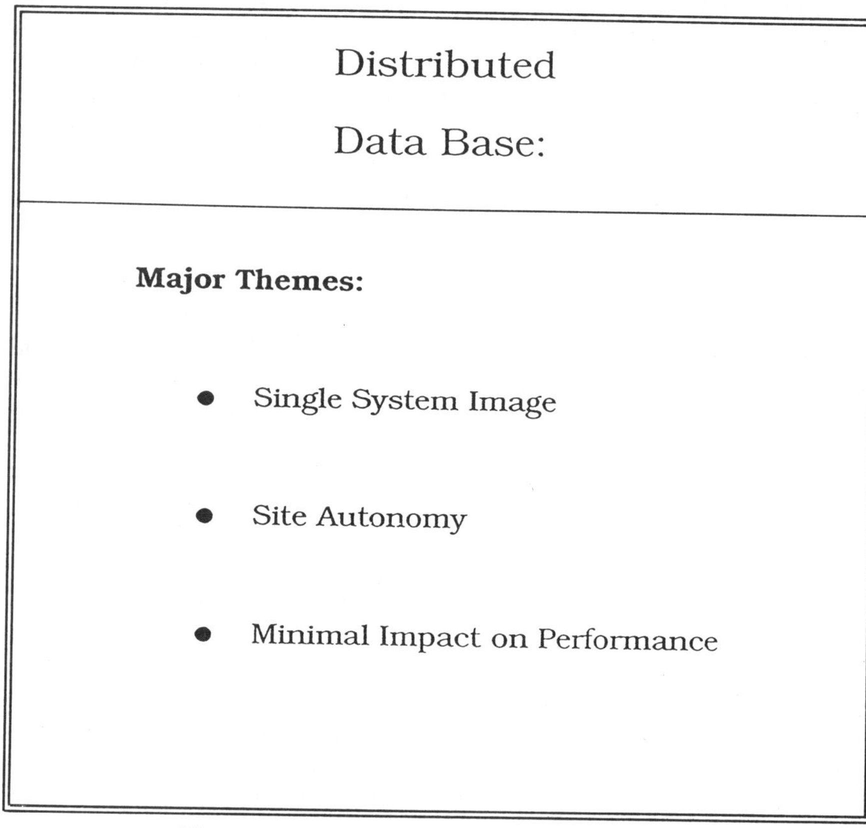

Fig. 2-6. Major themes of distributed databases.

Besides a single-system image, two important criteria are site autonomy and a minimal impact on performance. If anything, performance should be better than the environment before the distributed database implementation. Initially, when distributed database implementation goes live, the workload on the system is pretty light because the complete system does not go "live." It will be implemented in phases. People get used to a much faster response time and, as the workload builds and the next phases are implemented, they are going to complain, even if the overall performance of the new system is better than that of the older system. We get used to good things much quicker than to bad things. Again, it's psychological. It's not the technology that should be blamed. Management has to perform a decent "public relations" job so that the users' expectations are set at the right level.

Support requirements

One of the support requirements in the distributed database environment (see FIG. 2-7) has to be the means of locating data sets. The user doesn't have to know where the data is, but someone or something must know. That something will likely be the data dictionary/directory. Data dictionaries are used mostly by people, and a directory is used mostly by the system to determine the mechanics of accessing data.

A data dictionary/directory system (DD/DS) is a system that's designed to comprehensively support the logical centralization of data about data (*metadata*). It's not only capable of storing metadata (in the data dictionary); it's also capable of providing cross-reference information about the metadata (in the directory). The dictionary provides information about what the data is and what it means (logical); the directory provides information about where it can be physically found and how it can be accessed. It's an automated facility that supports the data administration (DA) function.

However, data dictionaries/directories are not taken seriously by many organizations. This is considered a mundane area and, as a result, creative and result-oriented staff don't like to work in the data dictionary/directory environment. Therefore, staff who prefer to perform only repetitive mechanical tasks don't want to rock the boat, and don't want to take any initiatives are assigned to data dictionary/directory projects. That doesn't create a nurturing environment for the project right from the start.

Keeping a data dictionary/directory accurate and current is an ongoing process. It's not a one-time event. A data dictionary/directory needs to be updated. Someone must be responsible for integrity of the contents. The distributed database environment is not going to be a solution to the problem of maintaining integrity, and it may even get worse. It's a matter of mapping and defining the data elements. In a distributed database environment, many processes access the databases, and consequently, one of the major support requirements of the distributed database environment is a defined level of consistency.

Implementing a defined level of security and authorization is also going to be a challenging task. In a distributed database environment, we consider microcomputers a part of the network. Microcomputers will store data downloaded from mainframes. In a centralized mainframe data processing

Distributed

Data Base:

Support Requirements:

- A means of locating the data
- A method of defining and mapping the data elements
- Control to ensure a defined level of consistency in the Data Base while allowing concurrent access by multiple processes
- A defined level of security and authorization checking for the Distributed Data Base

Fig. 2-7. Support requirements for distributed databases.

center, the much-talked-about glass house, there used to be very tight security. Microcomputers are not installed in a glass house. Many times, data from microcomputers is stored on a diskette that is inadvertently left overnight on a desktop. Therefore, security is going to be a major management issue in the distributed database environment.

Restoration of a distributed database

In the distributed database environment there has to be a method of restoring the database to a consistent state after all types of failures (see FIGS. 2-8 and 2-9). Consistency is very important, as is data integrity and performance. In-

Distributed Data Base:

A method to restore the Data Base to a consistent state after failures of:

- a transaction in process in any of the nodes
- any of the components of a distributed data base
- any of the nodes

Fig. 2-8. Restoring the database to a consistent state after failures.

consistent information is sometimes worse than a lack of information. Performance will also be an area of scrutiny. If users are receiving one-second response time, then they expect it all the time. They don't want to have a half-second response time one day and another day have to wait two minutes. Users would like to have, let's say, one-second response time consistently.

A *transaction* is a sequence of steps that constitute some well-defined business activity. A transaction may specify a query, or it may result in the creation, deletion, or modification of database records.

In the transaction processing environment, a transaction in any of the nodes could abort. Any of the components of distributed database may fail. Any of the physical nodes could malfunction. There have to be capabilities to restore the hardware, the media (in any portion of the distributed database),

Distributed

Data Base:

A method to restore the Data Base to a consistent state after failures of:

- the hardware of any of the independent nodes
- the media in any portion of the Distributed Data Base
- communications between the nodes working on behalf of a transaction

Fig. 2-9. A method for restoring a database to a consistent state.

and communications. In order to be able to restore databases to a consistent status, a distributed database management system (DDBMS) has to supply some functions; communications components have to supply other functions, and the database implementors have to supply yet more functions. Unfortunately, a majority of DDBMS vendors have software development expertise, but they do not have sufficient networking or telecommunications expertise. An organization will have to make sure that there are people with networking experience to fill in.

Optimization in a distributed database

In order to support a single-system image and to provide consistent response time, it's necessary to implement optimization techniques. Let's assume we're referring to relational databases, and that most DDBMS vendors who come up with DDBMS products have some relational technology in their backgrounds. Let's also assume that many relations under a DDBMS need to be implemented. Let's further assume that some relations are replicated and partitioned, and some relations have been stored separately. Results could be obtained by combining relations from various locations. There could be many locations from which data could be retrieved. The best location needs to be determined, and that best location may change from time to time.

Some questions that need to be answered are:

- Case study: In the case of an insurance broker trying to receive a profile of a potential client, Ms. Joan Carroll, the broker is going to visit Ms. Carroll to present new products (new types of policies). The broker is going to visit the client from Las Vegas, and the broker wants to find out the following before visiting Ms. Carroll:
  a. Is Ms. Carroll an existing client of The International Insurance Company?
  b. If yes, what policies does she have with us?
  c. Has she submitted too many claims in the past?

In order to find out this information, the broker could possibly get connected to Los Angeles or to San Francisco. The DDBMS system has to determine which node the request should be sent to.

To make matters more complicated, let's assume that the Las Vegas insurance broker has his/her own database with information about the potential and existing clients in his/her territory. In the database there is information about the policies that Ms. Carroll has with The International Insurance Company. But there is no information about the claims submitted by Ms. Carroll. The table with data that includes information about Ms. Carroll's policies needs to be "joined" or connected with the table on Claims, either in San Francisco or Los Angeles. The DDBMS has to determine which "join site" should be chosen. (See FIG. 2-10.) It also needs to determine:

- How to select the appropriate join site.
- How to create an order to the joins of relations.
- Which method to use to join them.
- Which synchronization method to use to update redundantly stored data.
- In case of failure of a transaction, which *backout procedure* to use for backing out the changes made. (Backout procedure is a recovery technique that restores a database to an earlier state by applying "before images." It's also called *rollback*.)

Do we join the relations to see whether we find what was already looked for, or do we just perform a complete join to get two rows out of one-hundred-

Optimization in

Distributed Data Base:

(Distributed Optimization Algorithm)

- Join Site
- Order of Joins
- Method of Join
- Synchronization Method
- Backout Procedure

Fig. 2-10. Optimization in a distributed database: distributed optimization algorithm.

thousand rows? The optimization algorithm also has to determine which synchronization method should be used, as well as which backout procedure should be implemented.

Data dictionary/directory

The two main interfaces of a data dictionary/directory are the interface with people and the interface with software (see FIG. 2-11). An interface with people somehow translates into a number of printed reports. With the distributed database environment, we're not necessarily moving into a paperless society. Anyone who thinks we're moving into a paperless society has to observe the number of microcomputers and printers installed. The microcomputer is one

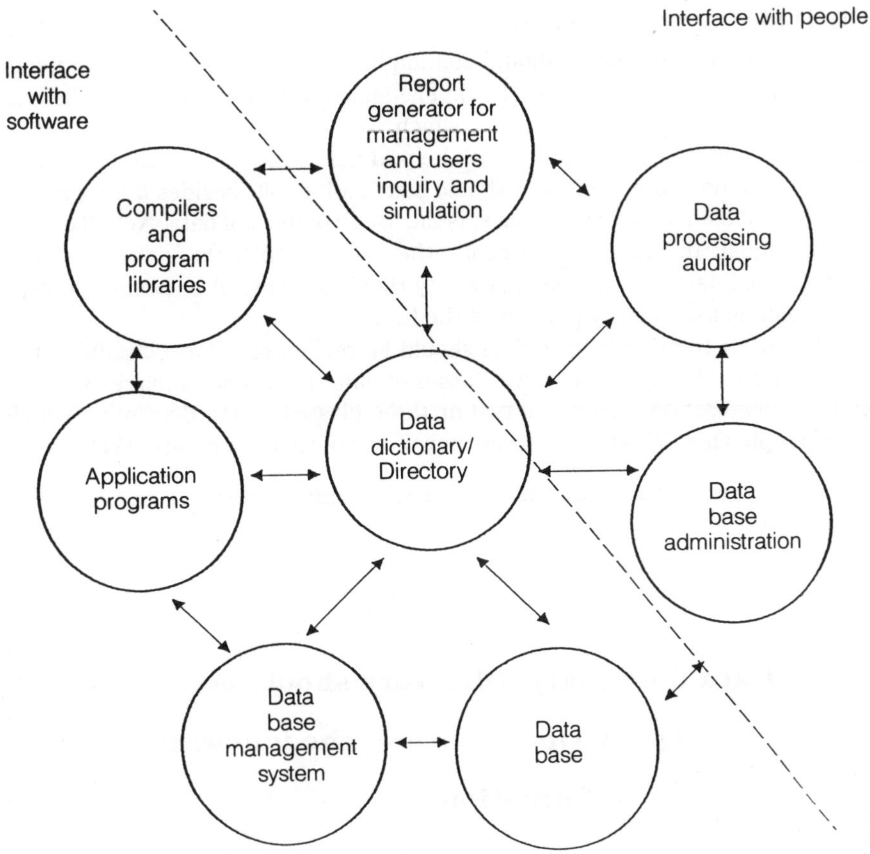

Fig. 2-11. Data dictionary/directory.

of the main components of any distributed database environment. We have many millions of microcomputers and printers. Almost every fifth microcomputer has a printer attached to it. What do we do with the printers? We print. On what? On paper, of course!

Another area we need to support with the distributed database environment, with the help of a data dictionary/directory, is the Executive Information System (EIS) or decision support system. The executives want from EIS "what is" and "what was" before going on to "what if."

Other people who need to interface with the DD/D are database administrators (DBAs), data administrators (DAs) and data processing auditors. The data administration function was, to begin with, a political function in a centralized place. In a distributed environment, we're referring to many locations to be coordinated. It's absolutely a politically charged environment, to say the least.

Interfacing with software is done with compilers and program libraries, as well as application programs and databases.

DD/D for query optimization

A data dictionary/directory should contain information on a number of items for query optimization (see FIG. 2-12). The speed of communication links will enable the dictionary to determine which communication links to use. The amount of data in each database will help to determine which database to go to. One area database designers should start looking at, besides taking inventory of the existing application base, is the usage pattern of data. Not all data is created equal. In most environments, the most recent data is the most frequently used data, and the eighty-twenty rule holds here also: twenty percent of the data is used eighty percent of the time.

The most frequently used data should be replicated. Start classifying the organization's data and make five classes of data. Five is not a magic number, and an organization may make two or three classes. Then determine which data is replicated. What is the frequency of use of replicated data? What is the

Data Dictionary/Directory

A Data Dictionary/Directory should contain, for Query Optimization, the following information:

- Speed of Communication Links
- Amount of data in each Data Base
- Which data is replicated where
- Frequency of usage of replicated data
- Speed of each machine in the Network

Fig. 2-12. Query optimization with the help of the data dictionary/directory.

speed of each machine in the network? These are just some of the criteria that could be stored in the data dictionary/directory, along with data elements, entities and processes. An optimization algorithm could draw on this information to make decisions regarding selection strategies.

The DDBMS has to provide transaction management (see FIG. 2-13), commit management, deadlock detection (before a deadlock occurs), system recovery, and object naming. Remember how you thought you had difficulty naming things with a centralized DBMS? Now just try a distributed environment. And the guidelines have to be fair; otherwise, they will not be followed.

A DDBMS has to provide for:

- Transaction Management
- Commit Processing
- Deadlock Detection
- System Recovery
- Object Naming
- Catalog Management
- Authorization Checking

Fig. 2-13. What distributed database management systems provide for.

The DDBMS also has to provide catalog management, and authorization checking has to be taken more seriously in a DDBMS environment. But security and authorization checking will require some time, which will be an overhead expense, and will probably result in performance degradation. This becomes a circus tightrope act when determining how much is just enough authorization checking and security so that performance is also adequate.

3

Distributed DBMS features matrix

This chapter describes some mandatory and desirable DDBMS product features and criteria for organizations considering implementation of a distributed database environment.

Hardware support

(See FIGS. 3-1 and 3-2.) For hardware support, the question is whether the DDBMS vendor offers support for the configuration of the particular organization. The number of operating system environments is enormous, even if an organization only buys from IBM. When putting together a strategic plan to implement a DDBMS, or any other new technology, information systems executives must first develop a baseline assessment of what architectures are currently used. Then it's advisable to "crystal ball" what other architectures might be deployed within the next five years. With that information in hand, an organization is better able to consider what software products fit the technological mix. In mainframe-based environments, management has purchased software based on the hardware they have installed. The trend with minicomputer-based environments is that the management selects prepackaged application software first and then selects hardware to fit that software. Depending on organizational need, the product should be available in an IBM version, a DEC version, or an IBM compatible microcomputer version. The product should also have IBM and DEC connection capability.

As far as IBM's mainframes and minicomputers are concerned, MVS/ESA, VM/ESA, VSE/ESA and OS/400 are SAA-conformant operating systems. (See SAA in the Glossary). IBM uses a variety of SAA terms: SAA participant, SAA compliant, SAA conformant. SAA conformant has a higher

Hardware Support
IBM Version
DEC Version
IBM-DEC Connection
IBM Microcomputer Version
IBM RISC-based Workstation

Fig. 3-1. Distributed database management matrix.

Hardware Support
Which Other Mainframes
Which Other Minicomputers
Which Other Microcomputers
Which Other RISC-based Workstations
Network Support ● Serial Ports ● Parallel Ports ● Asynchronous Transmission ● Synchronous Transmission

Fig. 3-2. Distributed database management matrix (cont'd).

level of SAA features than the other two. *SAA conformant* means that the product is developed on the SAA architecture specifications.

SAA participant means that some SAA-dictated features are implemented and some are not. SAA compliant is SAA compatible, but the product was not necessarily developed with SAA features in mind because it was developed before SAA came into existence. Features have been made compatible with SAA since the SAA announcement. SAA is described in a later part of this book (Chapter 5).

IBM would like to reduce the number of operating systems that it must support because it's an expensive endeavor. IBM has to maintain a separate support staff to provide systems maintenance for each major operating system and subsystem. The cost is tremendous, and IBM is looking to trim some of those expenditures. Maintenance includes the addition of features to keep up with technology enhancements, and SAA, with its standardized interfaces, provides a consistent vehicle for change. This assumes that IBM is successful in introducing and supporting the SAA-based software products.

On another front, we can't forget the huge installed base of MS DOS microcomputers, also known as *personal computers* or PC clones. These systems will be with us for some time and will have to be supported. The Graphical User Interface (GUI) is one of the main distinguishing characteristics of the microcomputing environment. A *GUI* is a user interface to the operating system. A GUI uses graphical icons, and there are a number of GUIs: Metaphor, Motif, NeXTStep, New Wave, Open Look, X-Windows and, of course, Windows and Presentation Manager.

Another architecture from IBM to pay attention to is RISC (Reduced Instruction Set Computing) and the Unix operating system for it.

In today's open environment with heterogeneous hardware, the DDBMS has to be able to support many manufacturers' equipment. Besides IBM, another major hardware vendor is Digital Equipment Corporation (DEC). The DDBMS should support the IBM/DEC connection. The DDBMS should support protocols to share databases stored on IBM and on DEC hardware. The major percentage of DEC installations are using VAX architecture. The DDBMS should also support Ultrix (DEC's Unix version on VAX architecture), as well as DEC's RISC-based workstation. A DDBMS should be able to support DEC's Gateway and other protocols in order to share the databases stored on IBM and DEC hardware without having to write major "bridging" programs.

A DDBMS should also be able to support the "same" applications running on either IBM or DEC systems with recompilation only, if necessary.

Areas for DDBMS installation

A DDBMS is potentially useful in a number of organizations. The following is a discussion of those organizations, in order of increasing complexity.

The first group will be organizations with several installations across the country. The organizations may have the same type of hardware. They may also have the same DBMS. (This homogeneity will be seldom found.)

The second group will be those organizations supporting a heterogeneous hardware connection, because there are many organizations that have hardware from several vendors. Governmental computational environments will be the first fertile ground for distributed database management system implementations. They probably are not using one and the same DBMS for the various machines used. Different DBMSs run on different hardware.

The third group will be those organizations supporting heterogeneous systems software with different operating systems. Even with one hardware manufacturer, there are a number of operating systems supported.

Users would like to access data stored on various hardware equipment without having to rewrite application software and without having to enter the same data over and over again. That's where substantial expenses occur. Frequently, data entry is a cause of new errors. Again, politics will possibly play a major part in a heterogeneous hardware environment. People using IBM hardware don't communicate well with people who have installed DEC equipment, and people from DEC installations dislike "IBMer's." It would mean tremendous savings if the same applications could run identically on IBM and DEC systems, and vice-versa, with only recompilation and without having to make any changes. But, as we all know, that's utopia. In data processing, as everyone also knows, any change, no matter how small, could result in a major expense.

For a DDBMS to be successful, IBM microcomputer versions running under MS DOS or a variation of MS DOS, especially PC DOS, are going to be a necessity because of the millions of MS DOS or PC DOS installations.

Major applications running under MS DOS or PC DOS in today's environment are word processing, spreadsheets and databases. The number one application is word processing, but a word processing document's life is usually two weeks at the most. The next major use of microcomputers is in spreadsheets. To support cooperative processing, some major spreadsheet vendors are announcing their products on multiple platforms. Lotus has 1-2-3 on IBM mainframes. It's also available on DEC hardware. Usually, a spreadsheet program's life is, at the most, four to six months. The third major use of microcomputers is in databases. Unlike the other two applications, a database created on a microcomputer could have a life span of two to three years.

Another question in a DDBMS evaluation is which other mainframes are supported. Especially in the government sector, there are mainframes installed from Unisys, Honeywell, CDC, etc. In Europe, there are installations of Honeywell Bull, ICL (acquired by Fujitsu) and Siemens. Also, in the mainframe area, the IBM Plug Compatible Manufacturers (PCM) should not be forgotten. The PCMs have a relatively respectable percentage of the market because of their attractive price performance, e.g., Amdahl and Hitachi Data Systems (HDS, formerly National Advanced Systems—NAS). For Amdahl installations, it's important to determine support for UTS, Amdahl's Unix version. Most of the PCM machines use IBM's operating systems. Most of the "other" mainframe manufacturers have their proprietary operating systems.

It's also important to review support for minicomputers. Other than IBM and DEC, support consideration must include manufacturers such as Hewlett Packard, AT&T, Data General, Prime, Wang and *Siemens Nixdorf Informationssysteme.*

Evaluate which microcomputers, besides IBM PCs and IBM PC compatibles, are supported. Apple is a major contender with its Macintosh line.

Another market segment for DDBMS implementation is workstations. Workstations from Sun Microsystems with SPARC architecture, Apollo (a division of Hewlett Packard), Hewlett Packard, DEC with MIPS Corporation's RISC (Reduced Instruction Set Computing Architecture) and IBM's RISC processors are a few to mention. Sequent is a mid-range Unix machine, but could be considered a "high-end" workstation. Pyramid is another mid-range Unix machine that could also be categorized as a "high- end" workstation. NCR and Alliant are among the other contenders. Unix versions that need serious consideration are AT&T's Unix V, OSF and IBM's AIX.

Unix is the dominant operating system in the workstation market and is very strong in design and engineering applications because of the popularity of the powerful single-user workstations for those applications.

One of the workstation application segments, besides Computer Aided Design (CAD), Computer Aided Manufacturing (CAM) and Computer Aided Engineering (CAE), is supermarket data processing. Supermarkets have to keep track of fast-moving brands because shelf space is limited. There are companies trying to identify retail shopping patterns, not only on a large scale, but in a granular mode. Supermarkets will try to keep track of the buying patterns of individual consumers' purchase of cereals, soaps, soft drinks, etc. Data will be stored on various types of computer installations because a consumer may be purchasing in various stores. Data collected in this fashion will constitute a distributed database.

Computer networking

Networking is a major component of the DDBMS environment. A computer network can be best defined as two or more computers, either all intelligent, or some intelligent and some "dumb" systems, connected to each other via electronic means for the purpose of exchanging information. Information could be in the form of a word processing file, accounting database, electronic mail, or customer records. A network may represent sharing common computer equipment, such as an expensive laser printer or a plotter.

Various forms of networks

If the distance covered by a network is a few hundred feet, the network is called a *local area network* (LAN). The network could also be a *metropolitan area network* (MAN), or the network may span across the globe or a continent, which is a *wide area network* (WAN). The connected computers, intelligent or dumb, are called ports or nodes. Both terms are interchangeable. These nodes may transmit data bits serially, one bit after another, or in parallel, multiple bits in parallel streams. Consequently, parallel transmission is faster than serial. These nodes may be capable of connection to transmission lines that transmit either asynchronously or synchronously.

Networking should be one of the major criteria considered when purchasing any computer equipment today. Even if some of the computer equipment is not connected into a network immediately, it may be connected in the future. From now on, any equipment should be purchased with networking in mind, whether an organization is considering a distributed database, cooperative processing, or computing in general.

Network status transparency

Network status has to be transparent, and an application program should not need to know which links in the distributed environment are now available. In a distributed environment, transparency and a single system image have paramount importance as far as database applications and networks are concerned. A *single system image* means providing the impression that all data is at one location. A single system image should be implemented at all levels, so that the user avoids the burden of choosing optimal or available routes for accessing data.

Networks, however, like all technology, fail from time to time. A number of strategies can be implemented to lessen the impact of network problems. Redundant links, data replication and system backup files all contribute to system reliability. If a link fails, redundant links will provide alternate links to use. If, for some reason, certain data is not available, redundantly stored data can be used, either at the same node or at other nodes. And, in extreme cases, if redundantly stored data is not available, system backup files can be used.

Transparency of a distributed system should be similar to a telephone switching environment. To repeat our example, a telephone call from New York to San Francisco may be switched via Dallas on one day and via Chicago on another day, without the caller's knowledge or intervention. The DDBMS should be able to identify all available routes to access required data. And even if a link fails during the transaction, it should still be possible to complete the processing successfully if alternative paths are available.

But the DDBMS should also consider human factors—if there is some degradation in the system's performance, the DDBMS should inform the user. This feature should be a part of the optimization algorithm. The system should inform users about any possible problems, just like a telephone system tells callers to try again later. That message may not be particularly appreciated, but it's better to know, rather than trying numerous times and not getting through. It might be better to take a few minutes off and then try again.

Features similar to those of the telephone system should be available in a distributed database system, because most of the accessing of the distributed database will be done in an online mode. Human factors are more important now, because the user is not in the same building as system administrators and can't easily ask for reasons about a delay in providing the information. Most of the people asking for information will be cities apart, if not continents apart.

Data distribution support

(See FIG. 3-3) One of the major facilities required of a DDBMS is the capability of distributing data throughout the network. Distributing data is based on the assumption that not all data is created equal. This means that not all data is used with the same frequency. Fragmenting data would be important in the supermarket example discussed before. Week after week, huge amounts of data are collected about grocery purchases. It might be desirable to store local data at various locations. There could be many different ways of splitting large amounts of data, a process known as *fragmentation*.

Fragmentation of data is easier with relations. A *relation* is a two-dimensional table with rows and columns. Data could be physically stored as a rela-

Data Distribution Support
Horizontal Fragmentation
Vertical Fragmentation
Replication
Data Dictionary (Global)
Data Dictionary (Local)
Data Directory (Global)
Data Directory (Local)

Fig. 3-3. Distributed database management matrix (cont'd).

tion or as a number of relations. The relations may consist of millions of database records, and each relation may have twenty, thirty, forty, or even fifty fields. The fields are columns, and the records are rows.

A part of the table could be stored at one site and another part at another site. This allows a user to cut up a relation into several pieces and place them at different sites according to certain distribution criteria. When relations are cut up, they must be put together. The relation should not just be fragmented without a plan for putting it back together. The DDBMS has to allow the database designer to cut up a relation into multiple pieces and place them at multiple sites according to certain distribution criteria. But the user doesn't want to know about this "cutting and pasting" business.

Horizontal fragmentation Horizontal fragmentation is based on having the complete database record stored at one location. The relation is cut horizontally. Some rows (records) are stored at one site. Some other rows (records) may be stored at another site according to some separation criteria (e.g., store records with keys 1 to 100 at site 1 and all the rest at site 2). There could be many different ways of distribution. That means the designers have to understand the data and the usage of the data. A database tuner has to look at the database for six months to a year after the initial implementation, because the tuner will learn a lot about the usage during that time. It's always interesting to compare the expected usage pattern of data to the actual usage pattern. The two patterns are very seldom identical.

Vertical fragmentation Let's assume there are thirty fields. Out of the thirty fields, only four, five, or six fields are used every single time, or more times than the others. A consumer doesn't buy cereal every week, but maybe every other week, or every third week. But milk is purchased every week. Based on this observation, a database designer may want to split the relation vertically so that a few fields are stored at one place and other fields are stored at other places. Tables T1, T2, . . . , TK are uniquely stored at various sites S1, S2, . . . , SK, for example, T1 and T2 at S1, T3 at S2 and so on. Vertical fragmentation requires some fields to be used for interconnecting the "split" relations. Otherwise, the relations are going to be disjoined, and they can't be interconnected. A *join* is a relational operator that allows retrieval of rows from two or more tables (or relations) based on matching values of specific columns.

To fragment data vertically, the data must be separated such that the fragmentation is without loss. If a relation is split horizontally, it's not that sensitive to loss because complete records are stored at each location. But vertical fragmentation is more vulnerable because of the splitting of relations with a few fields in one location and some other fields at various other locations, according to some column separation criteria. An original relation has to be created from the vertical fragments.

Vertical fragmentation is more difficult to manage than horizontal fragmentation. That's why most distributed database management systems support horizontal fragmentation before they support vertical fragmentation. Two, three or four fields must be put together and, before doing even that, there must be some common field with which to link it together. All fragments must have a set of common columns that determine the values of all columns in the complete relation, or a virtual column needs to be created artificially by the DDBMS to enable a one-to-one match of the fragmented records during reconstruction.

Replication of data Besides horizontal fragmentation and vertical fragmentation, replication of data might also be necessary. Some data will be simultaneously requested by many locations, and instead of having to go to other locations, it might be advisable to keep the data at the locations where it's most desirable. Performance will improve if the data is at the location where it's requested. Usage patterns of the data change considerably over time. What the database designer thought of as the usage pattern is not the same as people actually using it. A DDBMS has to provide capability of changing the replication pattern.

Copies of tables might be stored redundantly and must be guaranteed as identical at all times, depending on the environment. A bank, for example, has to provide that guarantee to the consumers. This is a major implementation problem because of synchronization. To avoid synchronization problems, data may be stored at only one place, but performance could be a significant problem when the same data needs to be accessed from various locations. For better performance, data has to be replicated. But, replication brings the problem of synchronization. A two-phase commit protocol supported by the DDBMS is necessary to provide synchronization of updates. *Two-phase commit* is a protocol that's used to insure uniform transaction commit or abort between two or more participants (transaction manager and database management system). The protocol consists of two phases: the first, to reach a common decision, and the second, to implement this decision. One participant is defined as *coordinator* and manages the execution of the two-phase commit protocol.

Replication transparency or copy transparency All copies have to contain the same value so the DDBMS can access the nearest copy. This has to be done by the optimization algorithm. The optimization algorithm could be a potential field for an expert system. An *expert system* is software that captures the knowledge and experience of a human expert, in the form of facts and rules, so as to aid others in decision making. As time goes by, the optimization algorithm "learns" more and more about the usage pattern. The optimization algorithm should "determine" the route to be taken for transmission, depending on the "congestion" of traffic, the same way as the switching mechanism of a telephone system routes calls. If the nearest copy becomes unavailable for any reason, it will be correctly updated once it's again available. It's conceivable that updates are made to the data at one location, and the same data is stored at another location, but is not updated yet. The data has to be updated once the system comes up.

Should the updates be done immediately, so the data is also available immediately, or could the updating wait until the end of the day or the end of the week? That means there need to be different data update strategies. A

DDBMS will not know the update strategies by magic; it will implement strategies stored by the analysts. Just like an application program, a DDBMS will do what it's told to do and not what a user wants it to do.

To keep the updates under control, it's desirable not to store more copies of the same data than are necessary. The adequate number of copies has to be determined by the database designers and by the database implementors. If a site is down, the user should still be able to access the data. Performance may not be optimal, so the user should be informed about a possible delay. Take human factors into consideration; users appreciate it if they are kept abreast of the situation and not left in the dark.

If data is replicated at various sites, read operations can be directed to any convenient copy, while writes must update and lock all appropriate database records. With write comes locking, and with locking comes deadlocking. Once the write is committed and completed, locks have to be released. Locking and unlocking could take quite a bit of time, resulting in performance degradation. The DDBMS has to ensure that either all copies are updated or none is updated. To support this feature, the DDBMS must provide a "two-phase commit" facility.

Two-phase commit is a necessity for a multisite update. The drawback of the two-phase commit is the doubling of messages. Local transactions will turn into distributed transactions, implying a much slower response time. Future distributed DBMSs may contain algorithms with improved capabilities so that distributed objects are updated inside a transaction. And crash recovery services will ensure that copies are consistent—either all or none are changed.

This algorithm, however, has a serious performance problem. Consider, for example, a person in New York who wants to cash a check. With a single local copy of the account information, the transaction could be processed locally within a few seconds. If, however, there is a second copy of the checking account information in London for reliability reasons, then that same transaction would require at least two roundtrip messages to London to commit the transaction. The first trip is to find out that the balance of the account to be updated is "up" for updating, and the second trip is to perform the actual update. Therefore, a response time of a few seconds is very unlikely.

As can be seen from this example, copy algorithms turn local transactions into distributed transactions, thereby causing much slower response times. A solution to this predicament must be found, possibly by applying application-specific semantics. Hence, it's expected that future distributed DBMSs may contain several multiple-copy algorithms, each appropriate to specific circumstances.

DBMSs should be able to support the snapshot facility. When a user wants to look at certain data to understand some trends, if that data keeps on changing, it will be very difficult for the user to identify the trends. A *snapshot* means that data is kept static for a certain timeframe. To support a snapshot capability, data from a relation is kept consistent, but not necessarily up-to-date.

Snapshots Snapshots are read-only and intended to provide a static copy of a database (e.g., last week's sales figures for all branches). Remember that most decision support systems have to provide not only "what if" capability, but mainly "what is" capability. Time series numbers are very helpful. An example of time series data is sales figures for all branches for the last quarter of each year for the past five years. To compare the numbers of the last quarter might be very helpful to a retail chain that makes 50% of the year's sales in the last quarter because of holiday sales. The snapshots are not updated when the base relations are updated. They may, however, be periodically refreshed by recopying the data from the base relations (e.g., every Friday at 6 p.m.). Snapshots could be very helpful in improving response time for certain types of applications where data supplied doesn't have to be accurate up to the second.

Data dictionary/directory

A data dictionary/directory system is designed to support the logical centralization of data about data (metadata). It's not only capable of storing metadata (data dictionary), but it's also capable of providing cross reference information (directory) about the metadata. The dictionary provides information about what the data is and what it means (logical); the directory provides information about where data can be physically found and how it can be accessed. It's an automated facility that supports the data administration (DA) function.

A data dictionary/directory should support horizontal and vertical fragmentation, as well as replication of data. A data dictionary itself is a database or several databases that may be made up of many relations. A relation could be stored locally, just like any other database, and the data could be viewed locally or globally. A data dictionary itself should be both a local and global facility.

A local data dictionary stores information about data, applications, users, security features, etc., locally, at the node where the data dictionary is stored.

A global data dictionary stores information about data, applications, users, security features, etc., pertaining to a number of remote nodes.

In order for a DDBMS to support a local and a global data dictionary/directory capability, the designers have to design the databases so that it's easy to store information about remote nodes and so that updates of remotely stored information can be done easily. DDBMS data distribution support is accomplished by supporting stored data in tables that are dispersed, replicated, or partitioned. Combinations of these could also exist. This means that partitioned data could also be replicated. Various combinations of partitioning and replication could be implemented with the help of a DD/D (data dictionary/directory) because the DD/D will keep track of the location of data.

A data dictionary is used mostly by people. People need to know about the location of data as well as about the availability of it. A data directory is mostly used by the system for optimally accessing data objects. A data directory is just like a telephone directory: it tells how to get to a certain number based on the way it's put together. The yellow pages are put together differently than the white pages, but there is some scheme that provides fast, or rather optimal, access. The data dictionary "tells" the user what the data means and the directory "tells" the user how to get to it. Callers read the name of the person or the company to call and look it up in the directory. The name and the telephone number are read, and the "dictionary" stored in a person's head understands what it means. The telephone directory helps a user find the items desired, and the dictionary helps decipher what they mean.

Naming conventions

The naming problem is one area that could get very political, and, again, could become very annoying for many people, because people get pretty "emotional" when it comes to naming. If somebody has called a field "employee name," and it's suggested that it be called "name of employee," it may not be appreciated. The naming problem in a distributed system is to allow data sharing without undue restrictions on the user's choice of names. For site autonomy reasons, it's not desirable to have a global naming system, nor will the users comply with such a system. Furthermore, adding a new site with an already defined database to a previously established network will lead to terrible renaming problems.

But most installations have some type of naming conventions. And naming conventions usually remain as mere guidelines and are not always implemented religiously. A suggested naming scheme might be: system-wide name consists of

USER_ID USER_SITE.OBJECT_NAME BIRTH_SITE

The user supplies only OBJECT_NAME, and the system puts together the rest of the components. USER_ID is known to the system because the USER has "signed-on" or "logged-on" to the system. USER_SITE is known to the system because the USER is using the system at a certain SITE. BIRTH_SITE should have been recorded with the OBJECT at the time the OBJECT was created for the first time. It's possible that an OBJECT was created at a certain site, but the ownership of the OBJECT is transferred to another site. There should be a guideline for transferring the ownership of the OBJECT and, with it, the most current BIRTH_SITE will be recorded with the OBJECT.

The OBJECT is either created or retrieved. A USER should be allowed to change a name only if it has been created by that USER. If the same object needs to be called differently, alias names or synonyms should be provided. That means there will be a BIRTH_SITE of the original object and a BIRTH_SITE of the alias. It's possible that both BIRTH_SITES are one and the same. But it's more likely that they aren't.

In a relational environment, a data dictionary is logically a single table that can be fragmented. This allows dictionary entries to be replicated and distributed among the data sites. However, this also implies that local objects may have their dictionary entries at a remote site, which could be their BIRTH_SITE. For these objects, data definitions might have been performed at remote sites which are their BIRTH_SITES.

Catalog is the term used in relational DBMS lingo. A *catalog* is a directory of all data in a database. In a distributed database, the catalog will contain the locations of each database fragment. A systemwide directory could be called a catalog, much as IBM calls DB2's dictionary a catalog. For faster access to the contents of the catalog, some part of the catalog could be stored in the buffer, which is a part of real memory. It's sometimes referred to as the *cache*. Of course, the hardware has to support cache memory.

In a distributed database environment it would be desirable to support a distributed data dictionary/directory. The system could then locate the objects with the help of systemwide names. A DDBMS may implement this capability for local relations (accessible from a single site) and global relations (accessible from a number of sites). The name of every global relation is stored at every site. Creation of a global relation involves broadcasting its name (and location) to all sites of the network, but cached catalog entries may be supported. However, a global catalog may restrict site autonomy and complicate system growth.

In a distributed catalog environment, catalogs at each site keep and maintain information about objects in the database, including replicas or fragments stored at that site. The catalog at the birth site of an object keeps information indicating where the object is currently stored, and this entry is updated if an object is moved. Cataloging of objects is done in this totally distributed manner to preserve site autonomy. An object can be located by the system from its system-wide name, and no centralization will be necessary.

For the catalog entry for an object, the following items should be entered: object's system-wide name, object type, object format, access paths available to reach the object, mapping in case of a view to lower level objects, and various statistics that assist query optimization. To find an object's catalog entry, the path taken could be local catalog, possibly local cache, birth-site catalog, and then the site shown by the birth-site, in case the ownership of the object was changed since the time the object was created.

If an object is stored at multiple locations, it probably will be accessed faster if the local copy of the object is asked for. But if the local computer, on which the copy of the object is stored, is out of service at the time of retrieval, it might be faster to access a copy from a specific location at one time and from another location at another time. This type of information has to be plugged into the optimization algorithm.

The optimization algorithm should not have information only about the available access paths to reach the object, but also about the "best" access paths. Lower-level objects will need to be mapped to higher-level objects to create views.

A view may or may not exist physically; a *view* consists of different combinations of physically existing relations. Data from a number of relations is put together to create a view. The view is considered to be at a higher level, and physical relations are considered to be at a lower level because the view is derived from the existing physical relations. Views can be created in many different ways. A view usually lasts as long as the user is signed on the system.

Consider two tables (or relations), PATIENT and SURGERY (see FIG. 3-4). A view asked by a physician could be the names of all people on whom "Open Heart Surgery" was performed between January 1, 1992 and March 30, 1992.

PATIENT TABLE		
Patient Number	Patient Name	Patient Address
1111	John White	15 New Street, New York, NY
1234	Mary Jones	10 Main Street, Rye, NY
2345	Charles Brown	Dogwood Lane, Harrison, NY
4876	Hal Kane	55 Boston Post Road, Chester, CT
5123	Paul Kosher	Blind Brook, Mamaroneck, NY
6845	Ann Hood	Hilton Road, Larchmont, NY

SURGERY TABLE				
Patient Number	Surgeon License Number	Date of Surgery	Surgery	Postoperative Drug Administered
1111	145	January 1, 1992	Gallstones removal	Penicillin
1111	311	June 12, 1992	Kidney stones removal	---
1234	243	April 5, 1992	Eye cataract removal	Tetracycline
1234	467	May 10, 1992	Thrombosis removal	---
2345	189	January 8, 1992	Open heart surgery	Cephalosporin
4876	145	November 5, 1991	Cholecystectomy	Demicillin
5123	145	May 10, 1992	Gallstones removal	---
6845	243	April 5, 1992	Eye cornea replacement	Tetracycline
6845	243	December 15, 1991	Eye cataract removal	---
5123	467	March 11, 1992	Open heart surgery	---

Fig. 3-4. Patient/Surgery table.

There is no physical table with the field Patient Number, Patient Name and Date of Surgery. A view created for the user (the physician) is shown in FIG. 3-5. This view is created by combining the two tables on only a few fields, such as Patient Number (a common field) of both tables, Patient Name and Date of Surgery. Contents of the surgery field are created for "Open Heart Surgery." Since the view doesn't exist as a physical table, no updates can be made to the view. If, in the future, the DDBMS would allow updating the view, the updates will have to be transferred to the physical tables. On occasion, there might be a number of tables, more than two, participating in creating views. Updating of a view is allowed if the columns of the view are identical to a physical table.

Processing support

(See FIGS. 3-6, 3-7.) A single-system image is the main theme of a distributed database environment. To present a single-system image, some aspects of

Patient Number	Patient Name	Date of Surgery
2345	Charles Brown	January 8, 1992
5123	Paul Kosher	March 11, 1992

Fig. 3-5. View created from physical Patient and Surgery tables to satisfy the request of finding the names of all people on whom open heart surgery was performed between January 1, 1992 and March 30, 1992.

Processing Support
Single System Image ● Query Transparency ● Update Transparency ● View Transparency ● Performance Transparency
Read Only
Read from Multiple Sites/Updates from a Single Site
Delete from a Single Site
Delete from Multiple Sites
Locking (Update/Delete), Granularity

Fig. 3-6. Distributed database management matrix.

computing have to be handled transparently, such as: query transparency, update transparency, view transparency, and performance transparency.

Query transparency means that a user should be able to ask the query the same way, no matter from which location it's run. The user from Chicago, asking for information about insurance policies when in New York, should be able to ask the same way as if he/she were in Chicago. *Update transparency* means

Processing Support
Two-Phase Commit
Query Optimization ● Local ● Global
Single Point Sign-On
Views Supported ● Transparency of Location of Data
Distribution of ● Application Functions (Local vs. Global) ● Resources (Local vs. Global) ● Responsibilities (Local vs. Global)
Site Autonomy

Fig. 3-7. Distributed database management matrix (cont'd).

the same as query transparency, the only difference being that instead of just querying, the person wants to update the tables.

View transparency means that if the Policyholder table (or file or relation) is physically stored in Chicago and the Claims table (or file or relation) is stored in New York, the user from Chicago should be able to ask the query the same way whether in Chicago or in New York. The view created with the two tables, Policyholder table and Claims table, should provide the user with the same view, whether asked in Chicago or in New York.

A user should be provided with the capability for read-only or read-from-multiple-sites and update-from-a-single-site. This is the minimum basic capability provided by a distributed database management system. Reading from multiple sites and updating from only one site is available with most of the DDBMSs. Update operation from multiple sites is extremely involved and, therefore, difficult to implement.

Delete is the most "expensive" operation because the DDBMS must first find out what it's deleting, and where the record to be deleted is pointing to, before the database record is deleted. Delete-from-multiple-sites, just like update-from-multiple-sites, is extremely complex and difficult to implement. As a result, most of the DDBMSs provide delete-from-a-single-site only.

The updates and deletes require a locking mechanism. Some DDBMSs don't let user "B" read the record that's being updated by user "A." Sometimes it might be advisable to let user "B" read the record with its older contents, depending on the type of record it is. If it's the balance of an account being updated, it might not be advisable to let "B" read the old contents while "A" is updating the balance. But, if it's the name of the person being updated, it might be advisable to make it available to "A" while "B" is updating it. This type of read is called a "*dirty read*." Dirty-read capability improves performance because "A" doesn't have to wait until "B" is finished with the update.

The mechanism of not letting anyone look at the database record while it's being updated or deleted is called "*locking*." Locking could be done to the entire database, or to the memory pages containing the database records, or to the fields of the database records. This is called "*granularity*" of locking. Field-level granularity is said to be the deepest. The DDBMS has to be sophisticated to handle a deeper level of granularity. But the deeper the level of granularity, the better the performance of the transaction. One transaction doesn't have to wait until some other transaction (or transactions) releases the lock on the memory pages containing the database records, or on the entire database.

Because of locks, there could also be a "deadlock." A *deadlock* is a situation where two or more units are competing for the same resources, and none may proceed (contention) because each run unit is waiting for one of the others to release a resource (a table, index, record, etc.) that has already been claimed.

Deadlock resolution is handled in a number of different ways by various vendors. When a deadlock is detected, some DDBMSs abort the transaction that is a participant in the deadlock situation, if it has performed the least amount of computing. Some DDBMSs abort the transaction that detects the deadlock.

In summary, locking may be an update lock or a delete lock. It could be "no read and single update," or it could be "multiple reads and single update." *No read and single update* means that when someone is updating a database record, no one can even read it. This is sometimes called *exclusive update*. *Multiple reads and single update* means that while someone is updating a record, multiple people can read it. There are many variations of locking and releasing locks. Let's look at some deadlocking scenarios and how the DDBMS may handle it.

A request to the DDBMS is given a transaction number that's made up of the site name and a sequence number (local time of day may be better). Each site is unique, and the sequence is increased for each new transaction. Therefore, the transaction number is unique. Uniqueness is necessary for identification purposes, for acquiring resources, for breaking deadlocks, etc. Another

tion purposes, for acquiring resources, for breaking deadlocks, etc. Another example is if a transaction starts at site A, sends work to site B, which in turn sends work to site A. Then it's necessary for A to know that both pieces of work are on behalf of the same transaction, so that locks on data objects can be shared. If such locks can't be shared, a deadlock will occur and make processing the query impossible. Ordering is used to provide a means of knowing which transaction to abort in the case of a deadlock between different transactions. A DDBMS should probably abort the youngest, largest numbered transaction. It's the application designer's responsibility to determine the transaction mix to have the least amount of deadlocking. If transaction A is asking for a printer used by transaction B, and transaction B is asking for the disk drive used by transaction A, a deadlock is going to take place when transaction A doesn't release the disk drive until transaction B releases the printer, and vice versa.

Transaction processing

One of the main functions performed by a DDBMS is transaction processing. A DDBMS, in particular, has to handle transactions from multiple sites.

What is a *transaction*? A transaction is a recoverable sequence of database actions that either commits or aborts. It has to be recoverable. The database actions could be creating, reading, updating or deleting database records. These are the four major database actions that either commit or abort. That means either the transaction is committed because either reading or updating was accomplished successfully, or the transaction was aborted.

Each transaction may be split into multiple transactions. Both synchronous and asynchronous execution can take advantage of parallelism and pipelining during the compilation and execution of the transaction.

Pipelining or named pipes (as used in microcomputer lingo) is a vehicle for passing data from one application to another. If the data is to be passed from one application to another on the same machine, e.g., in a multitasking mode, "anonymous" pipes can be used. In a multiuser mode, when data needs to move from one use to another, "named pipes" are used.

It might be desirable to find the information about somebody's buying patterns for groceries, such as produce or dairy products. The transaction for dairy products could be split into cheese types or milk to create two transactions.

Query transparency

To emphasize once again, the main themes of the distributed database environment are single system image and location transparency. That means an application doesn't need to know explicitly where a data item (set, record or field) is physically stored (the location) when it wants to access it.

With location transparency, data location can be transparent. If data location is transparent, the DDBMS knows where an object is currently stored, and there is no requirement for a user or an application to specify the data location in an SQL statement. If a table is moved to a different site, the name of the table doesn't change and, therefore, SQL statements that access the table don't have to be changed. The DDBMS should provide the features and specific mechanisms for accessing data items at remote sites. The DDBMS must be able to plan how to get to the requested item. It should be able to activate a create, read, update or delete of the data item. The user should be able to submit a query that accesses distributed objects without having to know where the objects are. There should not be a need to know the remote system's hardware, software environment, or the installed DDBMS.

Response time is the actual time that the user has been waiting for the system to respond. The perceived response time by the user is from the second the user pushes the enter key until the user gets something back on the screen.

To provide transaction transparency, the optimization algorithm preparation consists of name resolution, authorization checking, access path selection and optimization. An *optimization algorithm* is an algorithm that takes various parameters into consideration in determining how to access the database records requested. Let's assume that the Policyholder (automobile) tables and Claims tables are stored redundantly in New York City and in Chicago. A query for the names of policyholders (automobile) and claims in excess of $20,000 was asked from Dallas. The optimization algorithm has to make a determination whether to retrieve database records from Chicago or from New York City. Depending on the communication traffic as one parameter, a determination could be made to retrieve the records from Chicago. But the same query asked the next day may be performed by retrieving database records from New York City.

In a distributed database environment, concurrency control, deadlock detection and resolution, as well as logging and recovery, become important issues. Each transaction needs to receive a unique identification which will survive for the duration of the transaction.

Update transparency

A user should be able to run an arbitrary transaction that updates data at a number of sites. The transaction should behave exactly like a local one—the ultimate effect is that it either commits or aborts, and no intermediate states are possible.

To support transaction transparency, a distributed DBMS must support concurrency control and crash recovery for multisite transactions. A transaction that's split into multiple transactions to be run at various locations (or nodes or sites) is a multisite transaction. Recovery of a multisite transaction after a crash is, of course, more complex to perform than a single site transaction. In a distributed database environment, some data, such as the Policyholder's table, will be retrieved by many transactions. Concurrency control becomes a major issue to handle. All commercial products now use some form of dynamic locking in order to perform effective concurrency control. Setting locks at local sites within the local data manager and taking time out for deadlock detection will solve the global deadlock detection problem.

Crash recovery, however, is a much more complicated subject. Simply stated, a two-phase commit will help make sure that a distributed transaction is committed everywhere or aborted everywhere. With a two-phase commit, a distributed DBMS can successfully recover from all single and multiple-site failures. All commercial distributed database systems are expected to implement this concept.

The only drawback to the two-phase approach is that it requires an extra round of messages in the protocol. The first round is in polling all necessary nodes, and the second round is the actual commit. So a price is paid for this crash protection, because there is a trade-off between the level of service and the cost. Hence, several crash recovery schemes offering varying levels of protection might be included in distributed DBMSs. Urgency of crash recovery is dependent on the importance of the database records from the databases that have "crashed."

View transparency

View transparency effects a user directly. The view may or may not exist in the identical physical format. The view is created just for that slice of time while the user has logged on. For the user, that's the real world. For the user, that "make-believe" world is the real world, because the user has no idea that the view may or may not physically exist. If the user updates the view, that update may cascade into updates of many relations, because it's possible that vertical distribution (or fragmentation), partitioning, and/or horizontal distribution (or fragmentation) were used in implementing the distributed database.

Because of complexities involved in updating views, most DDBMS vendors don't support updates or deletes of database records from views unless the view is identical to a physical table.

Performance transparency

The distributed optimization algorithm is a major area for current research and development in distributed database environments. Since there are many ways for accessing and updating data, performance transparency is very complicated and, as a result, very difficult to handle for DDBMS vendors. There is also a major database design concern regarding replication of data for better performance.

Vertical and horizontal distribution

Vertical distribution or *vertical fragmentation* means splitting a table across different sites by columns. It allows columns of a single table to reside at different sites of a distributed database network. *Partitioning* is a method of distributing data in a network whereby only a subset of the entire database is located at a user's node. *Horizontal distribution* or *horizontal fragmentation* means splitting a table across different sites by rows. It allows rows of a single table to reside at different sites of a distributed database network.

If the most frequently used data is stored at multiple sites, accessing the data at these sites will provide better performance than storing that data at only one location. One aspect of data that needs to be remembered is that not all data is made equal. Not all data is accessed with the same frequency. The 80-20 rule holds here too; 20% of the data is accessed 80% of the time. In a distributed database environment, a user should be able to sign on at a single point, and the DDBMS should take over for the rest.

A *distributed query optimizer* finds a heuristically optimized plan to execute any distributed command. This simply means that a query can be submitted from any node in a distributed DBMS, and it will run with comparable performance.

A distributed query optimizer should keep track of the queries performed, the paths taken to access the databases, the order in which the tables are combined, etc. The "best" performing paths will be stored and will be used to undertake the next queries. That means the optimizer starts to get "smarter or more expert" in accessing and retrieving database records. This way of getting smarter is called a *heuristic approach.*

To provide performance transparency, a distributed DBMS should include a distributed query optimizer. This module is responsible for formulating an efficient plan to solve a distributed query, regardless of where it originates or how many sites have relevant data. In constructing an optimal plan, the distributed optimizer generalizes the query optimizer in current commercial relational systems by including communications, CPU and I/O costs. Although current distributed optimizers are quite sophisticated, they still require substantial improvements. Those improvements will have to come in the areas of load balance, nonuniform networks, administrative constraints and disk space restrictions. More and more organizations are interconnecting networks of various vendors. Networks from one vendor are not homogeneous, let alone networks from various vendors.

All of this means that real-world commercial optimizers will have to become much more complex than the ones in today's products. Furthermore, to generate optimal paths when multiple local data managers are present, the distributed optimizer has to deal with the local ways of handling data. Data available locally is accessible faster than having to transmit over communications lines. Policyholder data about New York policyholders should be available to New York brokers locally, and that of Chicago policyholders should be available to Chicago policyholders locally.

The final complication for a distributed optimizer concerns the enormous search space of plan possibilities. While it's feasible to do an exhaustive search of all possibilities in a local DBMS, this process quickly gets out of hand in a distributed DBMS. Techniques to cut down the search time are needed. This area will remain in the research and development realm for many years to come.

Two-phase commit protocol

Whenever transactions involve more than one database site, the DDBMS must take special care to be sure that the transaction termination is uniform. A transaction either commits or aborts. Either all of the sites commit or all sites abort.

The "two-phase" commit protocol is used to ensure uniform transaction commitment or abortion. It's a protocol that's used to ensure uniform transaction commit or abort between two or more participants (transaction manager and distributed database management systems). The protocol consists of two phases: the first, to reach a common decision, and the second, to implement this decision. It allows multiple sites to coordinate transaction commit in such a way that all participating sites come to the same conclusion, despite site and communication failures. There are many variations of the two-phase commit protocol. But in all variations, there is one site, called the coordinator, which makes the commit or abort decision after all the other sites involved in the transaction are known to be recoverably prepared to commit or abort, and these other sites await the coordinator's decision.

When the noncoordinator sites are prepared to commit and are awaiting the coordinator's decision, they are not allowed to unilaterally abandon or commit the transaction. This has the effect of tying up the transaction's resources, making them unavailable until the coordinator's decision is received. Before entering the prepared state, however, any site can unilaterally abort its portion of a transaction. The rest of the sites will also abort eventually. While a site is prepared to commit, local control (autonomy) over the resources held by the transaction is surrendered to the commit coordinator.

Some variations of the two-phase commit protocol hold onto resources longer than other variations. These protocols require all sites other than the single active site of the transaction to be prepared at all times. The linear commit protocols have a commit phase with duration proportional to the number of sites involved.

If the two-phase commit uses a presumed-to-commit protocol, the number of messages required in the usual two-phase commit protocol is 4(N – 1), where N is the number of sites involved in the transaction. But, by assuming that the commit succeeds, the number of messages can be reduced to 3(N – 1).

The first round of (N – 1) messages occurs in asking whether every node is ready to commit. (N is the number of nodes and one less is the coordinator node.) The second round of (N – 1) messages occurs when the commit is issued. The third round of (N – 1) messages occurs when the commit is successful. If the commit is not successful, the third round of (N –) messages conveys that the commit failed. And in the case of the failed commit, the fourth round of (N – 1) messages occurs to retract the changes made at some nodes.

If a failure requiring transaction abort occurs, then all 4(N-1) messages are needed. The improvement is obtained by removing the need for acknowledging the commit message. The coordinator logs the start of the transaction commit processing and then sends messages to the other sites (called apprentices or participants) involved in the transaction. An *apprentice* is a site that does work at the request of another site, which is then called the master.

Each apprentice still has to log its decision and reply to the coordinator, who logs the resulting decision. Therefore, the apprentice has to await commit/abort instructions from the coordinator, during which time its resources are tied up. Lost commit messages are detected by a time-out, but to avoid the very long outages that could occur if a network breaks down, operator intervention must be permitted. This presumed-to-commit protocol minimizes the duration of the commit protocol. Other variations provide mechanisms for circumventing the delay caused by coordinator failure. These variations send extra messages (to nominate a backup coordinator), which prolong the commit phase in the normal case. It doesn't appear possible to completely eliminate the temporary loss of site autonomy during the commit procedure.

Site autonomy

Site autonomy is the ability to administer different database sites independently and to have single nodes in the distributed system operating when connections to other nodes have failed. Each site or node is responsible for its data and for its processing. With autonomy also comes responsibilities. Each site is responsible for locking, logging, recovering and restarting database records. The organization's culture will determine the extent to which site autonomy will be available.

Staffing needs must be considered when some responsibilities of managing databases at the node sites are taken away. If management thinks that only the central site will now have all the expertise, and all the other sites don't need that expertise, management is in for a big surprise. Data processing professionals prefer technically challenging work. When everything is working smoothly, it starts to get boring for them. It's exactly the opposite for those users who are bankers or insurance people. Most of them don't want to get involved with the intricacies of technology. However, some users who have started to use computer technology think they know everything about it.

With site autonomy there should be no central dependencies on the network, no central catalog, no central scheduler and no central deadlock detector when the site prefers not to use these centrally managed facilities. There should be an option of using or not using these centralized capabilities. Maximum independence is called site autonomy. The site should retain local privacy and control of its own data. Each location will probably have data that makes sense only there and to nobody else.

While converting to a distributed environment, another aspect that should be considered is that data is not only data. Over the years people have put intelligence into that data. In our example of the insurance company, the policyholders (automobile) that have submitted more claims than the average number of accidents fall in a high-risk bracket. These policyholders could possibly receive a special indicator attached to the policyholder number. That means the policyholder number is not just a policyholder number for faster retrieval. It has some intelligence contained in the number.

There is some intelligence in the relationships between data, even in the way database records are arranged. Data is not only absolute data, but it also says something to the owner of the data at a certain location, which somebody else at another location doesn't relate to. Local autonomy has to be provided as far as the meaning of certain types of data is concerned. If a systems designer were to ask the data owners to think about all the intelligence put into the data, write it up and put it in the system, is it likely they will do it? They will not do it, because not doing it gives them power. People don't give up power easily.

Change management

(See FIG. 3-8.) Most installations pay attention only to creation. Very seldom is much attention devoted to maintenance. In most organizations, time spent in creation is only about 20% of the total effort, and about 80% is in the maintenance phase.

Change Management
Insulation from Change in Programs at One Location
Insulation from Change in View at One Location
Insulation from Change in Local Dictionary/Directory

Fig. 3-8. DBMS matrix: change management.

With change management, the designer has to consider how changing some programs at one location is going to affect other locations, and how changing the view at one location is going to affect other locations. A single system image means the user doesn't have to know about locations of data storage as well as changes made either to the data location or to the views.

Support structure

(See FIG. 3-9.) An ideal DDBMS should support heterogeneous operating systems, heterogeneous access methods, and heterogeneous database management systems. In the average Fortune 500 company there are 2.5 database management systems installed.

Support Structure

Heterogeneous
- Operating Systems
- Access Methods
- DBMSs
- Protocols

Fig. 3-9. DBMS matrix: support structure.

Compatibility with other DBMSs, operating systems, networks, and hardware are of paramount importance in a distributed database environment. In many instances a heterogeneous environment is a result of acquisitions done by organizations. It should be possible to transfer data back and forth between DECNET, IBM's SNA, WANGNET, and other wide area networks.

It should be possible to exchange data between DB2 at one site, Oracle at another site, and Rdb at a third. DB2 is IBM's Relational database management system for MVS environments. Its key strength is the SQL interface which is now a *de facto* industry standard. It's a strategic product for general information storage. Rdb is DEC's relational database management system for VMS operating system, and Oracle is Oracle Corporation's relational database management system for Unix, DEC's VMS and various other operating systems. Its key strengths are the SQL interface and its productivity tools. Because most organizations have diverse needs and require different databases, the ability to accommodate existing data and programs with known interfaces is critical.

Recovery and backup

(See FIG. 3-10.) Another major issue for a distributed database environment is recovery and backup. A database designer will need to keep track of currency strategies. Currency means, at the time of breakdown, which site, which database, and which database record were dealt with.

There are two levels of granularity of currency. Recovery strategy involves,

Recovery & Backup
Currency Strategies • Local • Global
Recovery Strategies • Local • Global
Recovery of a Transaction in Process in Any of the Nodes
Backup of Any Transaction Failed & Rollback of Data Base to Condition Prior to Failed Transaction

Fig. 3-10. DBMS matrix: recovery and backup.

also, how a system should recover, first locally, and then globally. Can an organization set up a "wait to perform global recovery" after the local recovery is accomplished, or is the system not functional until local and global recovery is accomplished?

Backup and recovery management should protect the integrity of the data in the event of a central server or node failure. Synchronizing updates on fragmented data means all nodes must be available in order to complete the transaction.

Replicated data that must be updated synchronously requires a strategy for handling processor failures and line failures. Line failure poses a real threat to integrity, because two processors could, while a line is out, update the same data, perhaps creating values that could never be reconciled without human intervention. Those values could then spread throughout the system like a virus.

One recovery scheme for preserving integrity during a line failure specifies where processing can proceed and stops processing on the replicated data at all other nodes. This strategy completely synchronizes the databases as soon as communications are restored.

Another recovery scheme restores a database on an as-needed basis. This method, called *"lazy"* or *"casual" recovery*, relies on a time-stamp mechanism. Once a line fails, secondary processors update the replicated data and initiate a time-stamping process.

After the line is restored, the secondary processors compare the time stamps on any replicated data that's accessed. The secondary processors synchronize the data, if necessary, before initiating the current transaction.

In many instances "lazy" recovery is good enough. Many times it's really not necessary to recover everything immediately. Again, that needs to be understood by the people who are designing databases, regarding classes of data, applications, and the users' needs. It's a multivariate analysis. With lazy or casual recovery, the secondary processors that are allowed to update the replicated data initiate a time-stamping process. That means more could be accomplished in the time frame if recovery is not done immediately, every single time, after a crash. It's one of the principles of queuing theory that if there are many small transactions, more gets done than if there is one long transaction. More can get accomplished by quickly finishing smaller jobs than if there is one long job.

Performance monitoring/tuning

(See FIG. 3-11.) An individual has to be made responsible for performance monitoring of the network, performance monitoring of recovery mechanisms, performance monitoring of usage patterns, and performance monitoring for user complaints. Some aspects, such as optimization, have to be handled by the DDBMS vendor in the optimization algorithm. But if a database designer in an organization knows how to distribute the company data the way it should be distributed, performance improvement will be accomplished faster than relying on the DDBMS vendor for everything.

Questions for DDBMS implementation planning

Beyond the preceding considerations, there are several questions that anyone contemplating the possibilities of a distributed DBMS should consider in order to determine what sort of product is really needed:

- Should we distribute data, or do we need to distribute only the access to data, with the data itself remaining at the site?
- Do we have "decent" data administration? The database administration function needs more "sophistication" in a DDBMS environment than in a centralized database environment.
- Do we want ultimate authority over data definition and access handled locally, globally or both? What type of local autonomy needs to be implemented?

- When a communications line fails, how do we balance the need for availability with the need for data integrity? How do we balance the cost of recovery with the need for integrity?
- In updating replicated data, how do we weigh the cost of simultaneous updates vs. the need for data integrity?

An organization should be able to make compromises with regard to all of these criteria, plus response time, cost and reliability, and select the combination that best serves its environment.

Performance Monitoring/Tuning
On-Line Monitoring • Local • Global
Inclusion of Transmission Costs in Optimization Algorithms
Optimization • Provision of Various Options with Up-to-Second, Up-to-Minute, Up-to-Date Data
Optimization of • Order of Joins • Method of Join • Access Method • Join Site

Fig. 3-11. DBMS matrix: performance monitoring/tuning.

4

Forces moving users to distributed databases

The distributed DBMS environment is much more complex than a centralized DBMS, which is, in itself, complex enough. What, then, are the benefits that justify this additional complexity? We can identify four potential reasons that are worth further examination.

Data can be stored and accessed in a pattern that matches the organizational structure of an enterprise. Most operational systems in a business have a degree (often substantial) of "local" usage, with varying amounts of remote access requirements. Arranging to store data at the site that uses it most can be efficient and may ease control procedures.

In our example of the International Insurance Company, New York City brokers will ask more often for the database records of the policyholders from the New York City area than from the San Francisco area, and vice versa. It's advisable, then, to store New York City Policyholders' table in New York City and the San Francisco Policyholders' table in San Francisco.

Distributed data aids overall system resilience. Loss of one node doesn't make all data unavailable and, if replication has been used, may not result in any lost access. The price of this resilience is, of course, an added complexity in automatic recovery after a node failure. In extreme cases, there may also be an inability to recover automatically under all possible failures.

Distributed databases can help to manage very large data volumes. Once a single system's online database goes above a certain size, it becomes difficult to manage operationally. Partitioning into a number of smaller databases can assist with management and control tasks.

Distributed databases allow incremental growth in data volumes. Not all data sets or items exhibit the same rate of increase in volume. Distribution allows variable rates of growth to be catered to in a cost-effective manner and without disruption to the entire database. In order to plan for future growth, someone from the organization should look at the pattern of data usage.

Who distributes data?

With all these complexities involved in managing distributed databases, a legitimate question comes to mind: Are there any current examples of distributed systems? Yes, a wide range of organizations already makes use of the distributed approach to managing data, although in most cases, not all of the required features are in their DDBMS. Most of these current systems are very large and international in scope. Others are more modest, both in terms of the volume of data stored and the number of nodes involved.

Here are a few examples:

- Airline seat reservation systems are possibly the most sophisticated example that combines multiple enterprises, computer architectures, data management environments and wide geographical spread. The systems also support very high transaction rates (up to 200 transactions per second) against a large, partially replicated, data volume (perhaps 500 gigabytes). Such databases are partitioned. In the case of airline reservation systems, there is no specifically distributed DBMS product that is stamped as distributed, but the systems are distributed.
- Credit card validation and query systems are, arguably, an example with the largest online data volumes and are subject to very high peak-transaction rates. The highest transaction rates are achieved in the retail industry during the three to four weeks in December before the holiday season. Master Card, Visa, American Express and Diner's Club Card are some examples of credit cards with heavy transaction volumes.
- Central government departmental systems are the systems that tend to be partitioned, but are, by definition, distributed systems. The Department of Motor Vehicles is one potential candidate, keeping track of millions of drivers, cars, licenses and traffic violations. Federal and state tax collection agencies are other examples with possible distributed database implementations.
- Supermarket buying patterns analysis is a system developed by a major bank for finding the grocery store buying patterns of millions of consumers.

Single-system image

You may have distributed data, and you may have distributed functions, but you also want to have a single-system image. A single-system image is the main theme of the distributed database environment. These features are possibly implemented with a product that's sometimes not even called a DDBMS.

It's not desirable to just replace a centralized system with a replicated distributed environment. Sometimes a manual system is replaced with an automated system with all the manual system's errors. The same thing should not occur in the transition from a centralized to a distributed system.

A distributed environment is a set of related data processing systems in which each system has its own capacity to operate autonomously, but with some applications that execute at multiple sites. Some of the systems may be connected with teleprocessing links into a network in which each system is a node. The systems may operate on different hardware architectures or on different operational systems.

A distributed environment means that, for whatever reasons, a company's or enterprise's important data is located in different sites of a computer network. In this context, *site* refers to each instance of a database management system (DBMS) that participates in a distributed environment. Two distinct database management systems on the same processor are two sites.

A number of issues that need to be considered by the designers are: update processing, delete processing, concurrency control (because of multiple requests), locking, and backup and recovery, just to name a few.

Organizational forces

Large organizational structures can be implemented in a distributed database environment that is able to integrate access to existing, local databases. With local autonomy, responsibility can be provided to local authorities who can control formats, procedures, access control, and privacy.

Location of data storage can be determined through geographic affinity of data. That is called *locality of reference*. Each application represents a number of functions. Depending on which function should be run at which location, an application can be split into multiple applications to be run at multiple locations. As a result of local data availability, response time will be improved. Data on New York policyholders should be available to New York brokers locally, and data on Chicago policyholders should be available to Chicago policyholders locally. Distributing data locally should also limit the scope of failures and mask failures by redundancy of data in a replicated format. Furthermore, distributing data should improve disaster recovery.

Another major force propelling distributed database environments will be improved performance. Making many low-level database requests to a remote node is much slower than making one high-level request to a remote server. That process does all the low-level database accesses at that node locally (see FIGS. 4-1 and 4-2).

The retrieval strategies for the query could "make or break" the response time. The example depicted is an exaggeration of the extreme, but, hopefully, it drives the point home.

Distributed databases with different architectures and features provide

Benchmarks have shown that the processing time for the same query written using SQL can range tremendously in a distributed environment depending on the strategy for retrieval. In one experiment, the results ranged from one second to more than two days.

The study involved the following tables: S(s#,city)-10,000 tuples stored at site A, P(p#,color)-100,000 tuples stored at site B, SP(s#,p#)-1,000,000 tuples stored at site A.

The information desired was: "Get all supplier numbers for suppliers in New York who supply red parts". The SQL query follows:

```
select S.S#
from S,SP,P
where S.city = "New York"
and S.s# =  SP.s#
and SP.p# = P.p#
and P.color = "red"
```

Additional information:
Number of red parts = 10
Number of shipments of New York suppliers = 100,000
Data rate = 10,000 bits per second
Access delay = 1 second per message
Total time = number of messages + number of bits/10000

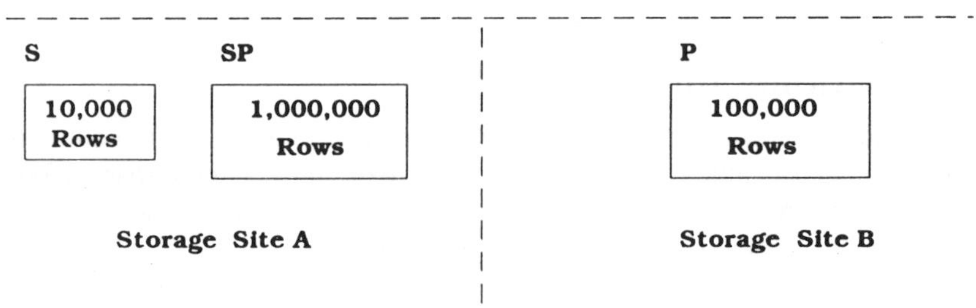

Fig. 4-1. Importance of optimization: managing processing and retrieval times. (Courtesy J.B. Rothnie, Jr. and N. Goodman. Proceedings of the 3rd International Conference on Very Large Databases, Morgan Kaufmann Publishers, Inc. 2929 Campus Drive, San Mateo, CA.)

high-volume online transaction processing as well as support of decision-support applications. These are the two major classes of applications.

There are a number of issues that need to be considered by designers of distributed databases, as well as by users. Issues for designers and users include:

- Query processing.
- Update processing.
- Concurrency control (locking is the major issue).
- Backup and recovery management.
- Structure management.

Let's consider these issues in more detail.

1. Join relations S and SP at A, select from the results for which city is New York. For each, check if part is red at site B. Time = 2.3 days.
2. Move relations S and SP to B and process the query at B. Time = 2.8 hours.
3. Move relation P to A and process the query at A. Time = 16.7 minutes.
4. Select red parts from relation P at site B. For each of these check site A to see if there is a related New York shipment. Time = 20 seconds.
5. Select parts that are red from relation P at site B. Move the result to A and complete the processing there. Time = 1 second.

The extremely wide range of results is from one second to more than two days.

Fig. 4-2. Various strategies for retrieving the data and processing it to satisfy the query. (Sentry Publishing Company, Inc.)

Query processing

Where should the query be processed? Complex queries can be split into a number of simple queries that can potentially be separately executed and, possibly, executed in parallel with a corresponding reduction in execution time. It must also be asked whether to move data (strictly speaking, a copy of the data) between nodes and, if so, how much data and to what nodes.

If data is being moved, it's temporarily being replicated. Replication is a method for keeping copies of a table at multiple sites synchronized. A local, read-only copy of tables is given to users (so response time is not subject to communications delay) and, when the source table is updated, the update is dynamically propagated to the other sites where the replicated tables are kept. What effect does this have on the currency of the content, and is this important to the query?

Update processing

It's necessary to ensure that an update to a data item or items is applied to all replicas in a consistent fashion. Note that this is a problem even in single-user systems because of the need to cater to possible partial failures of links or nodes. Concurrent usage additionally complicates the issue. *Concurrency control* is the DDBMS function that prevents interference between transactions when several users are updating a database concurrently.

Concurrency control

It's the DDBMS function that prevents interference between transactions when several users are updating a database concurrently. Several tricky problems come to the surface when it's necessary to break a complex update into a series of simple updates and avoid deadlocks. When interaction between updates and queries (concurrency issues) are considered, performance and partial failure recovery management must also be considered.

Backup and recovery management

In any distributed database environment with replicated data, backup and recovery management will remain one of the biggest challenges. As the distribution of data increases, these issues likewise increase. A backup is an image of the database, whereas a backward recovery is a recovery technique that restores a database to an earlier state by applying "before images." It's also called a rollback.

Structure management

There are a number of approaches to storing distributed databases. Each of these alternatives has an associated degree of cost that varies from option to option. Some alternative approaches where data is strictly partitioned, without replication, include:

- No replication of data or map. A road map is not roads. It only represents the location of the roads. Similarly, a map provides the location of each data item in the network. The map doesn't represent the contents of data, but rather, the locations of them.
- No replication of data, complete map at each node.
- No replication of data, single (primary) copy of map with partial map at each node.
- No replication of data, local maps only.

The alternative approaches where data may be replicated include:

- Master copy of data with complete replication at each node.
- Master copy of data with partial replication at each node.
- No master copy, partial replication at each node.

Cost considerations

As always, there is the consideration of how to keep the cost to a minimum. The answer is to distribute the data so that most accesses are local. Plan access strategies that minimize the amount of communications needed to respond to a query. This is to be achieved through query optimization, where the data access path is chosen based on the cardinality of the relations needed to respond to the query.

Cardinality of a relation is the number of database records of the relation, and is one of the major attributes to be considered for fast performance of join operations. A *relation* is a two-dimensional table representing data. Every column in a relation represents an "attribute." Every row in a relation represents a database record. A join is more than cross referencing between relations; it could be performed between two tables, three tables, or four tables by cross referencing and finding the common things for putting them together.

Let's consider our example of Patients and Surgeries from Chapter 3. For ease of reference, the same figures (FIGS. 3-4 and 3-5) are replicated as FIGS. 4-3 and 4-4. In order to find the patients' names with "Open heart surgery," it's necessary to "join" (or cross reference) the two tables from FIG. 4-3 on the Patient Number column of each table, and the entry in the Surgery column needs to be checked for "Open heart surgery" to find the database records that satisfy the value as shown in FIG. 4-4.

PATIENT TABLE

Patient Number	Patient Name	Patient Address
1111	John White	15 New Street, New York, NY
1234	Mary Jones	10 Main Street, Rye, NY
2345	Charles Brown	Dogwood Lane, Harrison, NY
4876	Hal Kane	55 Boston Post Road, Chester, CT
5123	Paul Kosher	Blind Brook, Mamaroneck, NY
6845	Ann Hood	Hilton Road, Larchmont, NY

SURGERY TABLE

Patient Number	Surgeon License Number	Date of Surgery	Surgery	Postoperative Drug Administered
1111	145	January 1, 1992	Gallstones removal	Penicillin
1111	311	June 12, 1992	Kidney stones removal	---
1234	243	April 5, 1992	Eye cataract removal	Tetracycline
1234	467	May 10, 1992	Thrombosis removal	---
2345	189	January 8, 1992	Open heart surgery	Cephalosporin
4876	145	November 5, 1991	Cholecystectomy	Demicillin
5123	145	May 10, 1992	Gallstones removal	---
6845	243	April 5, 1992	Eye cornea replacement	Tetracycline
6845	243	December 15, 1991	Eye cataract removal	---
5123	467	March 11, 1992	Open heart surgery	---

Fig. 4-3. Patient/Surgery table. (John Wiley & Sons, Inc.)

A *multistage join* means multiple relations are considered. Two relations are joined at a time, and the resulting relation is joined with one more relation, until all relations are taken into consideration. A relational system is a closed system. That means the result of two relations is also a relation, just like the number system. Addition or subtraction of two numbers results in a number

Patient Number	Patient Name	Date of Surgery
2345	Charles Brown	January 8, 1992
5123	Paul Kosher	March 11, 1992

Fig. 4-4. View created from physical Patient/Surgery tables.

belonging to the number system. When two relations are joined, the result is a relation. The order could be changed, and that order in itself could be a deterrent to system performance.

Let's consider our insurance example. Let's say that there are two files or relations: the policyholder file with 10,000 records (rows), and a claims file with 1,000,000 records (rows). We want to find all policyholders who have put in claims of $10,000 or more. Two operations need to be performed. A join needs to be performed on the Policy No. (number) of both relations, and a selection needs to be performed on the rows from the claims file with the contents in the claim amount column of $10,000. If the selection of rows satisfying the condition is done first, and then the join operation is performed between the resulting file and the policyholder file on the policy number, system performance will be much better than performing the join first and then performing the selection of the rows.

Some other parameters that affect performance are network traffic and disk access time. Disk access is still, as it has been, one of the big inhibitors to performance. The following are some other strategies that could be implemented with respect to minimizing the cost.

Data distribution Evaluate and distribute the data so that most accesses are local.

Communications costs A substantial amount of money will be spent on links, network control equipment, backup switching and other communications expenses. Plan the access strategies that minimize the amount of communications needed to respond to a query. This is achieved through a query optimization algorithm of the DDBMS considering the following:

- The data access path is chosen based on the cardinality of the relations needed to respond to the query. As explained earlier, cardinality means the number of database records, or rows, of a relation. In our previous example of a policyholder relation (with 10,000 records) and a claims relation (1,000,000 records), it's advisable to cut down the size of the resulting relation early in the query. By selecting the rows with claims > $10,000, we eliminate a large number of rows and then join the resulting relation with the policyholder relation.
- Distribution of the attributes or fields in the relations can be ordered

most effectively. The most frequently accessed attributes should be clustered on the left hand side of a relation when a person is, so to say, facing the relation. Database records or rows of a relation are stored on a disk in the manner that the left-most attribute is considered first, and then the next right one, then the next right one, and so on. Consider the policyholder relation of FIG. 4-5. The contents of the column First-Name is stored first, then the Last-Name, then the Policy-No. and then the Rep-No.

Policyholder File

First-Name	Last-Name	Policy-No.	Rep-No.
Thomas	Finneran	643489	2345
Joan	Carroll	856745	6748
Ann	Karel	679435	1367
Susan	Simon	468912	4589
Joan	Carroll	346512	6748
⋮	⋮	⋮	⋮

Claims File

Policy-No.	Claim-Date	Claim-Amount
643489	January 15, 1992	5,555.-
346512	March 30, 1992	12,250.-
856745	February 18, 1992	18,460.-
468912	April 11, 1992	25,560.-
643489	March 5, 1992	20,489.-
245867	February 8, 1992	120,560.-
⋮	⋮	⋮

Fig. 4-5. Policyholder and Claims files interrelated on certain fields.

- The size of intermediate results generated during a multistage join could be stored temporarily for later access. Joins don't need to be performed repeatedly with stable databases.
- An estimation of the network traffic involved is valuable. If it's possible, communications cost could be minimal by using "off-peak" times for transmission.
- Disk access costs could be minimized by keeping the most frequently used data clustered together.

Environment software Additional copies of the operating system, utilities and the DBMS will be required. While purchasing any software, it should be inquired whether the vendor has a network version of the software available. Instead of buying multiple copies of single user software, it's cost effective to buy a network version of the same software. Appropriate planning regarding this matter will save a substantial amount of software cost over the long run.

Applications complexity Since most available DBMS software does not yet provide all the management facilities required by designers, applications become more complex, more expensive to develop, and more expensive to maintain.

Operational procedures These are more complex in a distributed environment, requiring more technical support staff, more training and more time and effort to recover from failures.

Performance Achieving an adequate level of performance in all but the most trivial cases can require more of everything, including hardware, software, design expertise, application, database tuning and support.

Implementation issues

Identify the main functions. Don't try to implement the most visible function right away. In a number of large organizations, data is already distributed, and users would like to have access to the already distributed data. Integrate access to existing local databases. But keep in mind that most local databases are single-user systems, and in most instances, users are not necessarily interested in sharing "their" databases. Sharing is fine as long as the data belongs to someone else!

Features to be considered

How can distributed data maintain data consistency? How can communications costs be kept low? How is deadlock avoided? How is data synchronization handled? These are the major issues that have to be considered, as well as how and where local data should be stored.

How should the database fields be named? How should they be accessed, and how should they be updated, backed up, restored, protected and shared? Location transparency provides a single unified view. The users get their views and think that those views are only theirs. They don't necessarily want to share. Providing site autonomy with referential integrity, synchronization, partition independence, and replication independence are several of the issues that need further attention.

Data synchronization

This is the most complex feature to implement for a distributed DBMS, particularly when update or delete operations are to be performed. *Synchronization* means that replicated data at different sites must be identical.

Let's consider withdrawal of money at one site, and let's say it's a joint account. Money could be withdrawn in New York City and in Chicago on the same day and at the same time. A person withdraws money in New York City, and it's still not posted in Chicago. People could withdraw the money two or three or four times without its being posted. How is the balance kept up to date?

One way of synchronizing the common balance will be to lock accessing of the balance data item until it's updated at every node. Another technique used is two-phase commit.

Two-phase commit problems

While two-phase commit is highly valuable, there are significant drawbacks to be considered. A two-phase commit involves high overhead, more transmitted messages, and a greater volume of communications traffic. The traffic occurs among lock managers, data items and updating of nodes.

Each data item has to be assigned to a node for safekeeping. A node plays the role of a lock manager for each data item. During the message exchange, the data being updated is locked at all nodes involved, and it remains locked until all the nodes have completed their processing and communication exchanges.

Maintaining synchronized data is expensive, both in terms of the communication required by the protocol and the reduced availability of the data being updated.

Solutions for the overhead problem

Several strategies are currently available for overhead reduction. One solution is to decompose transactions that read and update multiple nodes. These transactions are broken into smaller, separate transactions, so they don't keep data locked for long. Another answer is to use a distributed DBMS that supports multiple synchronized updates within a single transaction. And perhaps the DDBMS vendor should invent a new synchronization protocol that consumes less overhead.

The main point, as far as performance is concerned, is that speed will depend a lot on where data is stored for given transactions. That means transactions have to be prioritized. There are a few transactions that will be run much more frequently than others, and the system should be concentrating on those. As a result, other transactions may not provide the best performance. The most important ten or so transaction types should be prioritized.

Local autonomy

Local autonomy should provide control of formats and procedures. In spite of these formats and procedures, there will be some discrepancies in the contents of the repeatedly stored data. Not every node, with its local autonomy, will follow the guidelines. But, if local autonomy can't be provided, there simply will not be a distributed database environment, because politically, it will not be implemented.

Functional decomposition and data placement

Data that's primarily for local use should be kept at the specific locations. That will minimize the transmission time and will provide a faster response.

Replication or partitioning of data

An alternative to the replication of data is data partitioning. With partitioning, a map of data location should be stored at each node. As the location of the data changes, the map has to be changed also. Another possibility is not to replicate any data and to keep a single primary copy of the map, with a partial map at each node. The partial maps would contain information that pertains to data stored at a particular node. It's also conceivable to keep a master copy of the data with complete replication at each node. That means you have ten centralized locations if everything is replicated in ten places. With that scenario, expenses need to be considered for hardware, systems software and people to manage it. As a result, in the beginning phase of the implementation of a distributed database environment, it will be quite expensive, compared to one centralized node.

DDBMS and related software

With software licensing agreements, you may have to pay for multiple copies, or you may have some licensing agreement where, beyond a certain number, you don't have to pay. Obviously, these aspects need to be considered. It will be too costly in the end if an organization uses illegal copies.

Applications complexity

Most available DDBMS software doesn't yet provide all the management facilities for designers. If functions and features needed by users are not considered during the design phase, then these features will have to put into the applications, which could be very expensive.

Consider a simple example where application complexity could be high if *referential integrity* is not supported by the relational DBMS. Each application has to code referential integrity in the programs. Let's assume that we have two tables, one is a customer table and one is an account table. A customer may have multiple accounts. You should not delete the customer record even if the customer is closing one account, because you have to see whether there are some other accounts of the customer in the bank. That means that integrity, in reference to the data that's stored some other place or places, has to be provided. This example relates to deletion.

Similar examples could be cited for addition and for updating of data. With personnel records, a worker should not be added to the employee table unless the employee is assigned to a department. That means the employee must be assigned to a particular department. These are the business rules. And these business rules have to be communicated to the DDBMS. Only then will the DDBMS be able to implement the rules. If these business rules are not implemented by a DDBMS application, programmers will have to implement them, making them very complex in the application programs. Operational procedures are more complex in the distributed environment, requiring more technical support, more training, and more time and effort to recover from failures.

Performance

Achieving an adequate level of performance, in all but the most trivial cases, could require more hardware, software, design expertise and other resources. The main consideration is to establish a scope for the distributed database environment, concentrate on some function, on specific applications to support the function, and on the automated facilities that people didn't have before.

Benefits of a DDBMS environment

A DBMS environment provides support of heterogeneous computing environments and better response time as a result of data's local availability. Distributed databases with different architectures and features could be separated into two areas: high-volume online transactions, and decision support applications. Most microcomputer-based systems are decision support systems. When a budget is prepared with a Lotus spreadsheet, it's a decision support system. It's possible that it's not classified as a decision support system, because Lotus doesn't bear that label on the box, but it's still being used as such.

Performance is an issue that needs special attention in a DDB environment when used with high-volume online transactions. Many low-level database requests to a remote node end up taking much longer than making one high-level request.

Availability and reliability

Some data access failures at certain locations could be masked by replicating the data. Data can be stored and accessed in a pattern that matches the organizational structure. This should be looked at more carefully, but not for matching data to the exact usage pattern of today. The usage pattern does change over time. The database designer has to see the pattern over time and then come up with some common denominator to fit the pattern of data distribution.

With a distributed database, system resilience can be provided. If one node is lost, it doesn't mean that all data is unavailable. Distributed databases can help to manage very large data volumes. Besides, the eighty-twenty rule should not be forgotten. Twenty percent of the data is used eighty percent of the time.

Major problems to be resolved

Some very challenging problems that need to be resolved are: how to distribute and maintain data consistency, how to keep the communications costs to a minimum, how to avoid deadlock situations, and how to handle data synchronization.

Organizational guidelines need to be established regarding how and where local or LAN data should be stored, named, accessed, updated, backed up, restored, protected, and, last but not least, shared.

Pitfalls of a DDBMS environment

Location transparency A customer is presented with a single unified view of both the data and the machine on which the data is processed. In a distributed environment, it would be unnecessary for a customer to wonder where the data regarding an employee's department name and location is physically stored. It may be, however, that in order to answer that query, a three-way join must be done on the host-based DBMS table containing location information and a workstation-based table containing departmental data. Since the results are the customer's only real concern in a distributed environment, this data can be retrieved without any knowledge of its location. In order to provide location transparency and adequate performance, database design has to be performed so that the most frequently accessed data is stored at as many nodes as possible so that access becomes local.

Site autonomy Sites in a distributed system should function autonomously. Site or local autonomy means local data is owned and managed with local accountability. All distributed data, therefore, belongs to some local database. Thus, such matters as security, integrity and storage remain in the hands of the local site. As a result, the "quality" of site autonomy will vary from site to site.

Referential integrity The DDBMS has to ensure that the correct "referential" state exists within the system among data that's represented. If an application program were about to delete a particular prospect from a prospect sales table, for example, that prospect's price quotes should also be deleted from the quotation table, regardless of where it's physically located. No further action is required on the part of the application program. Global application of referential integrity is not expected soon. However, referential integrity on a file server basis is within sight.

Partition independence A distributed database management system that supports partition independence would allow horizontal and vertical partitioning, but would behave as if the data were not partitioned at all.

Replication independence Copies of files could be distributed for local processing efficiency, but refreshed dynamically when updates are posted to the parent file. Even when a distributed application is ready for implementation, users will find that it will impose some restrictions on their data processing operations. Users may experience a decrease in processing efficiency. This may seem like a contradiction, but most distributed applications have tended to be CPU and network hogs. This condition may improve with the new breed of distributed database server concepts with gateway networking.

Users will have increased responsibility for data integrity and security. As more corporate data is stored on file servers and tape backup units, local sites will have to become more responsible. Such duties were traditionally thought to be the sole responsibility of data administration personnel in MIS, including such tasks as local and host backup, recovery and security. In a distributed database environment, these duties will have to be performed at many more nodes than just the central node.

5

IBM's distributed database direction

IBM is one of the manufacturers that people consider when evaluating the viability of any computer technology. Therefore, many companies want to adapt their strategic systems to distributed database technology if IBM is clearly supportive.

IBM defines five levels of Distributed Relational Data Access (DRDA):

- User-assisted distribution.
- Remote request.
- Remote unit of work.
- Distributed unit of work.
- Distributed request.

A brief discussion of each level follows, with a more in-depth look provided later. (See FIGS. 5-1, 5-2 and 5-3.)

User-assisted distribution

User-assisted distribution is the simplest of the levels and is best kept to occasional, well-managed instances. The user is aware of the data location and interacts with a remote system to obtain the information. The process is akin to passing another user a diskette containing a data file or software. Most of the mainframe-based computerized systems use this type of distribution.

Remote request

On the second level, remote request, an application at a site designated X can send a database request as an SQL (Structured Query Language) statement to

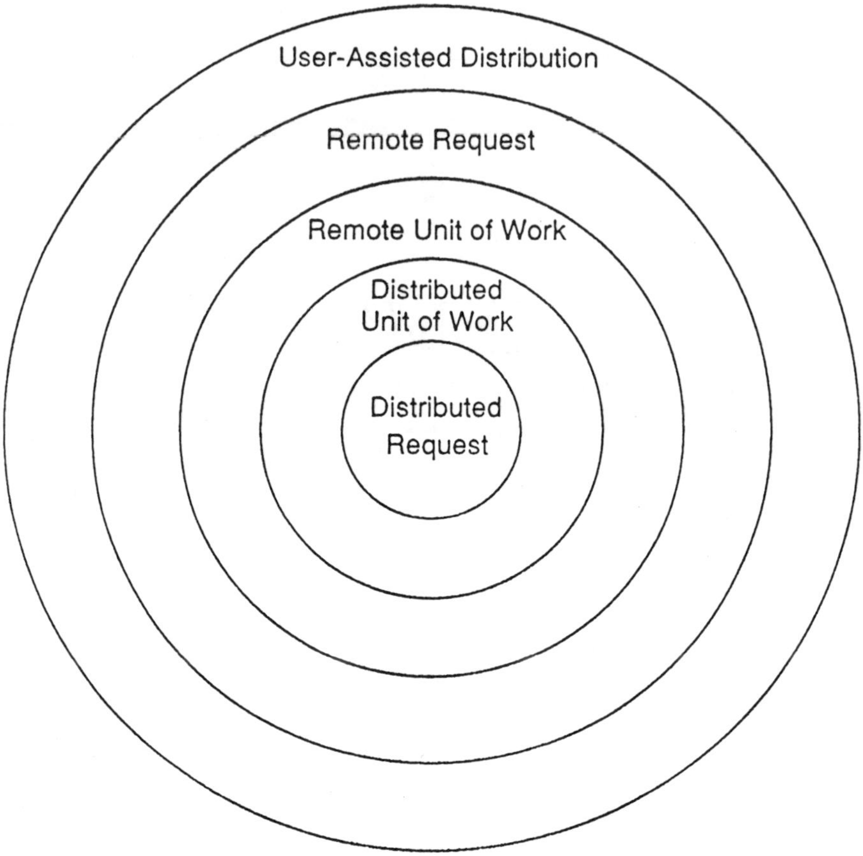

Fig. 5-1. Levels of distributed database management systems.

location Y, another remote site. The request is optimized, executed and committed, or rolled back, entirely at receiving-site Y. In some instances, the location X may not have a DBMS installed, and site Y may have a relational DBMS supporting SQL. Each SQL statement is independent. The application at site X can send another request to site Y, regardless of whether the first transaction was successful or not.

Only a single remote location can be specified in each SQL statement. In this context, "location" is a DBMS; one machine can have multiple DBMSs. Remote site doesn't necessarily mean physically remote.

IBM's Host database View (HDBV) and Enhanced Connectivity Facilities (ECF) provide remote request capabilities. HDBV provides the PC user with transparent access to the facilities of a VM or MVS system. HDBV may also be used to access host (or mainframe) data extracted by DXT. With ECF, a PC user can perform an SQL operation on host data. ECF enables implementation of the LU (logical unit) 6.2 protocol. From IBM's perspective, like or homoge-

- First Level of DDBMS
  - User-Assisted Distribution
    - ••User Intervention Possible
- Second Level of DDBMS
  - Remote Request
    - ••User interacts with an application running on the local machine to start the required operation on the remote machine
- Third Level of DDBMS
  - Remote Unit of Work
    - ••An application program executes on one system and uses the remote Application Program Interface (API) provided by another system. For DDBMS, any DBMS facilities available on local applications are available to applications running on remote systems.

Fig. 5-2. Various levels of DDBMS capabilities.

- Fourth Level of DDBMS:
  - Distributed Unit of Work
    - ••DDBMS finds out which system manages the data to be read or changed by each request. DDBMS coordinates updates at several locations in a single transaction.
- Fifth Level of DDBMS:
  - Distributed Request
    - ••All data location restrictions are removed. Whatever would be possible with all data local is possible in a distributed environment. DDBMS appears like one single DBMS.

Fig. 5-3. Various levels of DDBMS capabilities (cont'd).

neous distributed database capability means, for example, the access of DB2 database records from another DB2 database installation, or the access of SQL/DS database records from another SQL/DS database installation.

Remote unit of work

Remote unit of work, the third level, allows an application at one site, X, to send all of the database requests in a "unit of work" to another site, Y. All processing for the unit of work is performed at site Y. However, site X decides whether the transaction is to be committed or rolled back.

Remote unit of work is an interface implemented on a local system that allows SQL requests to be submitted (at the remote system) to a host (mainframe) where a DBMS resides. A DBMS doesn't need to exist on the local system, and the user or application at the local site doesn't need to know where the data is located, or use special procedures to move the request and the results between systems. Results are returned to the user or application at the local site.

For example, a remote unit of work on a personal computer might allow SQL requests to be made at the personal computer and executed on an MVS host (mainframe) running DB2. The results would be returned to the personal computer.

Distributed unit of work

With distributed unit of work (distributed transaction) level four, an application at site X can send some or all of the database requests in a transaction to one or more remote sites for execution. Each individual request is executed entirely at one site. However, different requests can be executed at different sites. Site X determines whether the transaction should be committed or rolled back. Within a single transaction or unit of work, objects that are the operands of SQL statements are allowed to span multiple sites. However, all operands of a single SQL statement are constrained to exist at a single site.

Distributed request

Distributed request, the fifth level, includes the capabilities of distributed unit of work. The most difficult of the levels, it also allows individual database requests to span multiple sites. A request or an application could be split up, and different pieces could be sent to various sites for execution. A request at site X can ask for a join to be performed between a table at site Y and a table at site Z. A more detailed description of the five levels follows.

Five levels of DDBMS capabilities

The first level of a DDBMS is user-assisted distribution. In this first stage of distributed systems, the user is keenly aware of the distribution process. For each distribution activity, the user is involved twice. For this stage, the user is extracting the needed data from one of the systems. He or she then physically takes the data to the system that is to receive the information. The user then loads the extracted data onto the second system. This is not necessarily an elegant way of transferring data from one system to the other. However, if this is a relatively rare event, it can be completely adequate.

Across some organizational boundaries, this may be the best way to get the job done. In fact, this is exactly the process followed when we install software on our systems at my company. A vendor creates an unloaded version of some software. We buy it and load it into our system. At this level of DDBMS, a user is aware of the process and can intervene when necessary.

Whether files, programs or database data are being distributed at this stage, the general processing flow is the same. In the next degree of distributed processing, the user is a little more isolated from the actual process and has less opportunity to adjust the process to account for differences between environments.

Second level of DDBMS: remote request

In the world of remote requests, life is a bit easier for the end-user. Instead of interacting with two different systems at two different times to move data from one onto the other, the user interacts one time with one system. At this stage, communications technologies are used directly by the systems to accomplish a user's task.

Remote request lets a user read and update data at a remote computer, but it doesn't allow for multiple requests to be grouped as a single transaction. Remote request is best suited to ad-hoc queries of remote databases.

Here's what happens. Generally, the user establishes a connection between his or her system and the system that has the needed data. This connection may be established automatically, but it's more likely that the user will invoke a procedure to log on to the remote system and prepare it to receive requests from another system. The user does this once, regardless of the number of upload and download requests to be made.

When the user needs data, he or she interacts with an application running on the local machine to start the required operation. This high-level request, such as an extract query, can be edited immediately before execution. The application at the user's machine composes the message that represents the user's request. The application then sends the message to the other machine, along with any data required to satisfy the request. The application at the DBMS's system receives the request and begins the processing necessary to do the job.

For a database extract, the application on the remote system will perform dynamic SQL operations to read all the rows of the target table and buffer them up. When the whole answer set has been collected, the application closes the cursor. The cursor is used for establishing the position in the database while reading it. After the records are read, it terminates processing with the DBMS. Finally, the buffered answer and status are transmitted back to the user's system. The user's application will then put the answer where the user requested. IBM's Virtual SQL (VSQL) processor in ECF performs SQL operations against DBMSs using this level of distribution.

ECF is a set of programs for sharing resources between IBM PCs connected to IBM S/370 host (mainframe) computers within MVS or VM operating systems. The functions available to the user by the Requester/Server program include: host data access, virtual disk, virtual file, virtual print, and file transfer. *Virtual disk* means that a PC can use a disk of the mainframe for storage. *Virtual file* means that a PC can create and maintain a file on the mainframe. *Virtual print* means printing could be done on the mainframe by the PC.

The application on the user's system is called the VSQL requester (or client) and the application on the remote DBMS system is the VSQL server. In this environment, the DBMS is really unaware that distribution is happening. As long as the database resources are held, no communication takes place. This allows use of communications facilities that might not notify the DBMS when failures occur and thus jeopardize availability of the data managed by the DBMS. All failures that matter to the DBMS are local, and the operating system ensures that the DBMS is informed.

In this environment, SQL statements (in VSQL queries) are sent to the remote system where the user is connected. There is very little opportunity for a systems administrator to intervene in this process; therefore, it's important that the SQL statements behave consistently, regardless of the target system. The user knows which system contains the data needed. The user can also have duplicate (but slightly different) queries for each system to accommodate language differences, though this is not desirable from the user's point of view.

In all the cases discussed so far, the distributed data is a copy of an original. Both the original version and the copy have lives of their own, and will diverge over time as updates are made. When this situation reaches a certain limit, the next level of distributed database handling is required.

Third level of DDBMS: remote unit of work

With remote unit of work, an application program executes on one system and uses the remote API (application program interface) provided by another system. For distributed database environments, this means that any DBMS facilities available to local applications are also available to applications running on remote systems.

Remote unit of work allows several requests to be grouped as a single unit of work. However, the requests to each unit must be on a single machine. Transaction-oriented production applications are possible.

One example of remote unit of work is transferring funds from a savings account to a checking account, where the savings and checking account tables are on a different system than the user. The transaction requires more than one request, and it must ensure that all parts of the transaction are complete before any update is committed. Since all data is on a single system, the database server on that system must be able to handle the full unit of program logic for the data. The requester is responsible for transmitting individual data requests and telling the server when the update should be committed. During a failure, the server is responsible for handling the backout procedures.

With the SQL language, all requests that change the database are tentative until committed by the application program. While the application is executing, database resources, including data, are protected with locks. This prevents interference by other users. While update locks are held, no other program is allowed to either read or update the data. While read locks are held, other programs can read the data, but they are not allowed to update it.

An application running on a workstation can gain read locks over large quantities of data by executing simple queries. These locks can interfere with locks required by others, and they will not be released until the application has released them. The SQL application program controls boundaries of the active unit of work or transaction through the use of commit and rollback requests.

This is essentially sharing in real time, as it was before any distribution was introduced; local users and remote users share the data as if they were all local. Application programs must do their job and then release the locks, which identifies a key requirement at this level: timely and reliable failure notifications.

Users have all encountered programs that don't execute properly. In particular, programs fail in a way that prevents them from doing a complete job, including releasing locks. For local applications, the operating systems provide notification of such application failures. The DBMS then rolls back the incomplete work and releases the locks held by the failed application.

In the distributed case, the operating system that sees the failure is remote to the DBMS. A mechanism for timely failure notification is a major new requirement as we approach remote API. IBM's SNA Advanced Program-to-Program Communication (APPC) and LU 6.2 provide a connection architecture that gives the timely notification required to allow remote applications to hold locks on database resources between requests without jeopardizing availability of the data for the rest of the users.

APPC is an SNA facility (based on PU 2.1 and LU 6.2) for general-purpose interprogram communications. APPC is a very significant enhancement, forming the foundation for IBM's future networking products. APPC is often used synonymously with LU 6.2 (LU 6.2 is the architecture, and APPC is the programming interface to it). IBM provides APPC applications for System/370, System/36, System/38, System/88, PC, RS/6000, AS/400, Display Writer, Scan Master, 3820 printer, etc.

From the SAA perspective, remote unit of work means that a program written, compiled and executed in one environment will be using an API provided by another system. (See FIG. 5-4.) Operating System/2 Extended Edition (OS/2EE) applications will access mainframe DB2 data using DB2's SQL API under the MVS operating system. As long as the application accesses only one DBMS at a time, it can adjust its logic to accommodate differences between DBMS environments. However, in a sophisticated environment, it's possible that the very same program may access local OS/2 data on its next execution, SQL/DS data on the one after that, and AS/400 data on the next. For this application to be successful, the APIs presented by all of these systems must

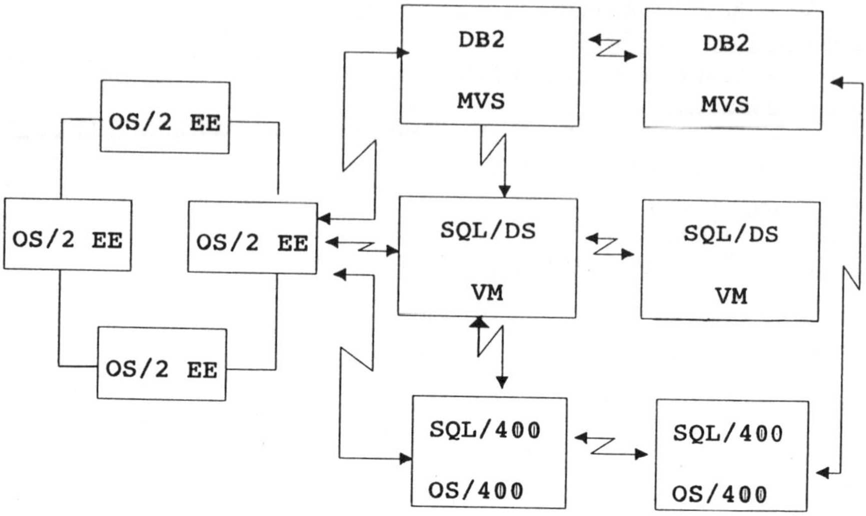

DRDA will be the basis for managing distributed data among VM SQL/DS systems and MVS DB2 systems, and then for OS/2 EE and OS/400 data base managers when distributed data base system support to multiple data base systems is available in those SAA environments.

Fig. 5-4. IBM's vision for its distributed database for like and unlike environments.

be the same. SAA SQL, as the database element of the Common Programming Interface (CPI), should provide a common API whenever IBM's SAA applications are available for these environments.

SAA, Systems Application Architecture, is designed by IBM to provide consistent interfaces across the products that conform to it. Although it was originally promoted by IBM as a way of achieving software portability, the real function of SAA is to provide an infrastructure for distributed and cooperative processing. The four pillars of SAA are: CPI (Common Programming Interface), CUA (Common User Access), Common Application, and CPI-C (Common Programming Interface: Communications).

SAA is a set of software interfaces, conventions and protocols. It serves as the framework for developing consistent applications across the future offerings of the three major IBM computing environments: S/390, AS/400 and PS/2.

As long as the data remains in one location and not too many locations are involved in any given set of processing, remote-unit-of-work processing is probably enough. However, if data starts moving on a regular basis or coordinated updates are required at more than one location, the next level of a distributed database is required.

Fourth level of DDBMS: distributed unit of work

Distributed unit of work, also called distributed transaction processing, provides two key extensions over remote unit of work. First, the DDBMS knows or finds out which system manages the data to be read or changed by each request. Second, the DDBMS coordinates updates at several locations in a single transaction. Within the scope of one transaction or unit of work, coordinated updates can be made to the database on the mainframe and to the database on a workstation.

Distributed unit of work eliminates the single-site requirements of remote unit of work. Requests in a single unit of work may span several machines, yet still be committed or recovered as a single unit. However, the tables requested in the query have to be resident at one and the same site.

One of the application areas where this is especially useful is data gathering from workstations into host systems, such as budget consolidations. Records can be moved from the workstation to the host without fear of loss or duplication.

Related updates at multiple locations can also be performed as part of a single transaction. As an example, consider removing an item from inventory at one warehouse's DBMS, showing the item in-transit at another's, and adjusting the financial records for both warehouses at a central accounting location as three related requests. As demanded by the semantics of transactions, no partial updates are allowed; either all of the related changes will be committed into the database(s), or none of them will.

From an architectural perspective, two-phase commit processing is required over the network of participating DBMS locations. Each must have a say in whether commitment of the transaction is possible or whether the operations must be rolled back. IBM's SNA LU 6.2 provides the architecture to allow this to occur.

From a practical perspective, the various warehouse and accounting systems may have been in existence prior to the introduction of the transaction in order to perform the coordinated update. In this case, aggregation of previously separate functions into a single, integrated function needs to be performed.

Another case involves a centralized system that has outgrown its machine, or one that is being decentralized to allow more local control at the remote locations. In this case, the old transaction programs that worked against local databases continue to operate, even though the data has been distributed from its original location.

In both of these cases, it's very important that the SQL language be the same in all of these systems. If the statements cease to execute when the data moves, or worse yet, they execute but produce different answers, the application programmer must constantly test and adjust the programs to accommodate changes in the environment. This is likely to become too expensive or impossible to manage.

With SAA SQL as a language, and the IBM relational DBMS products providing compiled and dynamic SQL, an operation called *binding* is performed. Binding is the process of linking an application program to its external schema or data description. *Binding time* is the instant in time when the data description is "assigned to" or "bound to" the code. The data description was previously separated (i.e., defined independently). Binding time has a direct effect on the level of control because, once data descriptions are bound to a program, the program is no longer dependent on the DD/DS for its metadata. Thus, the longer the binding time can be delayed, the greater the level of control for the DD/DS. The longer the delay, the bigger the flexibility in changing the contents of the data; but, at the same time, the worsening of the response time.

The DBMS examines the statements in the application, determines the location of all data accessed by the application, ensures that each location involved computes the optimum access algorithm to perform the operations required at that location, and prepares to coordinate execution of the transaction when requested. The whole process is automatic, and the user is unaware of the distribution that happens to satisfy the requests. Applications don't need to know the true location of data or how data is supported by performance improvements with the help of indexes. At this level of distributed support, the application must be sure only that the data referenced by any single statement resides at one location and doesn't have to be put together from several locations.

Some application statements may fail when data is moved from one location to another because the single-site-per-statement restriction is not honored. If this is a rare event, the application can be adjusted to avoid the problem, or selected data can be duplicated. However, if it occurs frequently, or the application can't be made flexible enough at reasonable expense, the next level of distributed database processing is required.

Fifth level of DDBMS: distributed request

In the distributed request environment, all data location restrictions are removed. Within a single SQL statement, relational data from many locations can be combined to produce the desired result. Whatever would be possible with all data stored locally is now possible in a distributed environment as well. The distributed database looks like one very large, single database.

However, the user still must consider the reality of the situation; there is no magic. If it would have taken a long time to perform the operation locally, it's still likely to take a long time in a distributed environment.

But, there are some possibilities for improved performance. For example, if local data at a workstation is stored remotely on a mainframe, the results can come back to the application faster; there is more CPU power available, faster DASD, etc. However, there are also possibilities for slower response. When communication channels are introduced between processing steps, delays are possible. Depending on the bandwidth of the channel being used and the amount of data that must flow, this may or may not be significant for the whole job.

Consider the following extreme example:

SELECT COUNT(•) FROM A,B where Col_from_A = Col_from_B.

The answer in this case will be only a few characters, regardless of the size of tables A and B. The SQL statement itself is under 60 characters. Neither of these sizes will significantly affect the time it takes to get an answer. However, if tables A and B are on different systems, the bandwidth of the path between them is crucial. If one of the systems is slower than the other, this could negatively affect the time required.

As they compute the fastest method of producing the desired result and having it delivered to the requesting application, the SQL DBMS optimizers can take into account all the various machines' speeds on which data is stored. This represents a significant leap in DBMS technology.

Distributed request removes the restriction that all the tables in an SQL request must reside on one machine. Distributed request permits an application to make an SQL request involving multiple tables on multiple machines.

Obviously, this optimization would be impossible if each of the SQL DBMSs spoke a different dialect of SQL with different semantics and produced results different from the others. To produce a result the user can trust, each of the DBMSs must be directly substitutable for the others in the sequence of operations required to produce the required answer. It can't matter which order the optimizer picks or how it divides the work between the DBMSs to get the job done.

There are four major protocols in the distributed database environment. The protocols include Distributed Relational Database Architecture (DRDA); a new level of Distributed Data Management (DDM) architecture; Formatted Data Object Content Architecture (FD:OCA); and Character Data Representation Architecture (CDRA).

DRDA umbrella

The DRDA umbrella is for distributed relational databases. It builds upon protocols in addition to LU 6.2 protocol. This applications services protocol allows a user to access distributed relational data wherever it resides on an interconnected network of host systems and programmable workstations that implement SAA. LU 6.2 is a session service that provides communication and transaction processing facilities needed for distributed relational data, including timely failure notification and propagation of security. SQL's power is extended to a network of systems from just a single system.

The Common Programming Interface (CPI) emphasizes portability from one system to another. These systems may or may not be interconnected. In most instances they will not be interconnected. Whereas the distributed database environment emphasizes interoperability and interoperability implies interconnection, DRDA prescribes commands, data descriptors, data, objects, communications, and statements.

Distributed Data Management (DDM)

DDM is an applications service that defines communications interfaces and manages routing of requests, replies and data. DDM includes a standardized relational database model and an SQL application manager. DDM has been around since the original definition of SAA.

PCs or PS/2s, System 36/38s, and AS/400s function by using LU 6.2 and APPC facilities (with CICS) to network processes on one machine with data on another. Thus, a PC user gets transparent access to data on another machine running the DDM software. But, commit and recovery facilities are not adequate. The DDM product is part of a wider initiative to enable the exchange of data between disparate machines. It's the base architecture for IBM's distributed database. DDM is an SAA product, but the relationship between DDM and SQL (which is meant to be the only SAA data access mechanism) is unclear. DDM is IBM's strategic architecture for distributed transparent file access across dissimilar file systems.

DDM lets systems work using LU 6.2 and APPC facilities to network processes on one machine with data on another. It defines communications facilities interfaces and manages the routing of requests, replies and data. For example, a COBOL application on one machine could read and write files on another machine. The "read" request is bundled on the request side of DDM on one machine and shipped to the server side of DDM on the other. Besides possible performance degradation, this shouldn't make any difference as far as a programmer is concerned.

The new level (Level 3) of DDM is extended to include a standardized relational database model and an SQL application manager. This is a high-level interface. The programmer doesn't have to program at the LU 6.2 level, which is a low level. Instead, the programmer can access data without writing LU 6.2-level code. A higher-level protocol is easier to use and program.

FD:OCA

FD:OCA (Formatted Data Object Content Architecture) provides users with a consistent way to describe and exchange field-formatted data. Data and its description can be packaged so that it can be understood by the SAA DRDA database manager. The description is intended to be attached to and transmitted with the data. This way, the receiver can interpret the data correctly.

This is critical because it's the method of passing data to the client from the server. FD:OCA is an extension to Information Interchange Architecture (IIA), which provides a consistent way to describe and exchange field-formatted data.

CDRA

CDRA (Character Data Representation Architecture) is supposed to ensure that all characters and symbols have the same representation across any pair of SAA DBMSs. With CDRA, IBM seems to be coming up with a reconciliation between two standards—ASCII (American Standard Code for Information Interchange) and EBCDIC (Extended Binary Coded Decimal Interchange Code). ASCII is used on most of the microcomputers, and EBCDIC is used on IBM's mainframes. Any time a user needs to take data from one database to another, if the databases are on two different platforms, a translation is necessary. ASCII must be converted to EBCDIC when uploading to an IBM host, and vice versa.

CDRA defines a method for data identification, providing an unambiguous interpretation of coded graphic characters for data that originates in SAA environments. IBM has added one more layer in between for easier interpretation by the system. Graphics is included in the character representation to make it into a more complete set.

With all of these efforts, it's obvious that IBM is very serious about implementing distributed database environments on the hardware platforms of the mainframes, midrange machines, workstations, and PCs.

Part II

Cooperative processing

6

Cooperative processing explained

Despite the widespread existence of microcomputers, or PCs, the majority of data handled by corporations, governments, and educational institutions still resides on bigger machines. But more and more of this data is being moved to microcomputers for faster decision making. The task of moving data from mainframes to microcomputers varies in complexity, depending on the software at either end and the format of the mainframe data.

In many cases, PC users have no control over the layout of the mainframe reports—it's up to users to accept the data as the mainframe generates it and somehow massage this into a format their PC application can use.

In a cooperative processing environment, portions of an application run on different computers, and data may be at various installations. One of the architectures used to implement cooperative processing is client/server architecture. In client/server architecture, user applications run on one or more client computers and work cooperatively with specialized applications running on one or more server nodes.

Cooperative processing is an architecture where two or more computers share the processing of a program. It's the ability to distribute resources, e.g., programs, files and databases, across the network. Cooperative processing should allow transparent access across any system so that users don't have to know if the resource is local or remote.

Some benefits of cooperative processing are:

- What the user sees on the screen is the system, as far as the user is concerned.

- By using a "friendlier" interface such as Windows, Open Look, New Wave, Motif or Presentation Manager, the microcomputer or workstation user can learn to use the application easily, and has a better chance of making fewer errors.
- Cooperative processing can reduce the amount of processing performed on the host or on the server computer.
- Work is distributed among servers and clients. Servers are usually "bigger" machines and clients are usually "smaller" machines.
- Per-unit cost of work done on a server is usually higher than on a client. This usually results in savings.

Various faces of cooperative processing

There are a number of ways to share a program between two or more computers. These include front-end processing, peer-to-peer processing, remote procedure call, and client/server architecture.

Front-end processing

A PC program can be written to run an existing host application without changing any code on the host application. This is done by writing PC code that issues calls to a PC-resident application program interface (API). The most commonly used API for 3270-based communications is the IBM High-Level Language API (HLLAPI).

In front-end processing, the host application runs as before, sending screen images to what it believes to be a dumb terminal. The PC program reads the host screen images by issuing calls to the API. The PC program then maps into its own fields the data from the 3270 map's fields. The PC program is then used to support the user interface and edit the data that is input by the user. When the user has completed working with the record, the PC program moves the data from the PC fields back into the 3270 fields and then asks the 3270 emulation program to send the map back to the mainframe.

Peer-to-peer processing

In a peer-to-peer processing application, two processors typically share the load of executing a program. Most of the time, one of the processors handles the task of presenting the interface to the user, while the other processor handles a more processing-intensive or I/O-intensive task, such as database maintenance. Peer-to-peer processing is also used to off-load a computationally intensive task to a processor that is optimized for such work, perhaps with a vector processing facility, parallel processing architecture, or a math coprocessor.

Depending on the environment and the nature of the peers, peer-to-peer processing is referred to as LU 6.2/APPC, remote procedure call (RPC), or client/server architecture.

LU 6.2/APPC

In commercial applications, many computers executing peer-to-peer processing applications communicate with each other using IBM's SNA Logical Unit 6.2 and APPC or CPI-C (Common Programming Interface: Communications). In this case, LU 6.2 is the low-level communications protocol, while APPC and CPI-C are the APIs.

Advanced Program-to-Program Communications is an SNA facility (based on PU (Physical Unit) 2.1 and LU 6.2) for general-purpose interprogram communications. It's a very significant enhancement, forming the foundation for IBM's future networking products. It's often used synonymously with LU 6.2 (LU 6.2 is the architecture, and APPC is the programming to interface to it). IBM provides APPC applications for System/370, System/36, System/38, System/88, PC, RS/6000, AS/400, Display Writer, Scan Master, 3820 printer, etc.

CPI-C (Common Programming Interface: Communications) is a super set of IBM communications verbs containing bits of APPC/VM and SRPI (Server Requester Protocol and Interface). It provides a high-level interface to APPC, and consists of calls available in SAA high-level languages and other SAA subsystems. CPI-C comes in two versions—a "starter-set" and "advanced function!" It's available on VM, CICS, IMS, TSO and OS/2. It has become an industry standard.

In IBM's SAA, APPC has been supplanted with CPI-C. CPI-C itself is functionally similar to APPC, but it's not syntactically identical. So applications written under APPC today will have to be rewritten when they eventually migrate to CPI-C.

Remote Procedure Call (RPC)

In the Unix and TCP/IP network worlds, RPC is used to implement peer-to-peer processing.

TCP/IP stands for Transmission Control Protocol/Internet Protocol. It's a set of protocols for network and transport layers of a packet-switched data network. It was developed in the U.S. for the Department of Defense Darpanet system, and it has become a *de facto* standard used by many vendors, particularly on top of Ethernet. TCP/IP is a protocol to keep an eye on if a mixed system is planned for implementation (especially if it involves Unix). TCP/IP is not a part of SAA, although IBM has stated that it plans to enhance CPI-C to include a TCP/IP interface.

TCP is the peer-to-peer protocol standard supported by the U.S. Department of Defense, and it is widely used in the minicomputer world. TCP provides session service and IP provides the datagram service.

RPC allows a program on one computer to call a subroutine that executes on another computer on the network. The code that is written for both the main program and the subroutine is exactly the same as it would be if the two pieces of code were on the same computer. The RPC tools provided by the network or operating system vendor take care of the communications work required to pass the procedure call to the computer that will execute the subroutine.

The primary difference between the RPC application and the more conventional peer-to-peer application is in synchronization. With conventional peer-to-peer applications, two programs run on separate computers. When one of these programs requires data or processing from the other computer, it opens a communication session and begins a conversation with the other program. At some point during the conversation, the program that initiated the link can go off and perform some other processing while the called program performs its assigned function. In effect, a peer-to-peer application implements a loosely coupled form of parallel processing.

With an RPC call, the processing of the calling program and the remote procedure don't overlap in this way. As it would if it were calling a local procedure, the calling program waits for the subroutine to execute. When it receives the data or the return code to indicate the results of the subroutine's work, the calling program continues processing.

Client/server architecture

In the PC LAN world, client/server architecture is most often used to describe how the current group of database servers operate. The database server programs split the data I/O task into two parts. The workstation program issues requests to the database server. A program on the server machine evaluates the request, retrieves the requested data, and transmits back to the workstation only the requested data.

While the term client/server architecture most often refers to this type of processing, there are some cases in which the task that runs on the server is not a database program. A more detailed treatment of client/server architecture is provided in Chapter 9. In a fully distributed database, the programmer or user will be able to use the tools of the database product on the local processor (PC or workstation) without knowing the physical location of any data. The database product will be able to find the requested data and retrieve it, or update it, even if it's stored on multiple dispersed processors connected over disparate network links. That capability is called *location independence*.

In addition to location independence, a viable distributed database should have no single point of failure. In other words, all data should be stored on more than one processor in case one of those computers breaks down. And the viability of each logical communications link between two nodes on a distributed database's network should not be subject to a malfunction in a single physical link. Logical communications links are established via common fields between the tables or relations. A logical link between the Patient and Surgery relations is Patient Number. There must be multiple communications paths so that, again, there is no single point of failure.

Cooperative processing, distributed databases and connectivity are all part of related capabilities belonging to the computing environment of today.

Much of the last few years' progress is dependent on the ubiquitous microcomputers. Microcomputers are positioned as a foundation for the distribution of processing load, providing less expensive computing power.

Systems with distributed database capabilities don't necessarily require cooperative processing as a prerequisite. However, cooperative processing requires some type of distributed database environment—or at least distributed access to data. A distributed database environment doesn't necessarily select computer types to optimize a specific type of processing. Most environments already have distributed data. Organizations would now really like to have distributed access to data. If an organization attempts to implement cooperative processing without providing access to data on the various platforms, the capabilities provided by cooperative processing will be limited. In cooperative processing we are distributing processing, whereas in distributed databases we are distributing data. But converting existing applications into cooperative processing will be very time consuming, because a major redesign will be mandatory.

Cooperative processing means developing the applications on an optimum platform and running them on optimum platforms as well (see FIG. 6-1). Cooperative processing is a subset of a distributed database and, in turn, a distributed database is a subset of connectivity and networking. It's necessary to have a distributed database or distributed access to data in order to implement cooperative processing. And to implement a distributed database, distributed access to data, and cooperative processing, networking has to be in place.

In an automated cooperative processing environment, the cooperative processing manager determines (see FIG. 6-2) on which platforms the specific application should run. Application Program Interface (API) is used to provide the same "look and feel" to the user. There may not be only three platforms to accomplish cooperative processing; there may be two platforms or four platforms or more.

In the distributed database environment (see FIG. 6-3) the application program is given to the distributed DBMS. The data dictionary's "intelligence" determines where the data is. Intelligence means having the information about where the data is stored, how to access it, who can use it, which applications use it, etc. The directory provides intelligence about accessing the data and applications. The cooperative manager determines on which platforms the specific application should run.

Cooperative processing is implemented among multiple levels of computers allowing a section of the applications to be directed for processing to the platform that is best suited financially, operationally, and organizationally. (See FIG. 6-4.) Cooperative processing refers to a type of multicomputer operation in which processing duties are assigned to specific types of computers because of the effective and efficient manner in which the processes can be performed on them. For example, editing of some input can be done on a microcomputer instead of having to send it to the mainframe. Financial reasons are the main incentive for people to downsize, and many companies will be downsizing

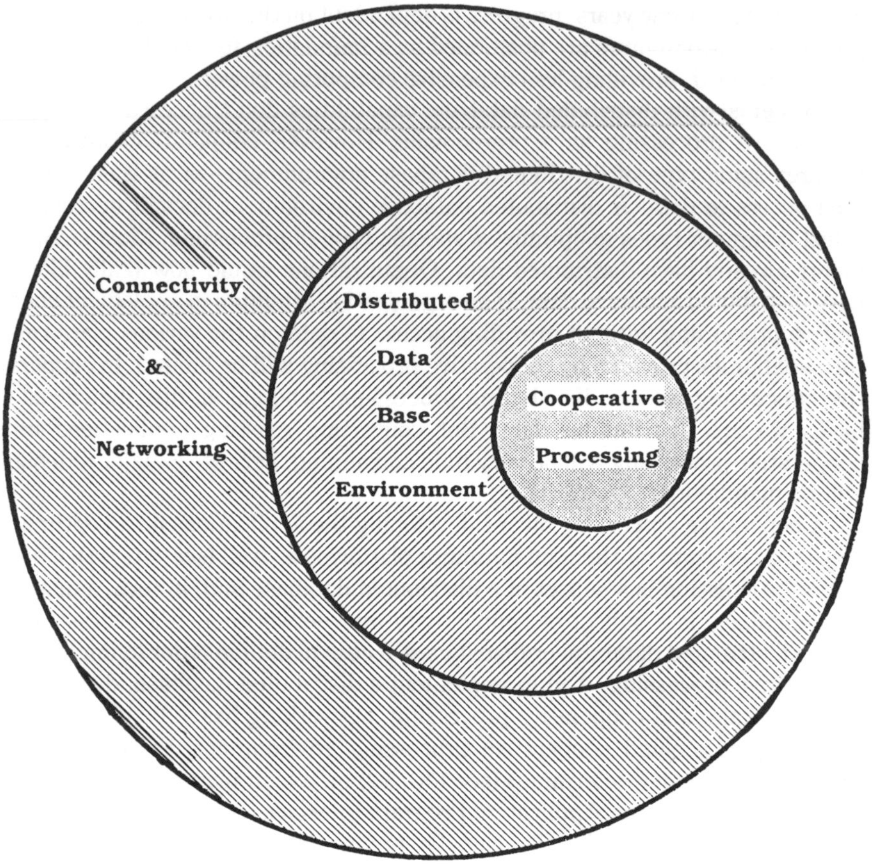

Fig. 6-1. Cooperative processing is a subset of a distributed database environment, which is a subset of connectivity and networking...in order to be effective in computing in the '90s.

application development. It would be ideal if maintenance could be downsized too. But, while the aim is to save money, the main obstacle to downsizing existing application systems is the expense of conversion.

Cooperative processing, on the other hand, does require a distributed database environment. Processing on "smaller" computers requires efficient access to local data for actual processing. In order for applications to be compiled, tested and run on "smaller" computers, these applications need data.

In cooperative processing, a mainframe could be a "super" server (see FIG. 6-5) or a "switchbox." The mainframe is sometimes referred to as a "giant" file server because it can support "giant" databases. A giant file server could also consist of a set of clustered minicomputers. By combining a number of DEC VAX machines, a user can approximate IBM's top-of-the-line mainframe power. But, every time a new cluster is put together, some percent-

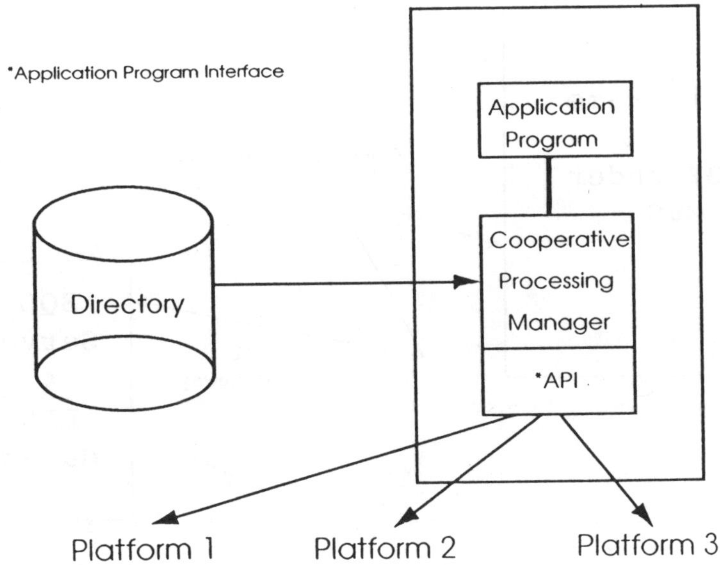

Fig. 6-2. Cooperative processing. (Xephon Technology Transfer, Ltd.)

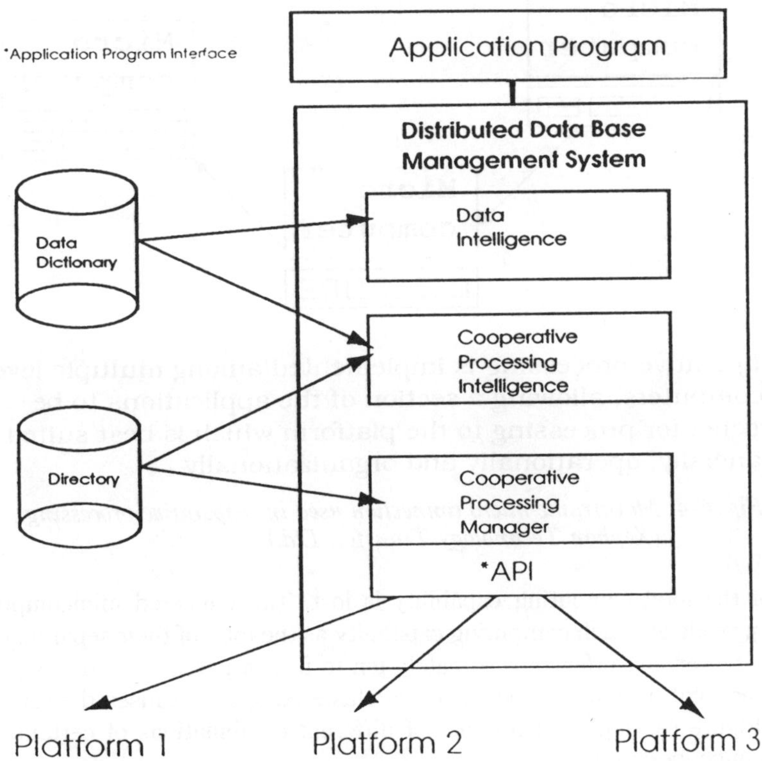

Fig. 6-3. Distributed database management. (Xephon Technology Transfer, Ltd.)

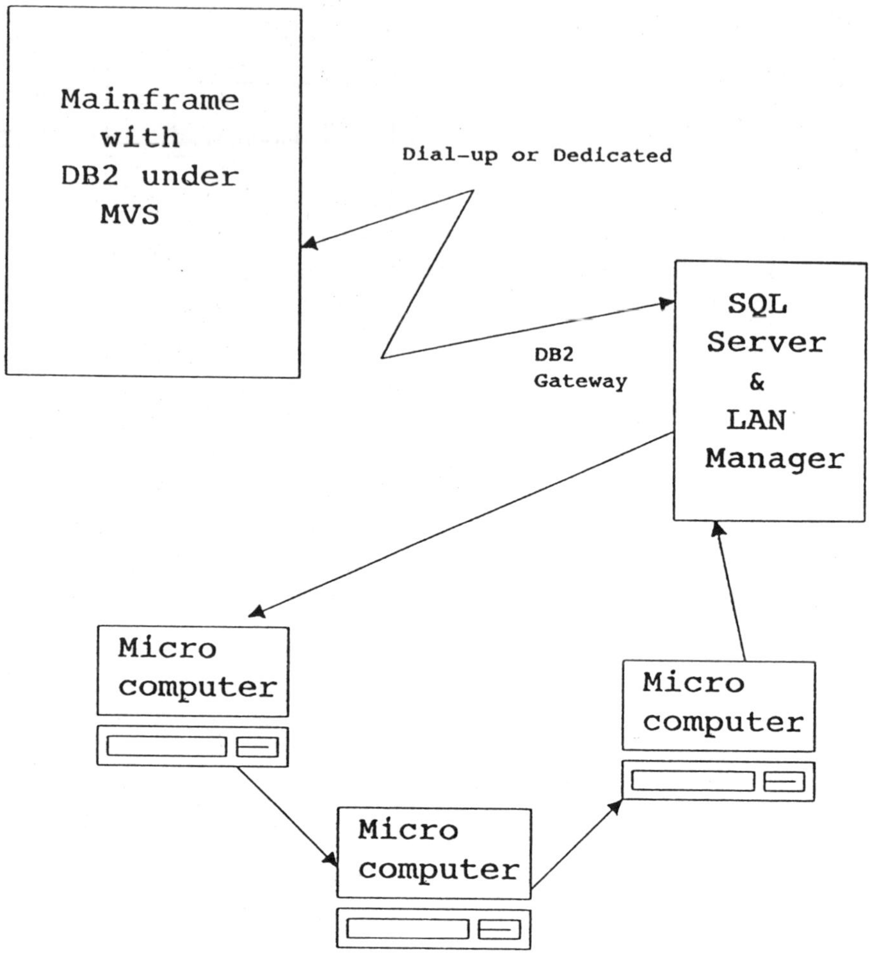

Cooperative processing is implemented among multiple levels of computers, allowing a section of the applications to be directed for processing to the platform which is best suited financially, operationally and organizationally.

Fig. 6-4. Mainframe-micro connection used in cooperative processing. (Xephon Technology Transfer, Ltd.)

age of the total computing capability is lost. Two clustered minicomputers don't provide as much computing capability as the total of their separate computing power, but offer approximately ten to fifteen percent or so less power than the total. Interaction between the clustered system causes the effective loss. Figure 6-6 depicts a number of different combinations of certain platforms in cooperation.

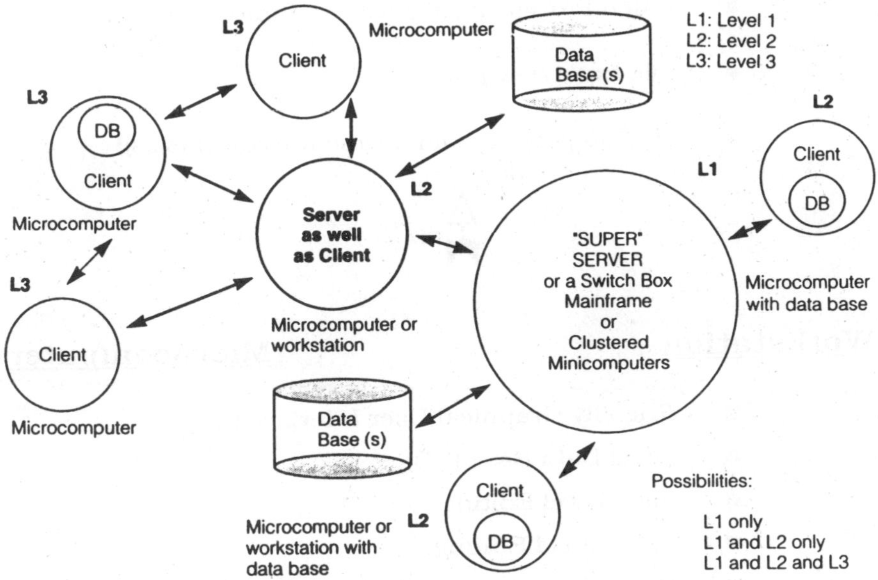

Fig. 6-5. Cooperative processing. (Xephon Technology Transfer, Ltd.)

- **Platform**

  Hardware, Systems Software (Operating System), Subsystems Software (eg. DBMS) and supporting tools (eg. Utilities) constitute a "**Platform**" on which stage Application Systems are "performed".

- **3 1/2 Platforms** (all combinations are feasible)

  - Level 1 Mainframe or Clustered Minicomputers
  - Level 2 Minicomputer or a "powerful" Workstation
  - Level 3 Workstation or a "powerful" Microcomputer
  - Level 3 1/2 Microcomputer

Fig. 6-6. Platforms.

Mainframe or clustered minicomputer roles

(See FIG. 6-7.) Batch processing operations, such as check printing, will still be performed on a mainframe or on clustered minicomputers if that is where checks were printed in the past. Some report printing will remain on the mainframe or on the clustered minicomputers, but not necessarily all. In the sixties,

- Batch Processing (e.g. Check Printing)
- File Input/Output
- Data Repository Management (Data Base(s))

Workstation or **Microcomputer**

- Friendly Graphical User Interface (GUI)
- Local Data Base (DB)
- Field Level Editing
- Cross Field Editing
- Help Screen Processing
- Error Processing
- Messaging
- Application Development & Unit Testing
- Application Component Processing
- OnLine Transaction Processing (OLTP)

Fig. 6-7. Mainframe or clustered minicomputers.

seventies and part of the eighties, most reports were printed on the mainframe because that was all that was available. Some "small" reports needed for "quick" decision making could be moved to the microcomputers. Large input/output files will probably stay on the mainframe or on clustered minicomputers. Such large volumes usually refer to gigabytes and terabytes of data. Data repository management with voluminous databases may also remain on the mainframe or on clustered minicomputers. The repository should have information about data location as well as access privileges. It should also have information needed by optimization algorithms and possibly the "intelligence" that we would like to have for network management.

IBM's cooperative processing strategy

Bring the power of the mainframe to the desktop; that seems to be cooperative processing in IBM's eyes. And it's not surprising. IBM would like customers to connect existing microcomputers to mainframes in order to fuel the sales of mainframes. Such interconnection will draw more mainframe power and, as such architectures and resulting applications grow, so too will the need for additional horsepower.

The mainframe-micro connection is not always as trivial as it appears on the surface. More hardware in the form of boards, more memory for the mainframe and microcomputers, more disk space at both ends, and communications software at both ends are necessary. Establishing and following guidelines for downloading data from mainframes to the microcomputers and uploading data from microcomputers to mainframes is not as easy as most of the vendors say.

Systems Application Architecture (SAA) is intended to nurture cooperative processing. Software products developed using the SAA communications protocols and interfaces should provide portability and interoperability of various hardware platforms. But these protocols and interfaces are IBM-proprietary. Parts of these protocols and interfaces are provided on an as-needed basis to the vendors that want to be SAA-compliant. SAA is supposed to provide portable software on heterogeneous hardware platforms. But when IBM says heterogeneous, they, in many instances, mean between IBM and IBM.

Heart of portability

One question that still needs answering is: how much portability provides real portability? Are the software products supplied by the SAA-compliant vendors portable so that it's easier for the vendors to port from one hardware to another? Or, will the applications written by the client organizations be portable? Are these SAA protocols and interfaces that the customers should be using in developing the in-house applications SAA-compliant? Can the SAA-compliant application software developed by an independent vendor be modified? Does SAA-compliancy also mean that the independent software vendors become IBM-dependent software vendors?

What about conversion? The already developed in-house application software base was written long before anyone even knew what SAA was or is. Besides, SAA is still evolving. Is IBM or another company going to provide some utilities to convert non-SAA-compliant applications into compliant applications? And, just as conversion utilities that convert "spaghetti" COBOL code into structured COBOL code don't take care of all possibilities, non-SAA to SAA-compliant utilities probably will leave small "details" nonconvertible. Besides, some applications that will be running only on one hardware and systems software platform should not be converted. Conversion still resembles "changing a tire on a moving car."

Everyone using IBM hardware should obtain SAA manuals and assign responsibility to an individual who is a practitioner and not a theoretician. That person should develop guidelines in the use of SAA protocols and interfaces for the soon-to-be-developed application base. Again, SAA's benefits are long-term benefits, as are those of CASE tools. A number of installations are disappointed in the use of CASE (Computer Aided Systems Engineering) tools because they expected instantaneously improved results. SAA is like CASE—a long-term strategy and not a "quick fix."

IBM's cooperative processing concept is embodied in its architecture aimed at support of the IBM environment. SAA is the blueprint for implementing a distributed environment in which programmable workstations (PS/2s) and a host (S/390 mainframe or AS/400) accomplish work through the coordinated or synchronized execution of functions. SAA is a collection of selected software interfaces, conventions and protocols that are thc framework for the development of consistent applications across the three major IBM

Cooperative processing in the IBM enviroment has certain definitive characteristics. They include:

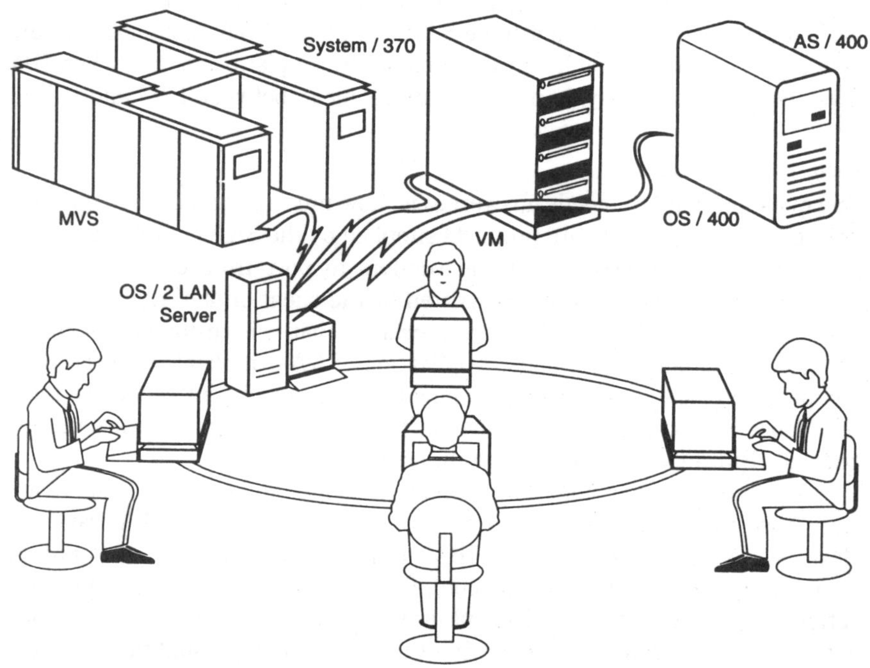

- A hardware platform of a host (AS/400 or mainframe) and PS/2.
- Offloading the presentation piece of the application from the host to the workstation.
- Increased networking requirements, such as 16MB Token Ring.
- Increased system memory, both on workstation and host.

Fig. 6-8. Cooperating with an IBM host. (Reprinted, with permission, from Datamation, *September 1, 1989. (c) 1989 by the Cahners Publishing Company, a division of Reed Publishing, U.S.A.)*

computing environments. IBM's S/390 machines and AS/400s are considered to be hosts (see FIGS. 6-8, 6-9, 6-10). The PS/2 is the workstation, with Presentation Manager providing a Graphical User Interface. IBM strongly recommends that the OS/2 operating system should be used on the PS/2.

IBM has realized that they have to join forces with other hardware and software vendors in order to remain competitive. As a result, IBM is entering

Some of the characteristics of the fledging client-server architectures for cooperative processing that use midrange systems today can include:

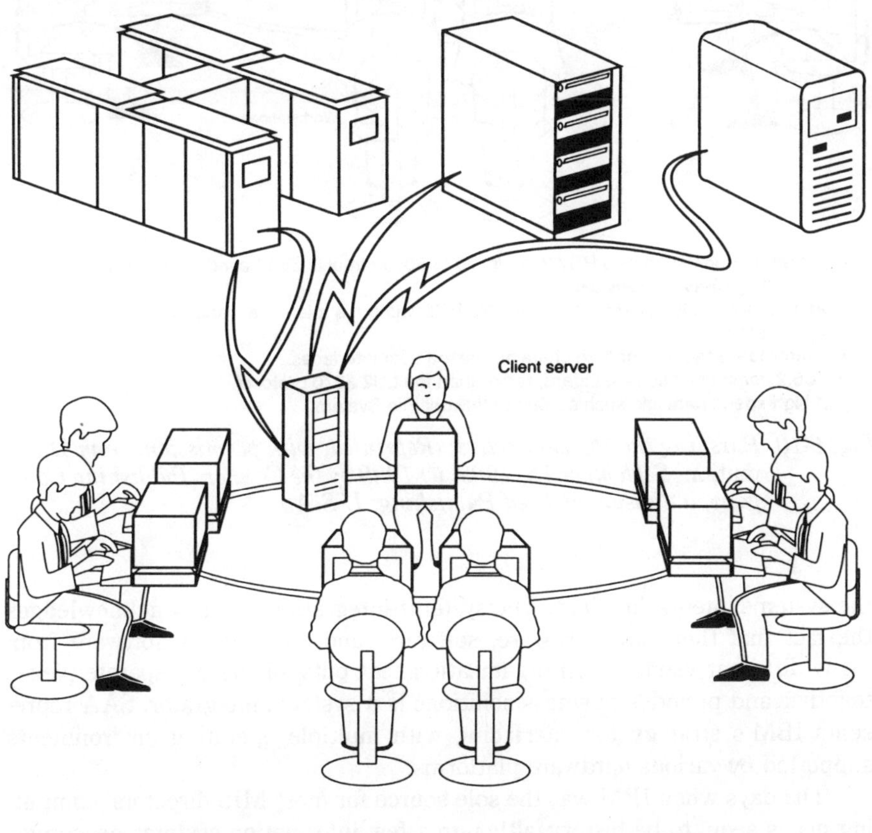

- The critically important business applications continuing to reside on the host and only user applications farmed out to the desktop.
- Migration tools that often are costly or dont make effective use of PC resources.
- The PC not recognized as a node on the network, to keep the complexity of managing the network to a minimum.

Fig. 6-9. A cooperative midrange. (Reprinted, with permission, from Datamation, *October 1, 1989. (c) 1989 by the Cahners Publishing Company, a division of Reed Publishing U.S.A.)*

The purist PC and workstation user believes certain technical attributes must characterize cooperative processing. These can include:

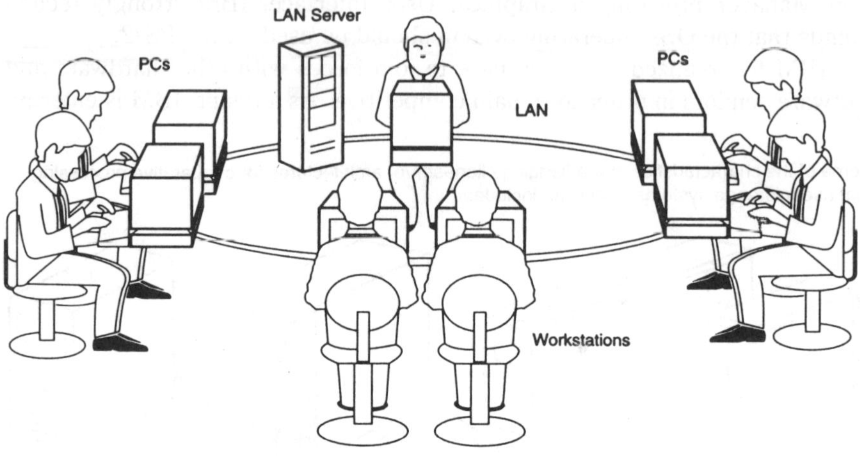

- A high-end-unit-such as a PS / 2 model 70 or 80, an Intel 80386-based PC or workstation (Sun, Apollo)-as the LAN server.
- An application distributed across multiple PCs, without a role necessarily being played by a central host.
- Graphical-based, rather than character-based user interfaces.
- LU6.2 communications standard, rather than the LU2 3270 protocol.
- A high-speed network, such as Sun's Network File System.

Fig. 6-10. Pursuing the PC perspective. (Reprinted, with permission, from Datamation, *September 15, 1989. (c) 1989 by the Cahners Publishing Company, a division of Reed Publishing, U.S.A.)*

the systems integration field. The systems integration strategy acknowledges the fact that there are hardware, software, and applications software from many different vendors. An organization that puts all these disparate pieces together and provides business solutions is a systems integrator. SAA represents IBM's strategy for interfacing with multiple operating environments supported by various hardware platforms.

The days when IBM was the sole source for most MIS directors' computing needs seem to be history, although a few information systems executives will continue to buy only through the world's largest computer company.

With SAA, IBM is trying to provide systems integration on IBM hardware platforms, and maybe in the future with "Extended" SAA, IBM may plan to provide systems integration on IBM and non-IBM platforms. Information warehouse seems to be that approach. An organization should be able to write applications on any of the platforms supported by SAA and should be able to run the applications on any other platforms supported by SAA. SAA should ideally provide the capability to transfer an application from any platform to another platform as long as both platforms are supported under SAA.

SAA (see FIG. 6-11) has four major components: common programming interface, common user access, common communications support and systems environment, which means operating systems environment. Common applications are applications either from IBM or from a cooperative independent software vendor, called an IBM business partner. The common applications are expected to use the Common Programming Interface (CPI). In principle, if the same CPI is used, an application written on AS/400 should be transferable to an IBM 370 or 390 or even to a PS/2 with no changes other than a recompilation. The CPI could be used to develop applications that can be integrated with each other and transported to run in multiple SAA environments.

What should the user see? The user should see Common User Access (CUA). CUA is the screen layout and program function keys that provide the same look and feel, whether an application is running on AS/400 or on a 370 or 390 machine, or on PS/2. These are the three hardware platforms currently supported under the SAA umbrella. CUA could be used to achieve consistency in panel layout and user interaction techniques.

Common applications consist of vertical software and/or horizontal software. Vertical refers to a specific industry: manufacturing, medical, banking,

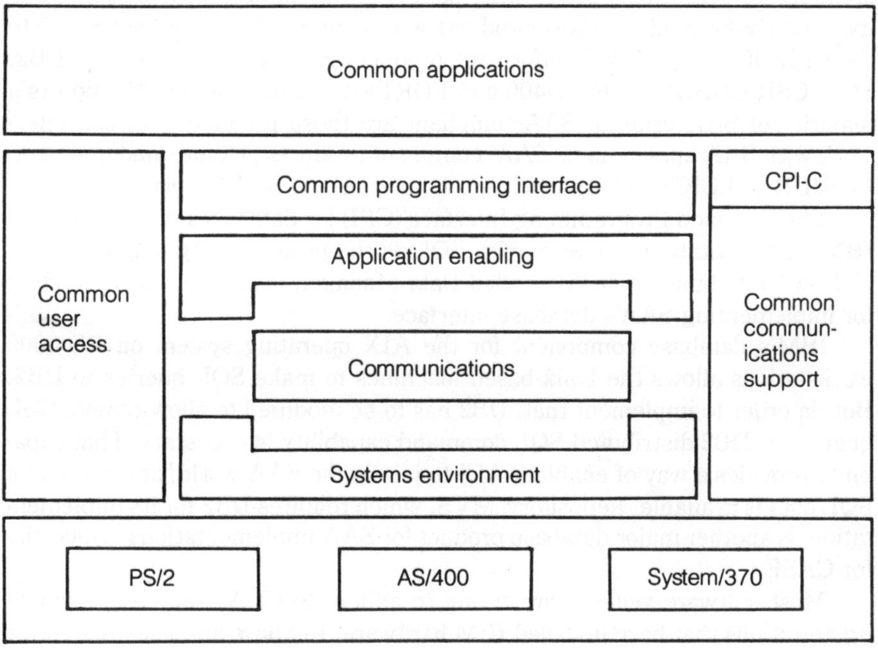

Fig. 6-11. Host environment.

and securities, to name a few. Some examples of vertical software are applications for medical claims processing and just-in-time manufacturing. Horizontal software could be used by multiple industries. Some examples of horizontal software are a DBMS, CASE (Computer Aided Systems Engineering) tools, spreadsheets and word processors. There are SAA languages and services defined for use by application developers working on in-house software projects.

The communications component, which is the connection to the outside world, is the Common Programming Interface for Communications (CPI-C). CPI-C could be used to connect applications, systems, networks and devices.

Dialog Manager is an important component of the database access language. Dialog Manager is a component of OS/2's Presentation Manager.

For communications services and the network application programming interface, there should be PC emulation of "dumb" terminals. There are four million 3270-type "dumb" terminals installed, and the systems supporting these terminals will remain in operation for some time. PC users should not be locked out of those mainstream applications, and they will require terminal emulation.

The various operating systems that are a part of SAA are: OS/2, OS/400, MVS, VM, with several versions available for the mainframe systems and a few others.

SAA has three levels, rating how completely a software product adheres to architecture definitions. SAA-conformant is at the highest level of SAA fidelity. SAA-conformant are those products whose internals are built according to SAA specifications. SAA-conformant products include, among others, DB2, SQL, CSP, COBOL, C, RPG/400 and FORTRAN. SAA-compliant supports a majority of SAA criteria. SAA-compliant are those products that can interwork with SAA applications. SAA- compliant products include, among others, IMS/DB and CICS. SAA-participant supports some SAA criteria.

The Common Programming Interface (CPI) for databases revolves around IBM's DB2 database software with SQL as the programming language. OS/2EE, with its bundled DBMS called Data Manager, is another major product for implementing SAA's database interface.

IBM's database component for the AIX operating system on RS/6000 workstations allows the Unix-based machines to make SQL queries to DB2. But, in order to implement that, DB2 has to be modified to allow remote SQL queries. A DB2 distributed SQL command capability is necessary. That capability provides a way of enabling AIX to join in the SAA world, at least where SQL data is available. Repository/MVS, which requires DB2 for its implementation, is another major database product for SAA implementations, especially for CASE.

Most software vendors are trying to adhere to CUA, and so too should organizations that have installed IBM hardware. In-house application systems should be written as if those systems are going to be marketed to the outside world. It would be advisable for organizations with IBM environments to study major SAA manuals. As mentioned before, one person should be delegated to develop one document out of all of these manuals as a companywide extract. New applications should be written using CUA, and CPI language should be supported.

Changing to a new or different programming language will be extremely difficult, if not impossible. A language is a very emotional issue. It's possible to convince newcomers to use a newly accepted language as the programming language of choice, because they are trying to look good in a new job and will not voice their reservations. "Old hands" will be reluctant to change.

CUA describes the way an application looks, feels, and behaves, and also defines a wide range of standards for workstation functions and for mainframe interactive terminals, which are referred to as "dumb" terminals. A user interface has to be defined for both Mainframe Interactive (MFI) terminals and for intelligent workstations. Intelligent workstations such as IBM's RS/6000 and PS/2, or single-user machines from Sun Microsystems and Hewlett-Packard/Apollo are widely used. A microcomputer also is an *intelligent workstation*. Any processor that can perform computing without assistance from another processor is an intelligent workstation.

There are some standard program function keys with Dialog Manager. The dialogs are supported with the help of action bars, menus, screen object definitions, a help facility and message handling. Recent college graduates and current college students are used to graphics-oriented systems. As they enter the business world, they will be the first ones to expect and use graphical front ends.

CPI defines how an application can access data management communications and systems control program services. CPI standardizes these means of access across all SAA-conformant development environments.

Advanced Program-to-Program Communication

In order to transfer data or various items from one application to another application under the same operating system or under multiple operating systems, Advanced Program-to-Program Communication (APPC) is needed. It's done with the help of the LU 6.2 protocol. APPC and LU 6.2 go together because tokens are transferred using LU 6.2 protocol. (Networking is covered in more detail in Chapter 8.)

IBM supports the Token Ring network with the LU 6.2 protocol. Tokens can be data or pieces of applications. IBM is beginning to use the terms "process" and "program" interchangeably in this key area. As a result, there is plenty of room left for confusion about what is allowed to communicate, or cooperate, at what level, among the various platforms.

What is APPC and how have we evolved to it? In order to receive the most benefits from cooperative processing, there should be communication between the programs written on various processors. Transfer of data between these hardware platforms is only one step toward true cooperation.

Cooperative processing

There are a number of ways that organizations are trying to implement cooperative processing. The first step is establishing physical connection between hardware platforms. Within the definition of cooperative processing, this means the physical connection between the mainframe or clustered minicomputers and the microcomputers. Although physical connection is a prerequisite to cooperative processing, the physical connection alone doesn't provide productivity gains—it's just the means to the goal. Thus, if you have only established a physical connection between a mainframe and a PC, you have not implemented cooperative processing yet.

Let's evaluate various ways of using the processing power of a mainframe and a PC working together. There are millions of 3270-type terminals installed. In most large organizations, "bread and butter" applications are run by these terminals. In the past decade, organizations have purchased PCs for end-user computing instead of 3270 terminals. Some of these PCs are connected to the mainframe in 3270 emulation mode. But access to host data from a 3270 screen is just a piece of the solution in an application problem. The 3270 only communicates with a mainframe, not with a LAN server or a midrange option. Terminal emulation is not a complete solution.

Another aspect of cooperative processing is providing the same "look and feel" of the application, regardless of which platform the application is executed on. That leads us to graphical user interfaces (GUIs).

Graphical user interfaces (GUIs)

On workstations or microcomputers, one of the major functions supported is going to be a friendly graphical user interface (GUI). Some of the field-level editing of local databases could be done on a microcomputer instead of sending it to the mainframe. The mainframe, with its faster speed, should be used for input and output, which is often the computing bottleneck.

Some other functions that could be performed by a microcomputer are (see FIG. 6-12): cross field editing between different fields, help screen processing providing "true" help to computer users, error processing with input messaging, application development, and unit testing.

There are software vendors now providing full-function COBOL compilers on microcomputers. In order to use a microcomputer as an application development machine, the power of an Intel 80386 microprocessor or equivalent is the minimum required. It should also have at least 4 Mbytes RAM and at least 100 Mbytes of hard disk capacity. In many large corporations this is standard equipment for a server. Depending on the server's functions and the number of clients served, much more capacity might be needed. Some application components could be developed in an online transaction processing mode to support client/server architecture. Client/server architecture will be explained in more depth in Chapter 9.

- **Action Bars**
- **Pull-down Menus**
- **Pop-Up Menus**
- **Messages & Prompts**
- **Dialog Boxes**
- **Forms**
- **Local File and Data Base Access**
- **Field-level Context-sensitive Help**
- **Optional Learning Mode**
- **Date Editing/Validation:**
    - **Date Type/Mask Checking**
    - **Range/Limit Checking**
    - **Date Formatting/Checking**
    - **Validation against Data Base Files**
    - **Required Fields**
    - **Zero out not Valid Fields**
- **Multiple Validation Points**
- **Dictionary and Form Documentation**
- **Panel/Form Painter**
- **Intelligent Editor (Language Sensitive)**
- **Integrated Compile/Link/Debug**

Fig. 6-12. Microcomputers' capabilities could reach this level of functionalities.

But cooperative processing is more of an organizational issue than a technological matter. In order for cooperative processing to be successful, "negotiating from above" is absolutely necessary. A number of users are reluctant to yield control over their personal computers by linking them to mainframes. They are apprehensive about losing their machines. Like car pooling, cooperative processing sounds very good in theory. There are many people who believe in car pooling, but very few people implement it. They just want to get into the car, turn on the ignition and go when they're ready. They don't want to wait for anybody. The same feeling is evident in the implementation of cooperative processing.

No one likes to have different screens presented to them when they switch from a terminal or a PC platform. The integration of the GUI and the host is usually through High-Level Language Application Programming Interface (HLLAPI) to an existing application program. With HLLAPI, the host sends the screen to the PC HLLAPI program, thinking it's talking to a display. The PC captures the screen with a 3270 emulator and passes it to a program written to imitate a terminal. Data is searched, manipulated and presented to the user with graphics, color and other GUI features. The user doesn't have to worry about the "bare bones" 3270 screens. The host is treating the HLLAPI application like a 3270 terminal. As a result of the additional manipulation of data, performance suffers. If the PC should function only as a PC and run programs written for a PC, all it needs is data. Data could be transferred between a host and a PC with the help of file transfer software.

File transfer

A file transfer program can be used to place application data on a PC. This doesn't necessarily increase application programmer productivity. The application programmer will be spending more time in managing the file transfer, converting formats and managing disk space. As a result, file transfer is not truly a cooperative processing environment. An advanced form of file transfer is providing distributed data access.

A relational database could be used instead of a file. The user's application can access local or remote relational databases transparently with the Distributed Data Access (DDA) product. But two major restrictions require that the entire application, run on the PC and the remote database, should be relational. Besides, sharing data is only one aspect of cooperative processing.

In true cooperative processing, both implementation data and applications need to be shared. An application program should share processing with another program. This is essentially a client/server model. The client is the program that initiates the request and the server is the program that services it. The model is often applied to PCs as clients and larger PC systems as servers. But any machine can be a client or a server. A client is a program, but servers can be customer-written programs, database managers or LAN managers that provide file and printer sharing.

There are different communication protocols supporting a client/server connection. One of them is IBM's APPC. APPC provides a set of rules and programming commands for peer-to-peer communication. Initiating a convention by a client with a server starts peer-to-peer acceptance. Because an application program knows that its partner is also an application program, information applied directly to the program logic can be sent back and forth.

Cooperative processing with APPC doesn't create a one-partner limit. A program can request processing from multiple servers simultaneously, regardless of their locations. Thus, the user sees a seamless transaction, one screen that executes more than one program at more than one location.

The disadvantage of APPC is that it gives peer-to-peer connections; whatever is coded at a PC program must have the mirror connection coded at the other end. This means development and testing must be coordinated with mainframe systems personnel. Common communications support defines the services that allow one platform to talk to another (the essence of cooperation).

Advanced Peer-to-Peer Networking (APPN) support is another major component of SAA that is important. APPN will determine how an application is going to react when the network topology changes, or there is a link failure, or traffic balancing tries to reroute the APPC request that is going to a compliant application on a specified node.

This is essentially the bridge between SAA and SNA (plus network management, presumably using NetView). Until the announcement of CPI-C, it was difficult to see how this component fit in with the rest of SAA. Now it's a little clearer, but there are bound to be more announcements in the communications area, particularly around application access to NetView services. This area remains critical. IBM has expressed intentions to begin implementing OSI network management standards.

The CPI, CPI-C and APIs, as an overall approach to application design standards, form an attractive idea, but one that assumes that designers exist who can bring together PC design techniques for non-PC-based application components. Designers in these two groups tend to have radically different views of the world and have often had problems converting from one to the other environment. To fully exploit the CPI in cooperative processing applications, we will need to develop a new breed of designer who is equally at home in both environments and who understands the requirements of efficient cooperative design. The moral is that in order to implement cooperative processing successfully, new skills have to be learned.

Digital Equipment Corporation's portability strategy is twofold. First, DEC's operating system VMS is portable from the smallest of DEC's machines, such as the Microvax, to the top of the VAX family. Another aspect is reflected in the architecture called Network Application Support (NAS). VMS and NAS make application porting easy.

There also remains the problem of how to design a cooperative application that needs, for whatever reason, to include a non-CPI compliant component. This currently includes IMS databases. This requirement is not going to go away soon, given the current investment in applications with such noncompliant components.

Cooperative processing strategies

How will mainframe programmers be convinced that future development will be done on microcomputers? Mainframe programmers who are used to IBM's JES2, JES3, and all other complex, intricate environments don't think of microcomputers as serious application development platforms. In order to convince them that microcomputers will be the major platform for their energies, the following steps could be helpful:

- Start a prototype. Application programmers, like anyone else, are apprehensive about change. A prototype environment will not threaten them.
- Install industrial-strength tools. Many first-time PC application developers choose the simplest tools because they don't require expensive hardware. But, if these tools don't provide functions and performance as the mainframe programmers expect, the mainframe programmers will not use these tools.
- Consider COBOL tools on the PC. Many companies are using PC-based COBOL products with a mainframe counterpart to make the transition to the PC. If your company has a sizable installed base of COBOL programs, COBOL tools can protect your investment and foster support among "older" programmers.
- Focus on debugging issues. Debugging on the mainframe takes days. PC debugging can be done on-site in just hours. Concentrate on projects that take advantage of PC debugging software.

Mainframe programmers can often get rid of their anxiety by test-driving PCs. Install an electronic mail program on a PC LAN, and let the programmers use it for messaging. Such experiences can familiarize them enough to accept the PC as a legitimate computer product.

7

Cooperative processing: downsizing

When people refer to cooperative processing, they're really speaking of downsizing, and vice versa. *Downsizing* is when much smaller computers replace one or more bigger computers. These smaller computers are mostly microcomputers. Quite obviously, one mainframe can't be replaced by one microcomputer. A number of microcomputers are necessary to replace one main frame. And, it's not sufficient to only have standalone microcomputers. One microcomputer could still play the role of a single user workstation. But, since in most organizations a number of people work in teams for developing application systems, it's necessary to network these microcomputers to reflect group dynamics. Networking of these microcomputers, and the computing environment as a result of networking, is implemented via a local area network (LAN). (Networking is covered in detail in Chapter 8.)

In any group of things, there are some "stronger" things and some "not so strong" things. Microcomputers and their networks are no exception. There are "stronger" microcomputers with faster speed, with more memory, and with more disk capacity, and there are other less powerful microcomputers. The stronger ones are capable of "serving" the weaker ones. Weaker ones can perform some tasks, but for some other tasks they have to request help from the stronger ones. As a result, the stronger ones are rightfully called *servers* and the weaker ones are called *clients*. This type of computing, where some tasks are done by clients and some tasks are done by servers, is quite naturally called *client/server computing*. (Client/server architecture is covered in detail in Chapter 9.)

Many organizations have made major investments in mainframes, minicomputers and surrounding peripherals. They have also invested a substantial amount of money in developing and maintaining applications. These corporations are not going to discard all of this investment overnight, even if buying processing power today in the form of microcomputers is much cheaper than minicomputers, let alone mainframes. Organizations will keep on running existing applications on the installed computer base, but they will try to develop new applications on microcomputers, either in standalone mode, when appropriate, or in a network, if necessary.

As a result of the last two or three decades of building applications and accumulating all types of data, "big" databases have been stored only on mainframe disks, clustered minicomputers or on standalone minicomputers. These databases typically have information about clients, orders submitted by these clients, their payment records, accounts owed by clients, credit records, parts that go into assembling bigger parts, warehousing, inventory, shipping, etc.

These databases are many times worth their weight in gold. That means the new type of computing, client/server computing, should be able to "stand on the shoulders" of work already done in building such giant databases. To support these databases, the role played by mainframes, clustered minicomputers, minicomputers and "high-end" microcomputers will frequently be as "database servers."

Another characteristic of today's computing environment is that not all of the processing is done at one central place. Before the advent of microcomputers, it was not possible to have a mainframe at every organizational location. Today, a courier mail company's truck driver can, upon receipt of a package, enter the data regarding the delivery just completed. The driver doesn't have to send pieces of forms to the central location for data entry. An insurance broker can get policy cost quotes right in front of a prospective customer. Downsizing with the help of PC LANs, and connecting these PC LANs with a wide area network (WAN), distributes processing power where the actual business transaction is taking place. PC LAN servers can handle critical database applications at headquarters and at plant sites, while users at standalone microcomputers can enter orders and policies directly via modem.

The overriding need is for the computerized systems capabilities that enable users to respond quickly and cost-effectively to the constantly changing business environment. The option of distributing the application load among various computing devices in the enterprise network can prove to be an effective tool for managing information technology investment and getting results at the locations where action is taking place.

If a number of items are shipped from a warehouse, it's advisable to update the inventory right then and there, instead of sending completed forms reflecting the change to the centralized computer. With this type of "quick" updating at the warehouse, the organization can keep track of "Just In Time" inventory.

Cooperative processing (see FIGS. 7-1 and 7-2) has been developed in stages. In many organizations, cooperative processing will be a prerequisite to downsizing because most of the "mission critical" computing was done on mainframe computers. If some of it should be moved to microcomputers, there

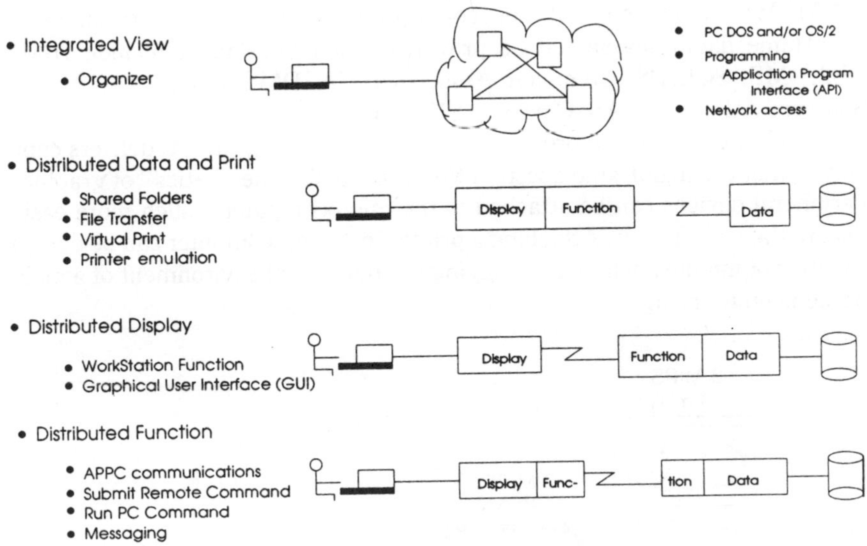

Fig. 7-1. Cooperative processing.

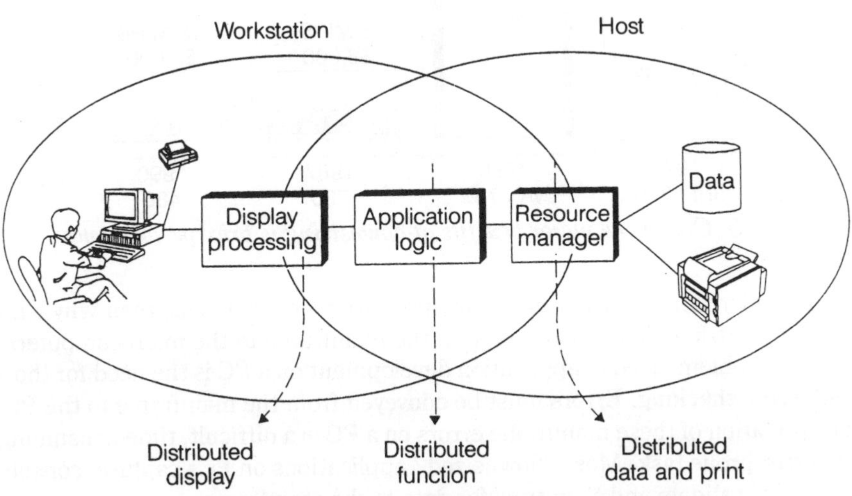

Fig. 7-2. Cooperative processing application model.

is a need for coexistence between the mainframes and microcomputers. First, there were only dumb terminals, then PC-to-mainframe terminal emulation, and then the ability for the mainframe and PCs to work as tandem processors. Now cooperative processing allows two processors to simultaneously execute the same application, each machine doing what it does best.

PC-to-mainframe cooperative processing is getting a lot of attention because it's a primary focus of IBM's Systems Application Architecture

(SAA). With a PC-to-mainframe connection, real-time access to all major mainframe databases should be provided. Such links must include IBM's DB2, IMS, SQL/DS; Computer Associates' CA-IDMS and CA-DATACOM, Software AG's ADABAS, Cincom's SUPRA and others.

In addition to cutting processing costs (see FIG. 7-3), the PC delivers capabilities that the mainframe doesn't offer, such as the "aesthetics" of graphics. Peripheral devices can be attached to the microcomputers much more easily than to the mainframes. Attaching a printer to a microcomputer can be done in a matter of minutes, whereas, changing the peripheral environment of a mainframe is quite trying.

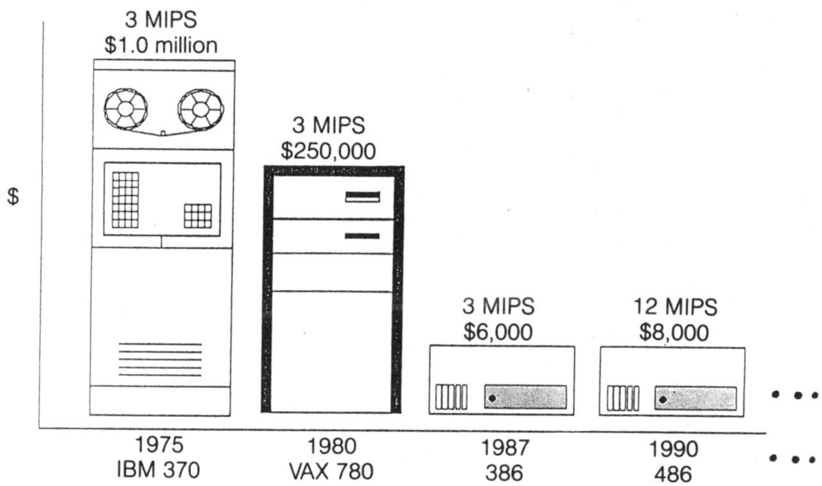

Fig. 7-3. One of the major benefits of downsizing is price performance.

If a microcomputer is a savior of application development, then why isn't everyone moving all applications from the mainframe to the microcomputers? One big problem faced in application development on a PC is the need for thorough error checking. Errors must be conveyed from the mainframe to the PC. Interpretation of these mainframe errors on a PC is a difficult, time-consuming and error-prone task. Most "downsized" applications on PCs capture, consolidate, edit, validate and then transfer data to the mainframe.

Downsizing is a relatively new technology that has generated more than its share of confusion. Everyone, users and vendors alike, agree on what downsizing is. But they don't agree on how to implement it.

Some vendors claim that their file-transfer products deliver downsizing, while others are convinced that software that automates communications does the job. But downsizing is more.

Downsizing typically involves offloading processing from a host to personal computers. There are a variety of reasons for doing this. First, PCs are more capable for some jobs, such as providing the user interface. Moving other tasks to the PC, such as data validation and editing, reduces the need for mainframe-to-terminal communications when a subset of the database from mainframe, periodically revised, is available on the PC hard drive.

The chief technologies for enabling downsizing in the IBM-compatible world are familiar: LU 6.2, peer-to-peer communications, and SAA. But these protocols don't themselves define downsizing. They establish conditions for downsizing to take place with IBM-compatible computers and software.

Communications standards

In downsizing, communications is an integral part of the application. Several processors work on parts of the application they are best at handling, some doing number-crunching, some presentation, some data moving and lookup, some high-speed parallel operations, and so forth. Each processor communicates with others at the highest level, the application level. In fact, communication in this environment is not itself considered an application, but instead, becomes a basic component of every application.

What is downsizing?

Downsizing is the process of migrating complete applications, or some functions of the applications, from centralized mainframes to networks of smaller decentralized systems. It's also implementing the latest technologies, resulting in reduced cost, improved user access, and greater flexibility.

With downsizing, organizations can move applications from big computers, such as mainframes, to smaller systems, most often to microcomputers on LANs. Even though downsizing is possible for many applications, it requires an up-front investment: purchasing a LAN and the corresponding software. Companies are reluctant to lay out money for the equipment, even though they may save many times that amount within a few years.

Downsizing, simply put, is delegating local processing tasks at sites that are down the organizational ladder, where they should be running to begin with. With a workstation, whether a PC or a Macintosh, instead of having a dumb terminal, you already have quite a bit of intelligence sitting on your desk. You might as well use it and perform some of the processing tasks. Software products that support this type of processing possibly save users money by delegating the processing away from an expensive mainframe. Table lookups, validation, and error checking could all be performed at the PC level. This can reduce communications overhead substantially. The cost of MIP on a mainframe is several hundred times higher than on a PC.

Even five years ago, any notion of replacing a mainframe with PCs was hearsay and considered impossible. PCs were not powerful enough. But as PCs get even faster and remain astonishingly cheap, more and more organizations are deciding that many of the functions performed by mainframes could be performed by microcomputers.

It's amazing to observe that it took PCs only about ten years to move into the corporate mainstream. The move is being resisted by most data-processing managers, who were reared in a mainframe world and don't want to slash their staffs. And it's viewed skeptically by many chief executives because, initially, there's going to be expenditure before the promised savings. Moreover, some companies with huge databases would be hard-pressed to break them into smaller chunks for PC networks. In other cases, the right PC software is still not available.

Main benefits of downsizing

The experiences of some organizations demonstrate that switching to PC networks is often feasible and highly cost-effective. However, dropping mainframes is not painless. In most transitions from mainframe-based systems to microcomputer-based systems, the staff gets reduced by almost two-thirds. More and more corporate executives, whether in data processing or not, are eager to control rising computer costs and are paying close attention to this fact.

A PC network's biggest advantage is cost. Microprocessor-based systems have at least a 100-to-1 cost advantage over mainframes, and it will soon become 300-to-1. Corporate executives and users are beginning to notice these price differentials. Computer hardware costs are only part of the story. PC networks require a much smaller number of computer experts. In addition, PC software is much cheaper to buy than mainframe software. Developing new programs on microcomputers takes much less time than it does on mainframe computers.

Mainframes are not flexible, particularly when applications have been developed in-house and maintained and modified for a number of years. Most of these applications were written under the assumption that the needs for which they were designed were going to remain relatively stable. These application systems were not built for change. As a result, change management is one of the toughest issues to handle with mainframe-based applications.

Downsized systems reflect the organizational structure more accurately than mainframe-based systems. A corporation is recognized as a collection of individual businesses, about which decisions are evaluated from that business perspective. Some business units are acquired, some are divested. Downsized systems could fit individual business units better than "big size" mainframe-based systems. It's extremely expensive to spin-off parts of mainframe-based applications when there are changes in the way the business units function.

With downsized PC-based systems, it's ideal to scale information systems to the scope of individual business units. Downsizing works better with departmental systems than with divisional systems, where a division consists of a number of departments. Coordination problems become more prominent in divisional systems, and more prominent still in corporate systems. But an application such as financial analysis for a department is an ideal application for a PC.

Another major benefit of downsizing is the software cost. The industry-average cost of PC applications versus mainframe application is nearing one-tenth. The average cost of PC applications versus minicomputer-based applications is nearly one-third. As a result, in many applications, it will take organizations a year to three years, at the most, to recoup the cost of downsizing. With all of these cost equations, it almost appears as if PCs have no limitations. But that is far from the truth.

PC limitations

PC networks still can't do everything. Mainframes remain best for programs requiring very large databases and 24-hour communication, such as airline reservations and automated teller machines. Switching complete software development to PCs is also slow, because PC software developers are still trying to match the capabilities offered by mainframe databases. Many mainframe and mid-range software developers are reluctant to supply PC software because of the much lower prices and lower profit margins. The microcomputer market has started to look like a commodity market. The big computer manufacturers, that in the past generally tried to sell more and more "iron," are trying to sell mainframes and minicomputers as "servers" for PC networks. They are also beginning to make PC network products. But a host of small hardware and software companies are also eager to provide what customers need.

We have reached downsizing through an evolutionary process (see FIG. 7-4). Centralized batch-based processing with hosts (see FIG. 7-5) advanced into centralized online host processing with data manager and video displays. It further evolved into distributed dialog management by transferring requests

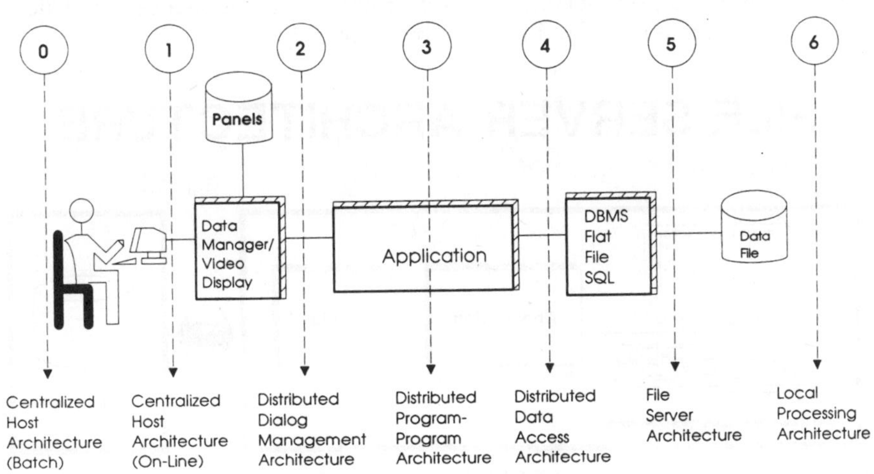

Fig. 7-4. Design of distributed systems.

HOST-BASED ARCHITECTURE

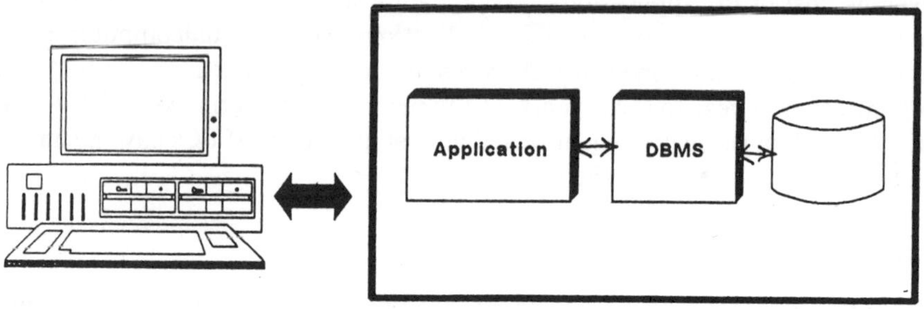

Fig. 7-5. The application and the DBMS run on a host computer and interact with the user through a terminal or display.

and data from the mainframe to terminals. This further provided the capability of one function to run on multiple mainframe processors. Data distributed on various processors could then be accessed.

File server architecture (see FIG. 7-6) enabled connection to the server (mostly mainframes that were the back-end) and transferred data files to the client (front-end), which had both the application and DBMS running. With database server architecture (see FIG. 7-7), the DBMS executes on the host server (back-end), providing data for the application running on the client (front-end).

Downsizing could also be implemented using client/server architecture (see FIG. 7-8). Portions of the application run on different computers. There are various types of servers providing application-specific services, such as data server, communications server, print server and computational server. (Client Server architecture is covered in detail in Chapter 9.)

FILE SERVER ARCHITECTURE

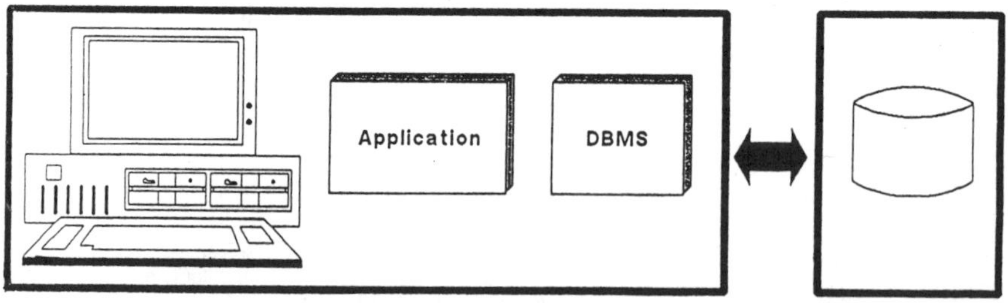

Fig. 7-6. The application and DBMS run on the client—entire data files must be moved from the server to the client.

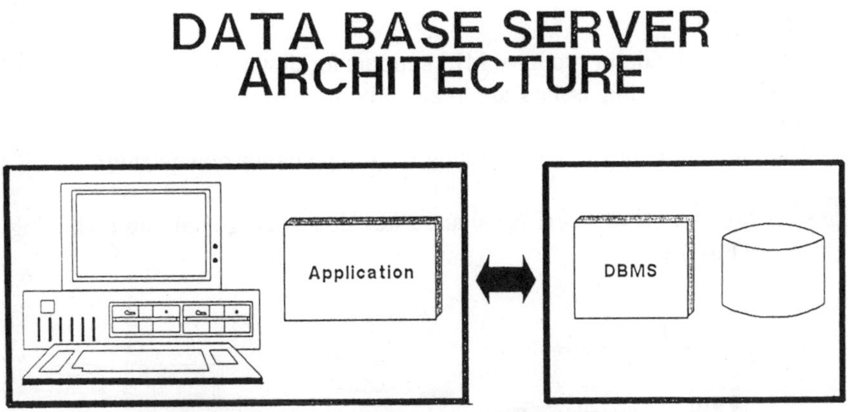

Fig. 7-7. The DBMS executes on the host server (back end), providing data for the application running on the client (front end).

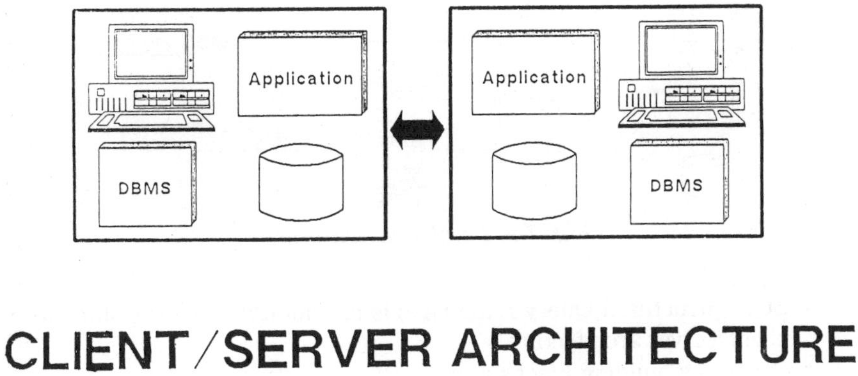

Fig. 7-8. Client/server architecture.

Cautions before downsizing

If existing mainframe-based systems are to be transferred to PCs, it will be very time consuming to transfer a major part of the system. The design of the mainframe-based system is quite involved. The best strategy is to carve out a piece that fits a department's needs. There should be a very good understanding of the problem and of the software to be used on PCs.

Downsizing needs technical support and hand holding, even after the system is installed. People don't appreciate the technical support they are receiving from their data processing department. If the mainframe doesn't work, the users blame MIS and wait until it functions again. If a PC doesn't work, the users often have to bring it to life. The technical knowledge required to make downsizing work is very seldom given enough thought.

MIS support

It's absolutely mandatory to have MIS support for downsizing. It will not work otherwise. Downsizing issues are really about management and not about hardware.

What are some of the key enabling technologies for downsizing?

- Local area networks (LANs) are a key downsizing-enabling technology (see FIG. 7-9).

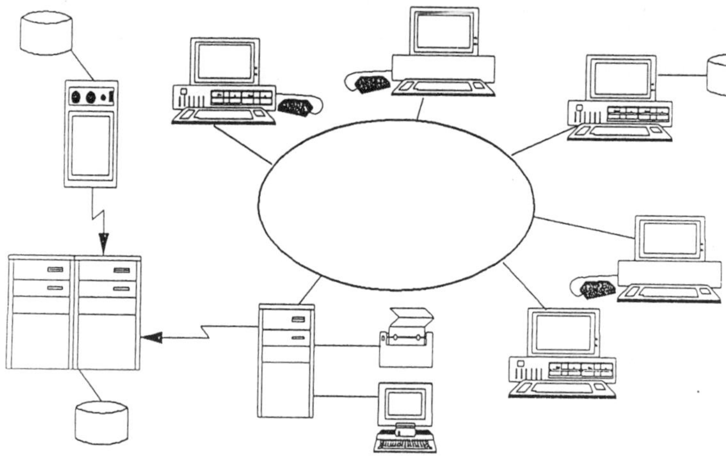

Fig. 7-9. Local area networks.

- SQL (Structured Query Language) is considered a *de facto* standard in client/server architecture.
- Other key building blocks are:
  a. Graphical user interfaces: A GUI provides the same look and feel irrespective of the platform used for the application delivery.
  b. Logical Unit 6.2: The LU 6.2 protocol is supported by IBM, and it's a very important protocol with IBM hardware.
  c. Open systems: This includes Unix and OSI from the International Standards Organization.

What is the organizational impact of downsizing?

Downsizing should be tried for new applications, not necessarily for the existing ones. It's not advisable to convert existing applications if no significant modifications are required. Like any other application development, if there's no organizational commitment, production quality applications, with backup, recovery, etc., can't be developed, because creating a production quality application is expensive.

Due to development on various hardware and software platforms, there could be increased system complexity, because people from various groups will have to work together. Professionals working on various computing platforms don't necessarily communicate well. It has been estimated that about 60% of the errors are a result of human communications problems. This may result in more "bugs" in software, if not properly managed. There could be increased managerial control problems, as well as increased security and integrity problems.

Which application is a good candidate for downsizing? Any system that doesn't need a great deal of intercontinental communications, and whose database fits in a LAN environment, is a good candidate for downsizing. It would be advisable to consider communications, data, and processes required by the application. If the application is communication and database intensive and light in processing, it might be more appropriate for a mainframe. If it's processing intensive and not so intensive in communications and data, the application might be more appropriate for microcomputers.

Without a doubt, microcomputing is here to stay. Most microcomputers are considered to be workstations. Individual workstations should be acquired with communications in mind. One of the major strengths of a mainframe is security, backup and recovery capabilities. Microcomputers have some distance to go in providing security and backup capabilities.

Some desirable aspects of microcomputers are their low cost, consistent response time, and availability and ease of use as compared to mainframes. Some difficulties in today's micro environment are the moving and sorting of large amounts of data. These two activities are time consuming. Thus, backup and recovery are tough to handle. Some of the DOs and DON'Ts of microcomputer-based applications are listed in FIGS. 7-10A and 7-10B.

How to be successful in downsizing

To create a successfully downsized environment within your organization, the following guidelines should be helpful:

- Wise choices. First, identify applications that will be easier and faster to implement. There's a learning curve, even for downsizing! Initial successes are extremely important and are useful when it's time to negotiate for other projects. Prepare an application portfolio to choose from.
- Management commitment. To ensure downsizing success, commitment of both corporate and line management is mandatory. Commitment translates mostly into budget approval and providing adequate staff support. In a downsized environment, departmental managers have more responsibility than in MIS application development.
- Appropriate technology base. Downsizing uses new hardware and software technologies. Some existing IS staff will have to be moved away from traditional COBOL and IMS environments and into the use of workstations and LAN tools. Some of the "old time" IS staff may not

Do

- Identify your users, their needs, where they want to go and their future support needs.
- Establish a list of software that you will support. Keep this list flexible depending on the number of users to be supported using a specific software product. If the numbers of uses of a specific product increases, move that product into supported products Category, and if the number reduces, drop support of the product, even if it was on the supported Products Category. This action is going to be more difficult to implement.
- Plan a phase-out policy that will place all users on fully graphically-oriented platforms as soon as possible.
- Make your volume-purchasing clout count for better software and support prices.
- Work with your software vendors to help them incorporate desired features in their product upgrades.
- Support sharing of documents across the company.
- Monitor applications currently run on your company's PCs.
- Frequently communicate with users concerning upgrades of supported packages and their advantages.
- Investigate the potential of asset management systems to help you know what hardware and software you have in place, and where.

Fig. 7-10A. PC application proliferation: do.

Don't

- Forbid users outright to use unapproved software.
- Arbitrarily refuse support for software without a common sense explanation to the user who requests it.
- Standardize software for various applications before the state of the art is fully defined.
- Add a non-networkable word processor, spreadsheet or DBMS software to your approved list of supported software.
- Attempt to standardize programming tools or applications that are not easy to use.
- Select software on purely technical grounds, without considering the staying power of its publisher.
- Select software that will not be compatible with installed applications in a groupware environment.

Fig. 7-10B. PC application proliferation: don't.

appreciate it and may leave the organization. Make sure that there are trained and experienced staff who can maintain the "old time" applications developed on the mainframe, because these applications will not be moved to a workstation platform in the near future. And, some of them never will be, until they die of natural causes—"old age."

- Realistic expectations. Don't promise too much, too soon. It may take one to three years for a small to medium-sized company to be "downsized." Remember, your users' and your management's happiness depends on expectations you might create in them!

Part III

Networking

8

Connectivity and networking

In a successful distributed database environment, connectivity and networking have to be in place first. Also, for cooperative processing, one of the major prerequisites is connectivity and networking (see FIG. 8-1). It will constitute a major part of the world of computing in the '90s. It's a growth industry on all fronts. A number of computer professionals will need to gain expertise in networking in order to support it. Both installation and maintenance need a high level of expertise for support. It's projected that networking will be growing at a very fast rate, and it will reach its peak of growth by 1998.

Connectivity

Connectivity is the manner by which one computer system is able to communicate with another using defined protocols. Connectivity could be viewed as a logical concept, and that concept is implemented physically with networking. Cooperative processing requires that transparent connectivity is provided so that each part of the computing system—that means the platform consisting of hardware, systems software, applications software, and utilities software—can be readily and easily available to all other parts without operator intervention.

There are various types of networks (see FIG. 8-2). Local area networks (LANs), metropolitan area networks (MANs) and wide area networks (WANs) are just a few ways of networking various distances between nodes.

We will discuss Integrated Services Digital Network (ISDN) as well as Systems Network Architecture (SNA), X.25 and Open Systems Interconnection (OSI) later in the chapter. *ISDN* is a new standard for building a nationwide, and possibly global, digital network. *SNA* is IBM's data communications architec-

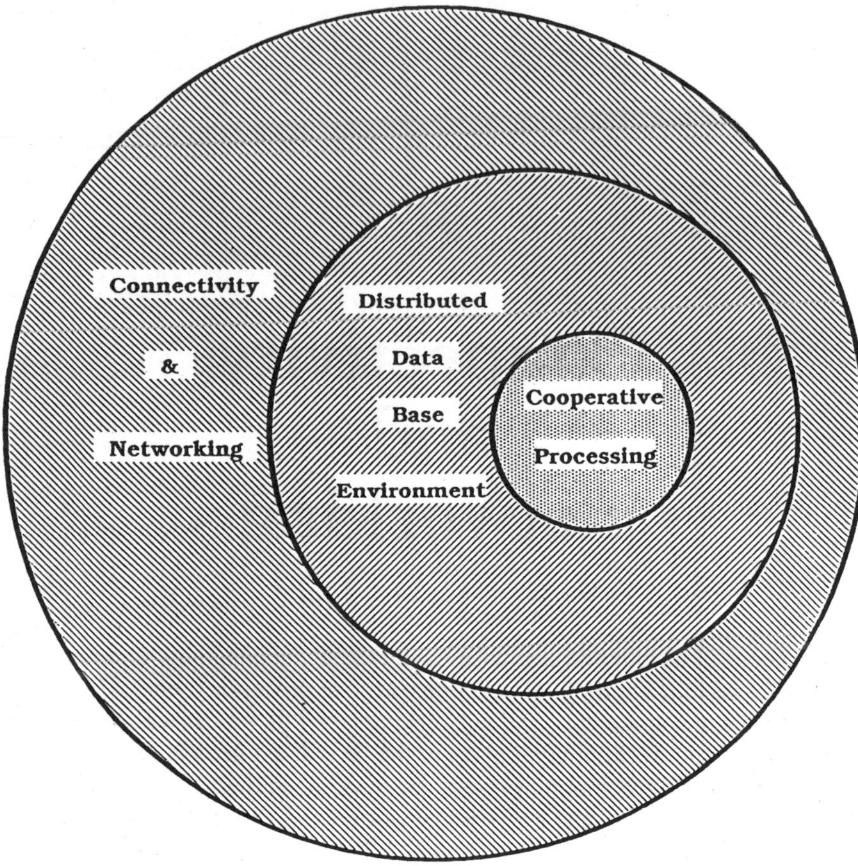

Fig. 8-1. Cooperative processing is a subset of a distributed database environment, which is a subset of connectivity and networking.

- Local Area Network (LAN)
- Metropolitan Area Network (MAN)
- Wide Area Network (WAN)
- Integrated Services Digital Network (ISDN)
- SNA, X.25, Open Systems Interconnect (OSI)

Fig. 8-2. Various types of networks.

ture defining levels of protocols for communications between terminals or workstations and application programs.

X.25 is an international, albeit non-IBM, standard for attachment to packet-switched networks. IBM support of X.25 has been more verbal than real, but inclusion of X.25 in SAA gives a new lease on life to X.25 within the IBM world.

OSI is a set of international standard protocols and services for communications systems, partially overlapping in function but incompatible with SNA. IBM affirms its commitment to OSI and has included OSI as a part of SAA. OSI is a seven-layer model for communications developed by the International Standards Organization (ISO). Working from software to hardware, the OSI model contains the following seven layers: application, presentation, session, transport, network data link, and physical. Each layer is responsible for a different communications function.

LANs are commonly used to connect personal computers in one building or on one campus. There are restrictions between any two nodes regarding distances. A major component of client/server architecture is a LAN.

MANs are commonly used to connect computers throughout a metropolitan area. Cities such as New York, Boston, San Francisco, or Los Angeles have a number of MAN installations. In most U.S. metropolitan areas, Bell Operating Companies (BOCs) are among the providers of MAN services.

WANs are commonly used for providing communication between geographically separated computers at distances beyond metropolitan regions, possibly constituting a global network. WAN technology has been in use over a much longer timeframe than LAN technology. As a result, WAN technology is more mature than LAN, as far as reliability is concerned. WANs are used mostly in conjunction with mainframes. We have had mainframes, with their associated dumb terminals, for many more years than microcomputers. There are a number of organizations that base their computer centers in the U.S.A. and communicate with London or Hong Kong via terminals. Most WANs use a mainframe.

Either the older analog or newer digital techniques are implemented to create a WAN. Digital networks have many more capabilities, much bigger bandwidth, and better transmission quality than analog networks.

IBM's WAN architecture is implemented with Systems Network Architecture (SNA). Another major set of standards for logical and physical networking, called Open Systems Interconnection (OSI), has been put together by the international standards body.

There are two major types of WANs. One is called packet switched and the other is T-1 multiplexing. Packet switched is popular with value added networks (VANs). Value is added to the network by providing some more information with transferred data packets. *T-1* refers to T-1 time division multiplexing.

Integrated Services Digital Network (ISDN) is the next evolutionary step for WAN technology. As a possible indicator of ISDN potential, Japan seems to be determined to get into ISDN much faster than the U.S. or Europe.

ISDN is a new standard for building a nationwide, and possibly global, digital network. With digital signals, a much larger bandwidth is achieved. With ISDN, data is still transferred over the telephone network, which is highly convenient because the telephone network is already installed in the walls. The providers of ISDN services are mostly Bell Operating Companies (BOCs) in the U.S. BOCs are in the process of installing fiber instead of copper wherever possible. Fiber provides a much bigger bandwidth and improves the entire public telephone network.

There are a number of different LAN architectures, but the major contenders are based on the following architectures: star, ring or bus (see FIG. 8-3). Among others, star architecture is supported by one of the major organizations, AT&T (American Telephone and Telegraph); ring architecture is supported by IBM, and bus architecture is supported by Digital Equipment Corporation (DEC).

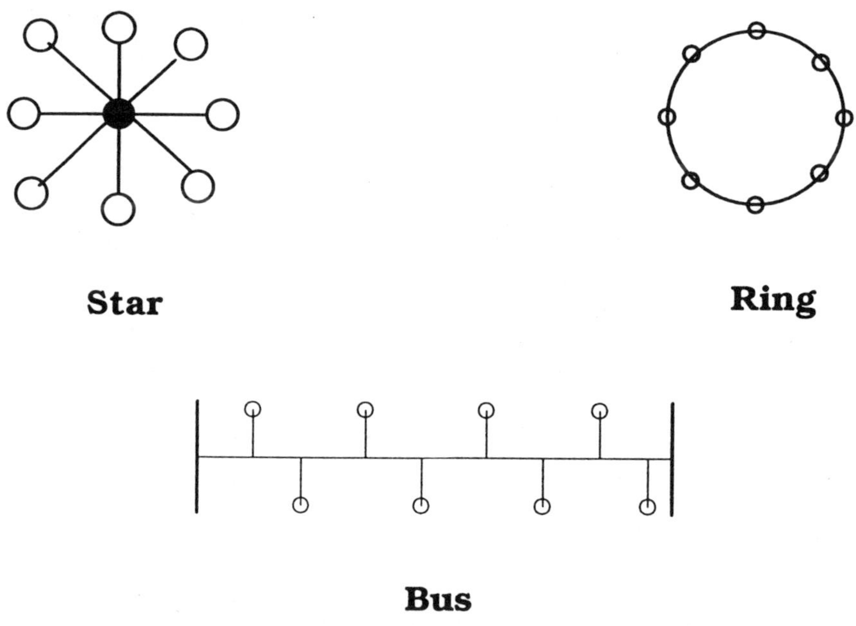

Fig. 8-3. Three alternative designs for a local area network (LAN). A LAN is defined as a group of microcomputers linked together by cables and networking software.

A LAN is a group of microcomputers linked together by cables and networking software. The part of LAN that has to improve its reliability is the network software and not the physical cables. In most computing, the hardware is much more reliable than the software. Hardware is tangible, whereas, software is intangible. Software has not reached the stage of engineering; it's still more art than science, and networking software is no exception.

In a typical LAN configuration, a PC-AT class or above machine is used as the *server*, which is the center of the network. Of course a PC-AT may work out fine as a server, but the server may become a bottleneck if attached clients are also PC-AT type machines. In order to avoid that, the server should be at least a couple of times stronger than any of the strongest nodes on the network. The server has to be stronger in terms of both processing and storage. Other microcomputers, sometimes called *clients*, are used as node machines that typically store executable files. That enables a person to turn off the connection with the network and use the microcomputer standalone. Data storage is usually delegated to the server, which should have a large hard disk storage facility.

Network topologies

Let's evaluate the star, ring and bus network topologies. (See FIG. 8-3.) New topologies are created by combining these three basic ones. In a star network, the server node is connected to each client node. The *star topology* has cables that radiate from the server node to each client node. A polling protocol is used in which the server node sends a message to each client node, in turn, querying if that client node has anything to send. If the client node has information to send, it sends the data at that time. The message goes back to the server node, and then the message is sent to the address specified by the client node. If a node has nothing to send, the server node continues around the star, querying each client node in turn.

The advantage of star topology is that it's easy to add more nodes to the installation. And it's simple to identify cable failure if something goes wrong because each node has its own cable. Star network is economical for a small network with close proximity.

There are several disadvantages of the star topology. One is that the central server is the single point of failure. If the server fails, the nodes will not be polled for data. Cost of installation also quickly increases as the network grows. A cable must be run to each individual node, even if there are multiple nodes located in a group far from the server.

The *ring topology* is laid out with a single cable running through each node, sequentially linked to the server. A token-passing protocol is used in which a single token is passed around the ring through the server node as well as each client node. This token carries a single packet of information at a time. Each time the packet passes through the node, the node has to see if the message in the packet is addressed to that node. If the packet is empty, it's a free token and the node can attach its own information packet for some other node to receive. Each node has to wait for a free token before it can transmit data.

Advantages of the token ring network include:

- Its deterministic nature. Rules are established to limit the length of time that each node can control the token before relinquishing control to the next node. This time interval makes token availability determinable and allows each node an equal opportunity to transmit data.

- Network failure. A variation of the token ring network can be established. Multiple nodes, besides being on a ring, could be connected to a node that then can be considered a multistation access unit, as in FIG. 8-4. This multistation access unit can act as a bypass to one of the nodes in the event of line disruption.

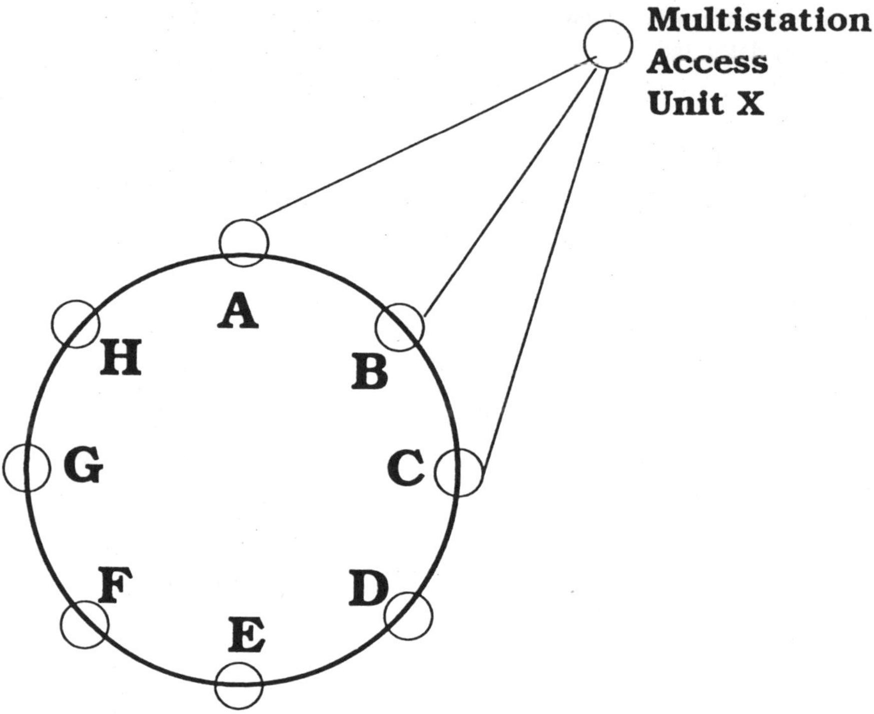

Fig. 8-4. A variation of a LAN is a multistation access unit, X. This access unit can act as a bypass to one of the nodes in the event of line disruption. If B fails or the line between A and C fails, A could transmit the packet to X, and X, in turn, can transmit it to C.

The disadvantage of the token ring is that network response time degrades as the number of nodes increases, because only one packet is on the ring at a time.

The *bus topology* is a linear network. A single length of cable is shared by all network devices. The cable is not connected at the ends but is closed at the ends with bus terminators.

The bus architecture uses Carrier-Sensed Multiple Access (CSMA) or contention protocol, which means that if the network senses traffic on the network, it doesn't send data. It sends data only in the absence of traffic. It's possible that two nodes may detect no traffic and begin to transmit at the same instant, resulting in a collision. When a collision occurs, the node will stop transmitting data and will retransmit the data after a random time period has passed. The random time is a variable every time. That's the reason it's random. Contention is resolved on a first-come, first-served basis. This type of protocol is known as probabilistic since the interval between transmissions is not controlled or determinable.

An advantage of the bus topology is its wiring simplicity. It's just one wire with two ends. Disadvantages include:

- The single point failure characteristic of the bus. If the bus fails, nodes past the failure point can't pass information to one another. At the same time, one bus line could end up as two bus lines. Where the line broke off, one end becomes the terminating point to one route, and the other end becomes a starting point to another route.
- Response time degrades with an increase in traffic and increase in number of collisions.

Basic and advanced LAN services

A LAN is not used just to connect microcomputers, but also to connect peripheral devices. Two or more microcomputers can share one printer or plotter. However, in a number of organizations, LAN services are extended beyond device sharing. It's not only the printers that are shared; corporate data is also shared via networkwide databases. One of the most widely implemented applications using a LAN is electronic mail.

In a competitive information-systems environment, as compared to simple device-sharing environments, security and fault tolerance are of greater significance. Applications are extended beyond printer sharing. Services such as electronic mail and networkwide databases are increasingly critical.

One application typically implemented with LANs is telemarketing. Telemarketers call potential or existing customers on the phone. The organization has installed a database on the server. Each marketer accesses the database from a client node. Information from the conversation with the customer, including when to contact the customer again, what was discussed, and any other pertinent information, is entered on a "scratch pad" on the server database. Everything is stored on the server disk so that when the same client is called the next time, the same questions are not asked. Everyone accessing the particular client's database record is informed of all previous conversations during a certain time frame, such as the past six months. Every morning, those who need to be called are tagged, and then all calls that need to be made are distributed among the telemarketing people. If they had not installed the LAN, the same client could have been called three times on the same day, and possibly conflicting or confusing information could have been given. Of course, this doesn't sit too well with the customer.

Major LAN architectures

The major LAN architectures encompassing overall LAN designs including hardware, software and rules for communication are as shown in TABLES 8-1 and 8-2.

Three major architectures implemented in the industry are Ethernet, Token Ring and ARCnet. They differ in how they send data through the network. They also differ in how microcomputers are wired together using any one of these three architectures. There's a difference in data transmission rate, a difference in error detection, a difference in maintenance, as well as a difference in priority management.

Table 8-1. Major LAN Architectures

Product	Comments
Ethernet	Developed by Xerox, DEC & Intel. Implemented mainly by DEC. (Bob Metcalfe, former Chairman of 3 Com Corp., is credited with the invention of Ethernet while working at Xerox's Palo Alto Research Center)
Token Ring	Patented (supposedly by Olof Soderblom of Willemjin Holding BV, Rotterdam, Netherlands. The patent is contested in courts. Implemented mainly by IBM.
IBM PC Network	Developed by Sytek. Implemented mainly by IBM & Sytek.
ARC NET	Developed by Datapoint and implemented by Datapoint. It is used in PC-only LANs.
StarLAN	Developed and implemented by AT&T.
LocalTalk	Developed and implemented by Apple Computer Company.

Table 8-2. Major LAN Protocols

Protocol	Comments
TCP/IP	Mostly used in Unix environment
DECnet	Developed by DEC and implemented at DEC installations.
Novell Net-Ware	Developed by Novell. It is one of the popular LAN protocols used.
OS/2 LAN Server/Manager	Co-developed by IBM and Microsoft. Marketed by both vendors. It is referred to as LAN Server by IBM and LAN Manager by Microsoft. Both vendors have made some modifications since it was developed jointly.
Sun NFS	Developed and implemented by Sun Microsystems, Inc.
ISO	Protocol standard put together by International Standards Organization.
AppleTalk	Developed and implemented by Apple Computer Company.
Banyan VINES	Developed and implemented by Banyan to connect heterogeneous equipment.
Net BIOS	Network Basic Input Output System

Carrier access method

Carrier Sense Multiple Access with Collision Detection (CSMA/CD) and token passing are the two most widely used carrier access methods. With Ethernet, if the line is clear, the node transmits its data. If the line isn't clear, the node waits and then tries again. With ARCnet and Token Ring, a sequenced method called token passing is used.

Two types of topologies used are logical and physical. *Logical* topology refers to the flow of data, and the differentiating factor is the carrier access method. Token ring architecture passes tokens in a ring, whereas ARCnet is a token-passing bus. *Physical* topology reflects the way microcomputers on a LAN are physically linked. Ethernet typically uses a bus topology; ARCnet uses a star or a distributed star, and token ring employs a star-wired ring. In a distributed star, which is sometimes referred to as a tree, a number of hubs are connected together. A Network Interface Card (NIC) is the microcomputer's passage to the network.

There are four types of cabling systems that are currently used: coaxial cable, unshielded twisted pair, shielded twisted pair and fiber optic. Each of them has its advantages and disadvantages.

- Coaxial cable. This type of wiring is used for connecting cable TV. It's relatively expensive. Ethernet mostly uses coaxial cable.
- Unshielded twisted pair. This type of cabling is used in regular telephone cabling. Since telephone lines are already installed in office buildings, unshielded twisted pair is the least expensive option for LAN installation. But at the same time, it's also the most susceptible to electronic interference.
- Shielded twisted pair. This wiring is the same type of twisted pair as used for the telephone wiring in the walls. The only difference being that it's shielded. It's used for token ring networks and provides a greater degree of protection against interference than unshielded twisted pair.
- Fiber optic. Pulses of light instead of electronic signals are used for this type of cabling. Fiber provides a very high level of security because tapping a fiber is not easy. It's also more reliable because lightning doesn't affect it. But it's the most expensive option, although cost is expected to decrease as fiber is used more, and as a result, prices drop. Because of its sturdiness, fiber is mostly used to implement a backbone. A backbone local network provides a high-capacity network that can be used to interconnect lower-capacity local area networks.

Protocols

A *protocol* is a way of communicating on the network. A protocol also plays a major role in communications between various types of LANs. Internetworking is a major challenge for the coming years.

OSI (Open Software Interconnection) plays a major role in internetworking. It's a seven-layer communications protocol intended to standardize network architecture. OSI implementation allows interconnection of disparate equipment and disparate protocols from multiple vendors. It will allow multimedia document transfer over a network.

How to choose a network

First of all, decide if you need a network. If you have two people sitting next to each other, when would you need a network for connecting their computers? A network is necessary if the two people are using the same large files. If the people in the organization spend more time swapping disks and trying to locate data than they spend working on their applications, then you need a network. That means you really have to study your organization first. Networks will not only improve communications between employees, they will also boost the return on computer investment. A network doesn't have to be a huge expenditure. The amount should include operating system software and some applications software. Training costs will be additional.

LANs, like microcomputer technology, are still maturing. Purchasing hardware and software because of offered discounts doesn't make sense, unless the organization wanted and needed the items to begin with. "Hoarding" discounted hardware and software will result in possessing older technology. Only whatever is needed should be purchased.

If all that's needed is communication among workers in the same department by a LAN, a WAN is clearly not appropriate, nor is a MAN. Several dozen independent software companies should be writing applications for a LAN under consideration so you can get more sophisticated software and have decent offerings to choose from. Buying network versions of software you currently use can also save money. If you have a 20-person network, but at the most only six people simultaneously use the spreadsheet, you will pay for only six copies, even though all 20 employees can use the program, though not simultaneously. You will want one standard program for each application, such as word processing or accounting, so that exchanged files are compatible. You will also need so-called utility programs that can find files that are lost or damaged.

When purchasing software for a network, it's absolutely necessary to find the maximum number of users it can accommodate. The vendor may say it runs on a network, and later on you experience that it only accommodates four users and you need networking for ten.

Managing a network

Make sure someone is in charge of the network. There are not that many people who have expertise in the technology. This is a position that's going to become more and more important in the nineties. You will need a network administrator who can do day-to-day housekeeping, monitor the system's security, provide backup and recovery, perform maintenance, and establish training procedures. If a network becomes a political issue because of tensions over who controls the corporate data, you may want to hire from the outside. But you will also need a high-level executive to monitor issues such as network security.

Managing today's and tomorrow's networks is one of the toughest challenges. Network management should not just be an ad hoc effort. Keeping cost reduction in mind, the network has to be modernized and serviced for maintenance. Besides planning and implementing the network, problem determination and problem resolution are two major activities. Watch for any recurring problems. Trends for repeat complaints should be established. Solve all problems as soon as possible, but especially the persistent ones. Work orders for network modification and repair have to be issued and tracked. Charge costs back to originating end-users. Network performance in terms of user needs has to be tracked and adjusted accordingly. Reports to users, operators and managers have to be generated.

Improving network management is a continual process, which has advanced from merely ensuring that necessary functions are carried out to monitoring which of these functions are performed efficiently and at the least possible cost. To improve the management process, network managers should:

- Automate manual processes only after optimization has taken place to reduce demands on scarce manpower.
- Where it's economically feasible, consolidate installed networks and nodes to reflect the way an organization runs.
- Hire and train network operation control centers staff to: install appropriate alarm and diagnostic tests to isolate faulty equipment and transmission circuits, keep track of work order and record keeping systems to document changes, assist users in network usage and outages, and document operational performance in periodic reports to management.
- Maintain workstation, facility and switch equipment promptly and properly.
- Use export systems to augment diagnostic, monitoring and control systems.
- Establish optimization systems that analyze the network, predict and adjust for traffic loads, and enable you to design optimal configurations based on carrier tariffs.
- Build configuration, pricing and tariff databases. Maintain records of circuits and equipment, as well as alarms and diagnostics associated with these elements. Maintain tariff databases to: verify invoices sent by the vendors, select optimum cost circuits when extending the network contract, and optimize the network with daily changes.
- Implement procurement management procedures. Develop equipment requirements; generate requests for proposals to vendors and evaluate responses.
- Watch and understand facility and equipment performance. Monitor the status of network elements, and generate reports to users, operators, managers and suppliers.
- Specify performance requirements; order transmission circuits and

equipment; test installations against performance criteria; supervise vendors and test against overall acceptance criteria.
- Plan the network. Determine requirements; plan architectures and configure equipment, facilities, and carrier services to minimize costs.

The network manager should come up with ten or fifteen of the most frequently occurring errors. Some problems are extremely trivial. The LAN manager should develop such a list and make it electronically available so that everybody sees it on the screen when they get started using the microcomputer and the network.

Training

Teach employees to use the network. Training is absolutely important, because once they have learned what could go wrong, users should be able to detect the problems themselves. The orientation or the main focus of training should be problem solving. Identifying a leader within each work group and giving that person time to work with others will improve acceptance of the system and may lead to good ideas on how to use it.

The LAN should make it easier for employees to communicate and could possibly save time by cutting down on meetings and enabling several employees to concentrate on solving the same problem. It can also cut software costs by eliminating duplicate purchases of software. There is a tremendous difference in the cost for twenty workstations or personal computers vs. terminals attached to a minicomputer or mainframe. Organizations vote with their wallets for LAN implementations with the client/server architecture for application development. Organizations are evaluating lower cost microcomputer-based systems and assisting development managers in implementing downscaled application development projects.

Comparison of Ethernet and Token Ring

The original developers of Ethernet were Xerox, DEC, and Intel. Ethernet is one length of a cable with two ends. Ethernet is used to connect a wide range of equipment. The nodes of the network have to contend for network resources by listening to the network traffic. Based on the traffic, a determination is made whether a message to a node should be sent or not. The potential problem could be: if two computers send data simultaneously, their data collides, and neither message reaches the destination. Ethernet's bus architecture dictates this type of a protocol. The Ethernet protocol precedes the IEEE standards.

IEEE stands for Institute of Electrical and Electronics Engineers. It's an international body that's quite active in developing standards for, among others, local area networks. IEEE has developed a standard called 802.3. This is slightly different from Ethernet. People who are using Ethernet will probably not switch to Token Ring; some users seem to have a "religious" attachment to Ethernet.

Token Ring (see FIG. 8-5) is a ring or a circle of cable. Token Ring is typically found on PC-only LANs, or where PCs are connected to IBM mainframes. In some implementations, it's technically a "star shaped ring," meaning that all the cable comes into a central location, but logically, it still behaves as a ring. A token is transferred from one node to the other. A node can send an electrical signal to another node or nodes if there's a free token. Because of the ring architecture, there are no collisions. IEEE's standard for token ring is 802.5.

The speed of a network is measured by how fast data can move under ideal conditions, and the *throughput* is the rate that data actually ends up moving most of the time. If a network is rated as ten megabits (ten million bits) per

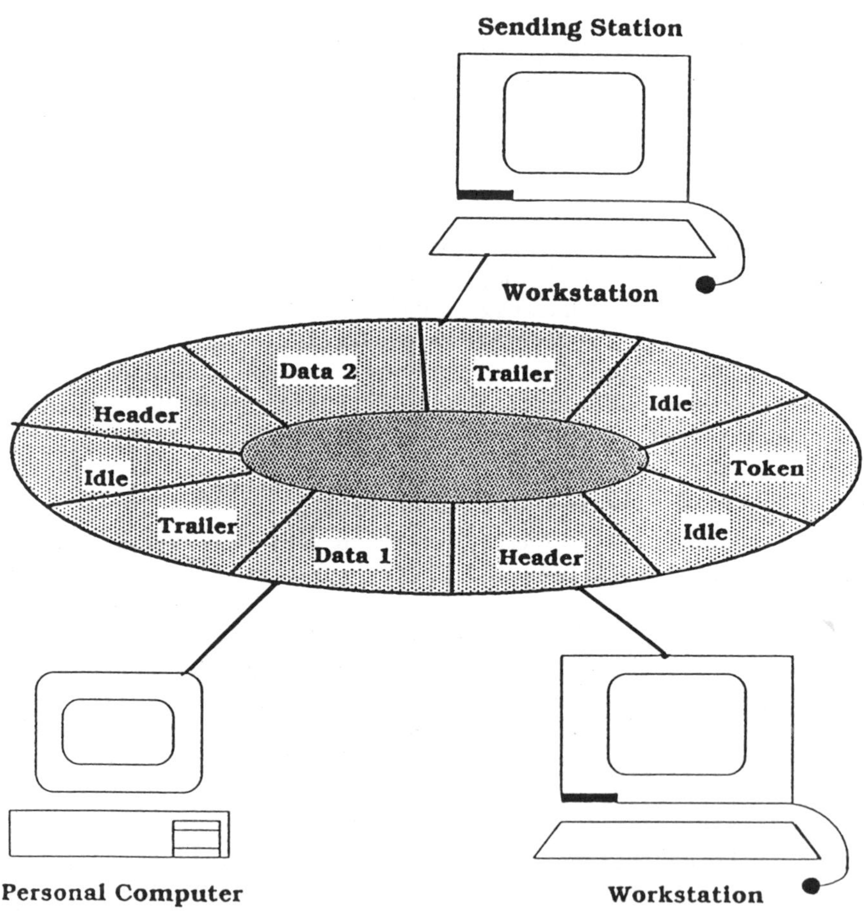

Fig. 8-5. IBM's 16 Mbps early token ring release. (UNIXWORLD, *August, 1989.)*

second, or sixteen megabits (sixteen million bits) per second, the resulting number could be 75 percent of the rate. It's just like a CPU; when there are 100 cycles it doesn't mean that all 100 percent of the cycles will be used for productive and tangible work. The same thing holds true with channel capacity. In most installations, when channel capacity is 45 or, at the most, 50 percent, it's said that the saturation point is reached.

Standard token ring networks are rated at four megabits per second, but IBM supports its sixteen megabits per second Token Ring LAN on twisted-pair cabling. But Ethernet is currently installed on more sites than token ring. First of all, Ethernet has been around for a longer time than Token Ring. But Token Ring is slowly catching up to Ethernet. Most installations with IBM mainframe and IBM microcomputers are implementing LANs supporting the LU 6.2 protocol, and then further installing SNA with SDLC (Synchronized Data Link Control) protocol.

LU 6.2 means Logical Unit Type 6.2. It's peer-to-peer data stream *cum* network operating system for program-to-program communication. LU 6.2 is IBM's strategic device-independent process-to-process protocol, and it acts as the session manager within SAA. LU 6.2's marketing term is Advanced Program-to-Program Communications (APPC). As a subset of SNA, LU 6.2 is designed for more sophisticated capabilities that are fostered in SAA and exploit intelligent workstations across distributed databases. *SNA* is IBM's data communications architecture that defines levels of protocols for communications between terminals or workstations and application programs.

SDLC is IBM's data communications protocol, used in SNA and covering the physical and link control protocol levels. SDLC has largely replaced BSC and async (start-stop) protocols.

Besides the three major architectures of star, bus and ring, there are various combinations of these basic architectures. There could be multiple tokens in a ring, as long as they're moving in the same direction, so they don't collide. Previously, a workstation had to wait until its data had traversed the entire ring. Now, a workstation can release the token immediately after sending its data.

IBM is also providing higher-speed transmission for shielded twisted-pair cabling. With token ring networking, the existing wiring in your walls can be used. That reduces the expenses considerably. Token ring networking is implemented with either shielded or unshielded twisted-pair cable, either of which is less expensive than coaxial cable. But Ethernet requires coaxial cable.

Users don't want to build a single autonomous monolithic network. They want several networks that can communicate with each other. And even if they didn't want several networks, they can't change it because there are several networks in existence. The networks are generally linked by a device designed specifically for that purpose: either a bridge, a router or a gateway, depending on how similar the two networks are and how complex the combined internetwork is. Subnetworks are linked to a master network called a backbone. For faster speed and better quality, fiber is the medium used.

Ethernet is easier to interconnect. Some kinds of token ring networks, such as that from IBM, are not as easy to internetwork as Ethernet networks. This is because IBM token ring networks require that each network knows how to route data through all the bridges.

There are not as many vendors that make token ring chip sets as there are for Ethernet. In the coming years, that may change.

Network failure and its remedy

If an Ethernet network breaks, it generally ends up as two smaller Ethernet networks, each of which continues to function. It's easier to recover from failure with an Ethernet server because it still has the same structure. But when a ring breaks it doesn't become another ring; it's just broken.

Computers on token ring networks circulate the token and their data around the entire ring; thus, if there's a break in the network, the network goes down. Some vendors have modified their products in recent years to help solve this problem. They have developed connector boxes. The box is actually on the network and the workstation links to the connecter box. That way, if a workstation fails or is disconnected, the connecter box remains on the network and continues passing messages to the next computer.

Alternatives to Ethernet and Token Ring

Ethernet and token ring technologies started to take shape in the late seventies, and then in the eighties they advanced further. They still have to advance even further in the nineties, but there's already something else on the horizon that will replace these. It's Fiber Distributed Data Interface (FDDI). FDDI represents the next generation of token-passing LAN technology. Some countries, like Japan, are skipping Ethernet and Token Ring and are going with FDDI. IBM is heavily investing in FDDI also.

Even if FDDI is a token-passing ring network type, it's not compatible with the token ring in use today. It's a dual ring, which improves reliability and performance. The major problem with FDDI is its expense. But another outstanding feature of FDDI is its speed. It will be able to transmit data at the speed of 100 to 200 megabytes (100 to 200 million bytes) per second. When more organizations acquire this technology, price per unit will be less.

When downscaling of development becomes more of a norm and mainframe applications are moved to the client/server architecture, that's when a robust network such as FDDI will be needed, because then you will be running many more applications on networks than you are running today.

There's another variation of LANs. If you don't have all the machines or all the nodes in one area, you could possibly get down to the LAN level. Users can access network applications via remote communications. Let's assume you have a PC somewhere just by itself. You don't want to install a LAN at that location. You could communicate with some other LAN and be part of the LAN even if you are physically remote. For companies with warehouses in distant locations, where there's no technical expertise, something like this may be attractive.

Security

Security needs to be considered much more seriously in a network environment than in a standalone case. Most of the time, though, security is breached, not intentionally, but because of sloppiness or stupidity. We are not treating security in any length in this book.

Wide are networks (WANs)

Private packet-switched networks enable the sharing of information between different types of computers in different locations. Packet switching is a method of formatting data from one computer into "packets" to be sent to another location. X.25 is an international standard used worldwide and a vendor-independent networking solution.

T-1 networks for voice and data communication offer a digital transmission technology that transmits digital information at a relatively high speed. Both digitized voice and data can be carried over the same T-1 network at the same time.

As far as IBM is concerned, SAA's cornerstone for communications is SNA (see FIG. 8-6), and IBM is concentrating on NetView as the implementation of SNA. With regard to SAA common communications support, there are five layers of software (see FIG. 8-7): data link controls, networking, session services, application services, and data streams. The communications protocol is SDLC (Synchronized Data Link Control), token ring for a LAN, and with X.25, the international OSI is supported.

With Physical Unit 2.1, IBM will be supporting Low Entry Network (LEN). IBM intends to support both non-IBM and IBM equipment. IBM provides Physical Unit 2.1 to support Logical Unit 6.2. As far as the communications are concerned, and as far as IBM is concerned, LU 6.2 is a very important protocol.

LU 6.2 and alternative plans

Interest in distributed application continues. But so far, LU 6.2-related product development has taken longer than anticipated, and vendors have not been expeditious in delivering off-the-shelf LU 6.2 application programs. Applications delivered by the vendors do seem to require substantial custom tailoring. When organizations require LU 6.2's advanced peer-to-peer processing capabilities, the protocol implementation will take off.

The LU 6.2 advocates are IBM's most loyal users, companies with IBM/390 mainframes running IBM's MVS operating system. Microcomputers with Microsoft Corp.'s DOS and Windows operating systems, IBM's OS/2, IBM

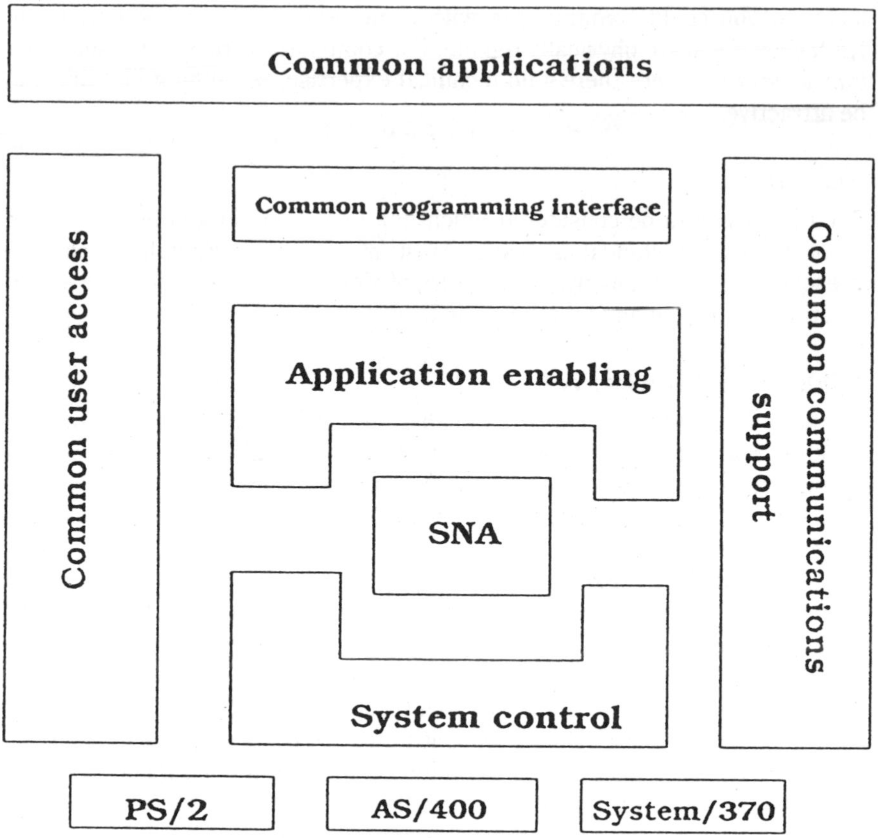

Fig. 8-6. The SNA mainframe is the core of SAA, but SAA explodes SNA into a new universe of networked load sharing, concentric to the mainframe. The impact on communications is a radical rethinking of existing SNA networks.

midrange computers, and Sun workstations are the most likely candidates to be connected to mainframes via LU 6.2. Because of some of LU 6.2 shortcomings, users have chosen alternate foundations to build their distributed applications. Unix servers, microcomputer LANs, and Transmission Control Protocol/Internet Protocol (TCP/IP) networks have become the core of distributed applications. Besides IBM's plans for networking, we have to look at DEC's plans for networking.

Digital Equipment Corp.'s NAS

Network Application Support (NAS) is DEC's title for its application integration program. It's very similar to IBM's SAA. NAS tries to set up the framework for running distributed applications across a DEC network, including systems from other vendors.

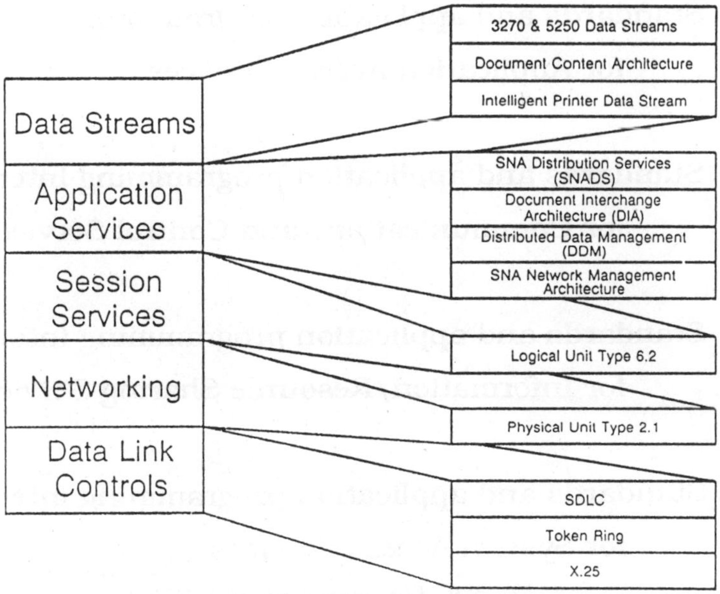

Fig. 8-7. SAA common communications support.

NAS lists standards and the specific application programming interfaces associated with those standards that DEC supports. Those standards and application programming interfaces fall into one of four categories of software-based services: application access services, which include user interface standards; communications and control services for communications between applications; information resource-sharing services, including DEC's Compound Document Architecture; and systems access services for operating systems.

What goes into NAS

(See FIG. 8-8.) DEC's operating system interface is POSIX, the Portable Operating System Interface, developed by the IEEE. Used extensively in the Unix world, DEC uses POSIX in its version of Unix called Ultrix. DEC will also include the interface to VMS, which is DEC's proprietary operating system.

Integrated Services Digital Network (ISDN)

Another very important network for the nineties is Integrated Services Digital Network (ISDN). ISDN is a new standard for building a nationwide, and possibly global, digital network.

ISDN calls for the implementation of a global, intelligent, digital network capable of transmitting voice, data and video information among not only the telecommunications companies of the world, but more importantly, among the world's end-user population.

- **Standards and application programming interfaces for Application Access Services**

- **Standards and application programming interfaces for Communications and Control Services**

- **Standards and application programming interfaces for Information/Resource Sharing Services**

- **Standards and application programming interfaces for System Access Services**

Fig. 8-8. The components of NAS.

ISDN consists of international standards drafted and adopted for use by the Consultative Committee International Telegraphy and Telephony (CCITT), a worldwide body that governs telecommunications and operates within the United Nations. These standards define physical interfaces, message formats, switching mechanisms, communications protocols and service capabilities. With these standards, telephone companies, computer and communications equipment suppliers, software vendors, and service organizations are able to design and develop systems that provide ISDN users easy-to-use, high-speed access to a new generation of network-based information services.

ISDN benefits

The following benefits go to telecommunications service providers, governmental and commercial organizations, and the home:

- Performance. The digital aspect of ISDN, with its higher bandwidth, provides for faster transfer times over lower-error-rate circuits.
- Plug and play. With the help of standardized interfaces, users can move, add and change devices on the network. A user may move locations and equipment with no disruption to the network or to the network's servicing of the user.
- Voice, data and video support. ISDN can carry and process all types of digital information streams. Most companies today operate two networks, one for voice and one for data. ISDN offers these companies a more efficient and comprehensive backbone utility.

- Cost effectiveness. ISDN allows for a much more efficient use of resources dedicated to networking an organization. By maximizing the use of the public network, private network investment can be more appropriately focused.
- Flexibility in network usage. ISDN service providers and consumers can tailor their networks.
- Reliability and redundancy. By consolidating facilities, implementing more advanced switching capabilities and broadening the reach of ISDN, the telephone companies of the world build a stronger, more resilient global network. The fear of downed lines and services is reduced.
- On-demand, advanced application services. The most exciting aspect of ISDN is its potential for multifaceted use by end users. Electronic directory and messaging utilities, voice/data processing and remote database access are part of the first wave of ISDN service activity. Automatic Number Identification (ANI), a service providing information on the calling party to the called party, has been at the forefront of ISDN application activity.

How is ISDN used today?

The trial sites for ISDN in the U.S. started in 1986. The McDonald's fast food organization is probably the most famous of the beta sites. The early subscribers include American Express, Chevron, Tenneco, Shell Oil, Boeing, American Transtech, Hewlett-Packard/Apollo Division, Shearson Lehman, NASA, Rockwell, 3M and Hershey Foods. Many large universities, such as West Virginia University, the Massachusetts Institute of Technology, Carnegie Mellon and Indiana University are also implementing ISDN.

Currently, most of these users look to ISDN as a utility network for providing voice and data transfer. American Express is one example of a user looking to ISDN as an advanced voice/data application provider. Through ANI, American Express is able to process customer inquiries more efficiently via its telemarketing service representatives. When you call American Express, your telephone number is passed through the network into an on-site private branch exchange (PBX). This number is then passed along to a database computer, where an application matches up your number with American Express' record of activity on your account. Information out of the database is delivered to your representative's computer terminal as he or she picks up the phone. Although this sounds like it would take a long time, it doesn't. In fact, due to ISDN's capabilities, your call goes through a number of times faster, allowing ample time to do the database processing. So the next time you call American Express, don't be surprised if the customer service person answers the phone saying, "Good evening, Ms. Smith. How are you tonight and how has your daughter enjoyed the *World Wonders'* book you bought for her in London last week?"

Why is ISDN taking so long?

ISDN is no panacea, at least not at the present time. The principal factor limiting ISDN use is incomplete standards. Without firm and fully complete CCITT specifications, the promise of seamless networking will not be met. ISDN standards are currently "fuzzy" in a number of key areas, limiting the ability of service providers and ISDN equipment and software vendors to build systems that are readily compatible. Among the drawbacks of ISDN are:

- Lack of popularity. Until ISDN is broadly available, its potential as the single most effective networking alternative is limited. This is especially true for those companies that are spread across numerous geographically dispersed locations.
- Fragmentation of the public network. The telecommunications companies of the world is not necessarily a one-decision family. Getting them to agree to standards is one thing; having them actually implement them is another. ISDN's ultimate success will be determined by the level of cooperation demonstrated in bringing ISDN products and services to market.
- Regulations. AT&T and the Regional Bell Operating Companies bear much of the responsibility for making ISDN a reality in this country, and yet the speed with which they offer new services is greatly influenced by regulating policies. The degree of implementation varies among the RBOCs.
- Limited ISDN equipment and services. ISDN hardware is just now becoming available, but it's expensive. A PC modem that connects a personal computer into the public telephone network can be had for a very small amount compared to ISDN.

What is the future of ISDN?

Work on the next phase of ISDN has started. This new broadband ISDN provides for even higher speeds and more intelligent services. Many companies implementing ISDN today look toward broadband ISDN as their true networking destination. The Japanese seem to be skipping ISDN altogether, choosing to use the much more technically advanced broadband ISDN now, so as to avoid the upgrade costs that would be excessive in the late 1990s.

This chapter is supposed to provide the reader with the basics of the field of networking. Unless networking is mastered at all levels, such as LANs and WANs, it's not possible to implement a successful distributed database installation. A number of organizations are implementing LANs with client/server architecture to implement distributed databases in workgroups. Of course, any network is only as strong as its weakest link.

9

Client/server architecture

When one processor requests a service from another processor, it's called *client/server computing* (see FIG. 9-1). The client is the generator of the requests, and the client is generally the home of the applications. Hardware architecture doesn't necessarily make one processor a client and another processor a server. The "bigger" processing power or "bigger" storage capacity of a processor doesn't automatically make it into a server. It's the function performed by a processor that determines whether it's a client or a server. A Cray Supercomputer can be a client if it requests a service from another processor.

Client/server computing is a form of network computing in which certain functions requested by "clients," typically individual workstations configured in a LAN, are serviced by the most suitable processors in the network, the "servers." A client can be connected to other workstations, also clients, on the LAN, or networked to a system of multiple servers with diverse performance levels as far as processing power and storage capacity are concerned. If there are multiple servers in the network, certain processing requests, such as printer services or electronic mail, may be routed to a workgroup server, which may be another workstation, on the LAN. Others, requiring greater computing power, such as an enterprise database or storage services, can be directed to a bigger computer.

The term server appears in many places and in many contexts. A server is used as a terminal server, a file server, a database server, a disk server, a mail server, a communications server, and a display server, to name a few places. A server is a server if it has clients; otherwise, whom is it going to serve? A client uses services offered by a server.

A terminal server is a conventional mainframe or a mid-range computer. Terminals, which are typically "dumb" when not connected to the mainframe or to a mid-range computer, provide information to the users with the help of

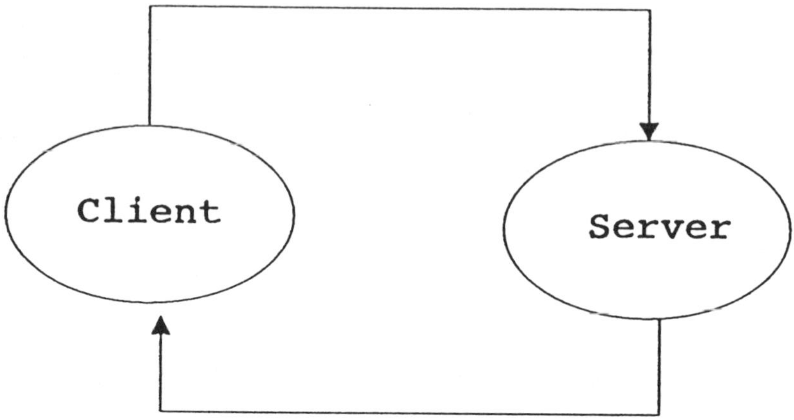

Fig. 9-1. Better communication between a requester of information (client) and provider (server) is necessary to provide "transparent" access.

applications that are already developed, in general, by data processing professionals.

In the file server model, (See FIG. 9-2), the client PC has installed on it the database management system. The client PC also has the user interface. The file server has the file manager software together with the number of files stored. The client PC requests a file or files. The file server only sends the contents of a file, and the DBMS at the client PC processes the contents. A file server enables users to share and back-up files centrally. Very fast disk drives and file access methods are a must.

In the client-server model, the client PC has the user interface. SQL queries are sent by the client to the database server. The database processing is done at the database server. Only query results are sent across the network.

A disk server is very similar to a file server, and it's sometimes easy to confuse the two. The difference is that file servers typically contain very comprehensive file record locking capabilities. With the help of the record locking capabilities, the file server can provide not only read-access capabilities, but also write-access capabilities to multiple users. A disk server often has shared read-access capability but very limited write-access capability because of lack of a record locking mechanism. As a result of the limited write-access capability, a disk server is usually substantially less expensive than a file server. File and disk servers need not be dedicated systems. They can be offered on a time-sharing system, such as a VAX, via software that permits the sharing of disk resources and of files.

A database server, which also can be either a dedicated system or software on a shared system, lets remote database applications access information stored on the server. A database server can be a piece of specialized database hardware with a database oriented instruction set such as READ, UPDATE, DELETE. If this piece of specialized database hardware can be connected to

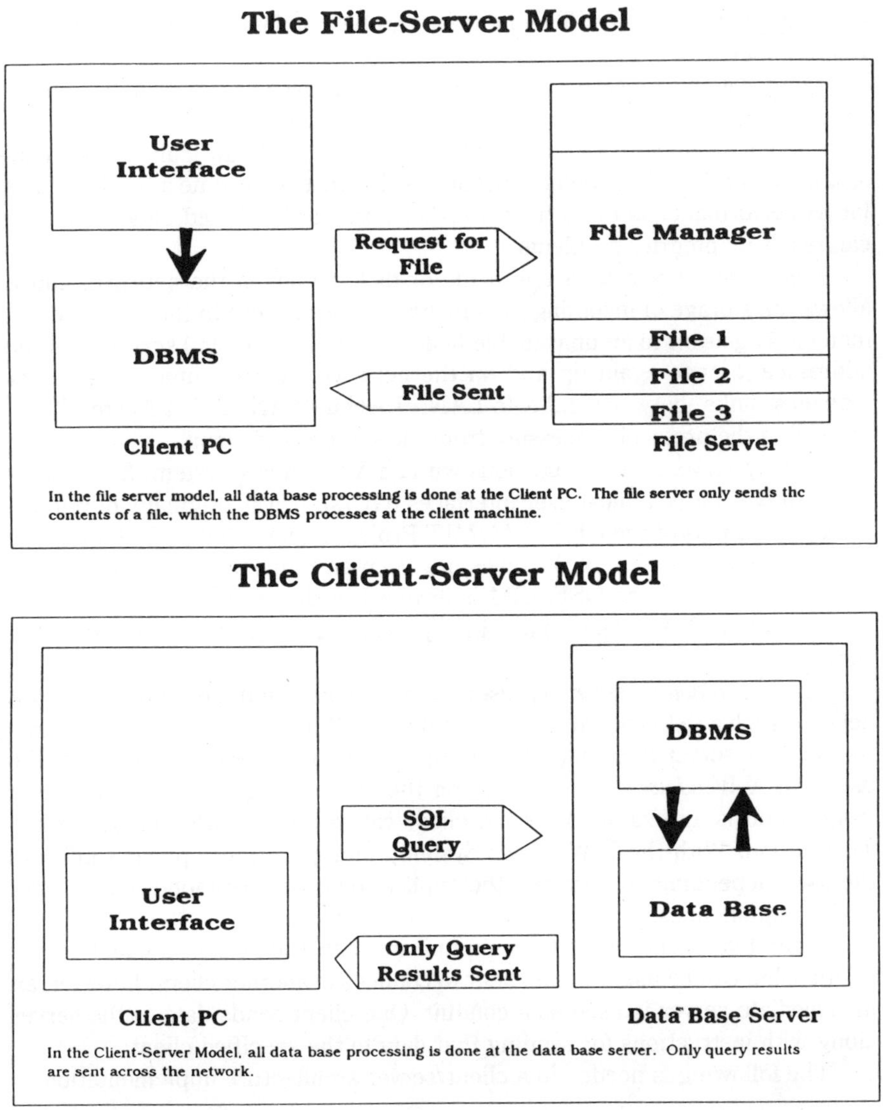

Fig. 9-2. Comparison of the file-server model and the client-server model.

another computer system, through which users can access the database, then this database hardware can be called a database machine.

Rdb/VMS on a VAX/VMS system can be a standalone database or a database server for Rdb/VMS running on other nodes connected via DECnet. It can also serve for dissimilar remote databases, such as 4th Dimension on the Macintosh, using the CL/1 interface to connect to Rdb. Database servers don't demand that all data required for an application reside on the computer system where it's to be executed. The database can be distributed across several networked nodes.

Many database servers provide or require the use of a common data dictionary, sometimes referred to as a *global data dictionary*, which may itself be fully distributed. A global data dictionary can be logistically difficult to keep consistent with regard to naming conventions. It can also become a bottleneck as far as performance is concerned. Furthermore, a distributed data dictionary can result in integrity problems.

A *mail server* is software in a file or disk server on the network, and it allows the storage of incoming mail messages for delivery to the addresses. A mail message sent to an unavailable node is stored at the mail server until the addressee is once again up and on the network. A communications server manages links between LAN-to-LAN, LAN-to-WAN and LAN-to-HOST, offloading the protocol processing from file servers and clients.

Display servers are synonymous with an X-Windows System. X-Windows is a standard for graphical user interfaces (GUIs). It was originally developed at MIT (as a part of the DEC/IBM/MIT Project Athena) but picked up by the wider Unix community. X-Windows has been an influence on the Motif GUI being developed by the OSF. IBM is involved in the evolution of X-Windows through the MIT X consortium, which provides a forum for discussion of the standard.

An *X-Windows server* represents the display and possibly the input devices, such as a keyboard, mouse or tablet. X-Windows clients are programs that use the server to display text and graphics and to receive input from the user. An *X-Windows client* can run on the same computer as the server (a workstation is an example), or the client can run on a different networked workstation. With the X-Windows System, all applications appear similar to the user, depending on how well the application developers followed the user interface guidelines.

When two clients want to communicate with each other, a client/server relationship can be used. For a client to connect to another client, however, an intermediate server is used as a conduit. One client sends data to the server along with instructions for sending that data to the specified client.

The following is needed in a client/server architecture implementation.

- A user-friendly graphical user interface resides at the client end.
- A significant portion, or all, of the application logic resides at the client end.
- The client/server system consists of networking capability.
- A client end and a server end should be distinguishable from each other, yet they should interact seamlessly.
- The client portion and the server portion may work on separate computer platforms, but they could possibly work on one and the same computer platform.
- The server is able to service multiple clients concurrently.

- The client end usually initiates actions. Particular actions, such as transferring money from reserves to a checking account if the balance goes under a certain amount, could be programmed to trigger by a database server.
- The database server should provide data protection, security, backup, recovery and SQL capability.
- If the client or the server hardware platform needs to be upgraded, it shouldn't be necessary to upgrade both. If the client hardware platform gets upgraded to a much stronger processor, performance of the server may become a bottleneck.

As far as the networking capability is concerned, the architectural components can communicate over a LAN. Some LAN configurations are increasingly being connected to MANS and WANs.

The client/server concept

The origins of the client/server concept are in the technology of database machines (see FIG. 9-3). Unlike process architectures, in which an application runs wholly on the host computer, server architectures enable the applications to run on computers separate from the database computer. In the sixties, seventies, and early eighties, a mainframe was a host with storage hierarchy.

Let's consider various levels of storage hierarchy. The processor has its memory. Some of the memory could be cache, the so-called processor cache, which is more expensive but faster than regular memory. The speeds of various levels of storage hierarchy are different. The next level is main storage, which is bigger in size than the processor cache. Main storage is less expensive and slower than processor cache. The next level of storage is mass storage. Mass storage, a permanent storage device, may consist of disk drives, tape drives and some others. These are different forms of memory. Data from disk storage is brought into main storage when the CPU asks for data. In a mainframe and minicomputer environment, disk storage is referred to as Direct Access Storage Device (DASD). In a microcomputer environment, disk storage is done on hard disk drives.

The next level of storage consists of the disk cache, which is set aside as a part of the disk. Let's consider various database environments. When someone refers to a host, the reference is probably to a mainframe or to a clustered minicomputer environment. The host has its main storage, which is also called real memory. Application code and systems modules needed from the database management system are loaded into main storage. Systems modules of the DBMS are stored on disk storage, which is virtual storage, sometimes also called *virtual memory*. Application code is brought into real memory from virtual memory on an as-needed basis.

An application program "tells" the database management system its data needs. The DBMS communicates with a disk controller regarding the needed

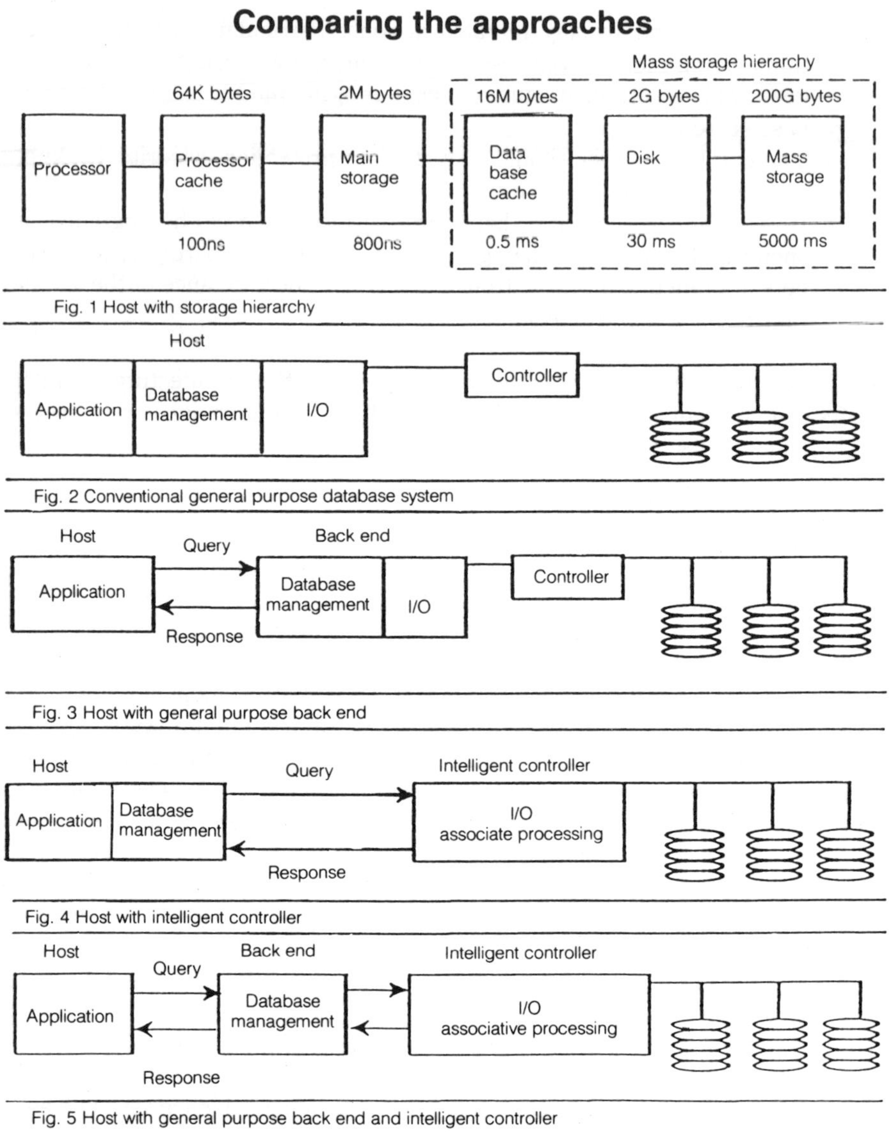

Fig. 9-3. Four approaches to a database computer, by George A. Champine. (Reprinted, with permission, from Datamation, *December, 1978.)*

database records. The disk controller searches for the database records, finds them, and presents them to the DBMS. That means the I/O processor interrupts the CPU in whatever the CPU was doing. That's the reason for calling it an I/O interrupt. The CPU has to put aside what it was doing, and go and take care of it if the interrupt has higher priority than what it was doing before. The DBMS has to look at those database records. Note that the DBMS and the application program reside in real memory. We know that the DBMS is I/O intensive. In order to minimize CPU interruptions, the DBMS component could be separated and put on a back-end processor. Only the application code remains in main memory, and I/O could be assigned to the back-end. That's a database machine.

Database machines

Database machines come in different shapes and forms. A database machine with a data-base-oriented instruction set is a true database machine. One of the early database machines was marketed by Britton Lee Corporation. Some of the concepts from the Britton Lee Machine were adopted by companies such as Teradata Corporation, who refined and added some of their own inventions and implemented those concepts further. One of the major problems with the Britton Lee machine was that it did not coexist with the IBM mainframe environment when it was introduced to the market. Up to the mid-eighties, most of the hardware manufacturers that wanted to be successful needed to coexist with the IBM mainframe. Teradata's DBC/1012 does that.

The concept of the database machine entered the client/server arena with microcomputers as clients. The server will have the database stored on it so that the server could possibly do some of the things that the client then doesn't have to do. Client/server architecture helps to divide the labor between clients and servers. If implemented correctly, client/server architecture could be the future of computing. We are separating tasks done by the server from tasks done by the clients. We have the database management back-end with the controller. Another variation could have an intelligent controller with some of the work done by the controller. That's the main concept of client/server architecture. Clients don't have to perform tasks that the server can do better, and vice versa (see FIG. 9-4).

Besides taking some concepts from the database machine, client/server architecture has also borrowed from fault-tolerant systems. The client/server

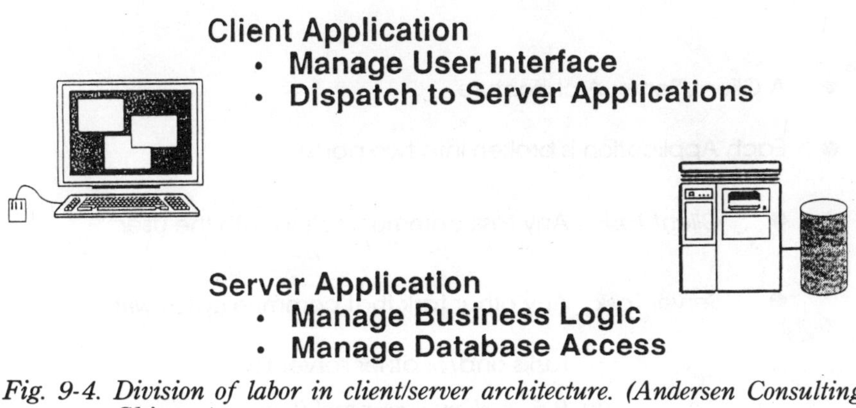

Fig. 9-4. Division of labor in client/server architecture. (Andersen Consulting, Chicago.)

architecture is a network, and in a network there should be a backup system if it's designed properly. One of the concepts of a fault tolerant system is that it has mirror imaging. Some data from server data should be stored with the clients, and it should be updated the same way as with fault-tolerant systems that provides a mirror image of the data. The main concept of client/server architecture is the separation of client and server tasks.

There could be different implementations of client/server architecture (see FIG. 9-5). Many clients could be networked with a server. The server, in turn, could be a client to another server. One of the major uses of the mainframe in the nineties is going to be the "giant server" as a switch box that's going to manage the "giant" databases. The mainframe may not necessarily perform massive processing, but it will maintain the data, transfer it, check the integrity, perform backup and recovery, and then transfer the data to workstations. There could be a number of client processes and server processes that could be transferred over a WAN or over a LAN (see FIG. 9-6).

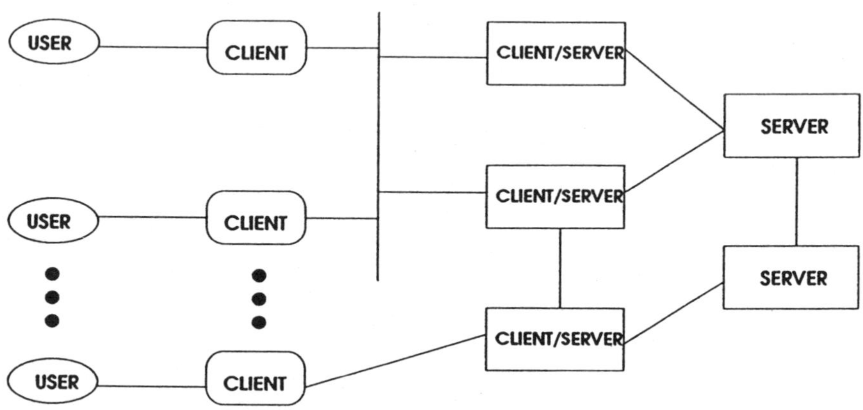

- A Client/Server Architecture
- Each Application is broken into two parts:
  - *Client Task:* Any task communicating with the user
  - *Server Task:* Any other task that communicates with client tasks and/or other server tasks.

Fig. 9-5. A client/server architecture.

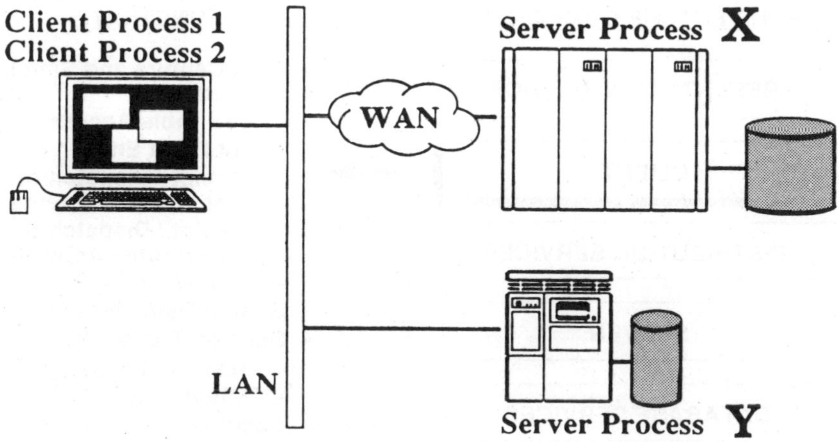

Fig. 9-6. Client/server processes. (Andersen Consulting, Chicago.)

A client/server environment has many components. Major services performed are presentation, client, distribution, server and database. Tasks performed by these components are listed in FIGS. 9-7, 9-8, 9-9, 9-10, and 9-11.

Let's consider what different types of servers we could have (see FIGS. 9-12 and 9-13). An electronic link needs to be established between different types of servers and clients. A printer is shared in many installations. There could be a print server that can distinguish between different types of fonts and do the "legwork" before the documents are provided to the printer for printing.

Another type of server could be the facsimile server. The fax machine has become an integral part of the office environment. If a fax-server could translate the transmission ahead of time, the actual transmission would be per-

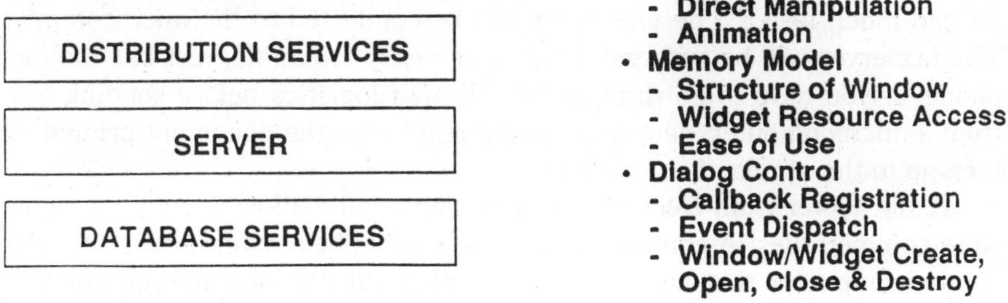

Fig. 9-7. Tasks performed by the presentation services component. (Andersen Consulting, Chicago.)

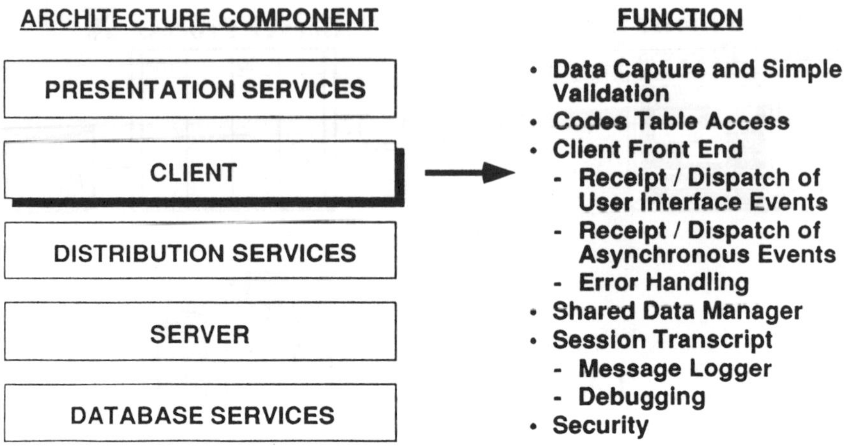

Fig. 9-8. Tasks performed by the client component. (Andersen Consulting, Chicago.)

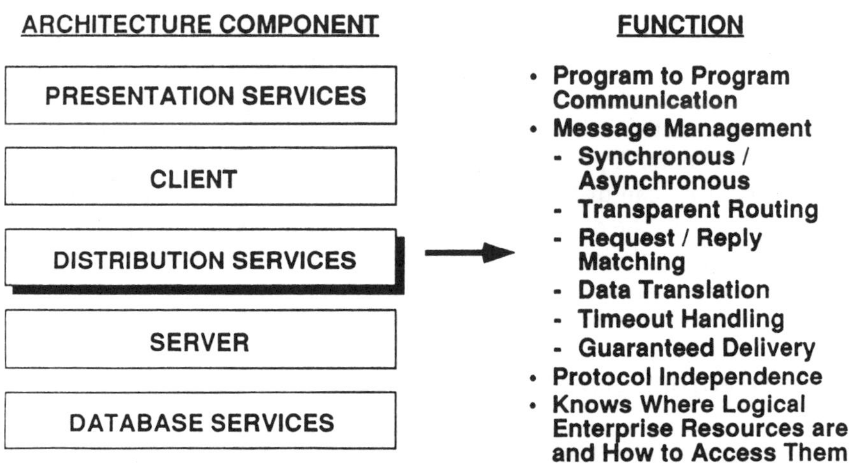

Fig. 9-9. Tasks performed by the distribution services component. (Andersen Consulting, Chicago.)

formed much faster. The fax-server will be connected to the microcomputer. The faxserver will be successful only if it's easy to handle, just like dialing a phone. If you have to go through complicated logistics before sending a fax from a microcomputer, people are just going to get the document printed and then go to the regular fax machines.

A file server is an electronic librarian and could allow users to share and store common files. A computational server could be a mainframe or a cluster of minicomputers that can perform complex calculations at high speed. A communications server can connect one network to another, have some intelligence in finding which nodes are not functioning, and ensure that the network

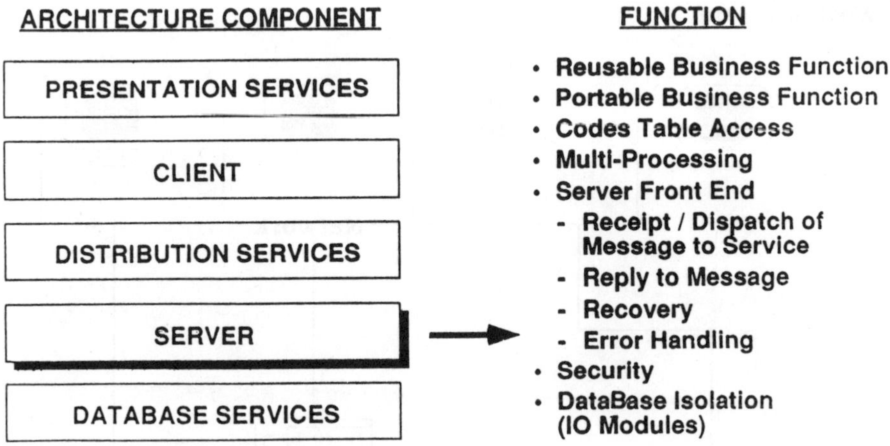

Fig. 9-10. Tasks performed by the server component. (Andersen Consulting, Chicago.)

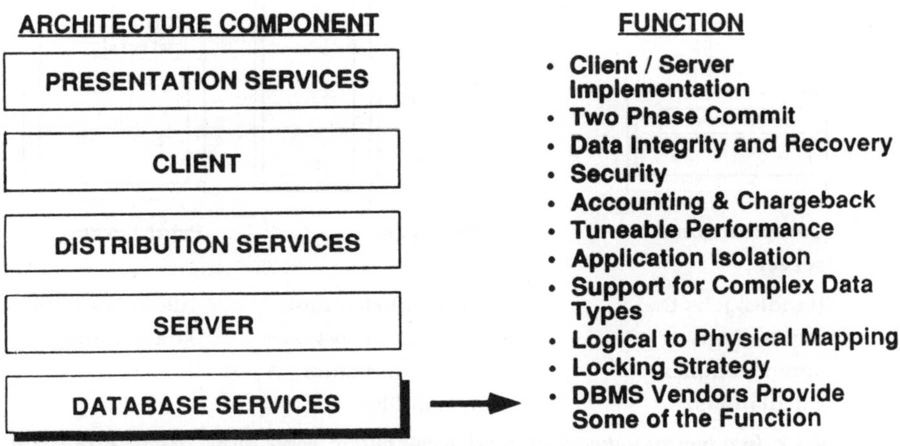

Fig. 9-11. Tasks performed by the database services component. (Andersen Consulting, Chicago.)

runs smoothly. An applications server could possibly run a number of applications that are not run on clients; an applications server also works in tandem with databases. It's not necessary to have a server for each different function. Some functions could be combined in one server.

This is the new division of labor in tasks that need to be performed (see FIG. 9-14). An application program is the front end and a database server is the back end. The front end takes care of forms design, presentation, application logic, data manipulation, and query tools providing menus and utilities. The server should support many client tools simultaneously. Clients should work with many servers simultaneously. Data location should be transparent to clients. A back-end server is the database server that takes care of the storage,

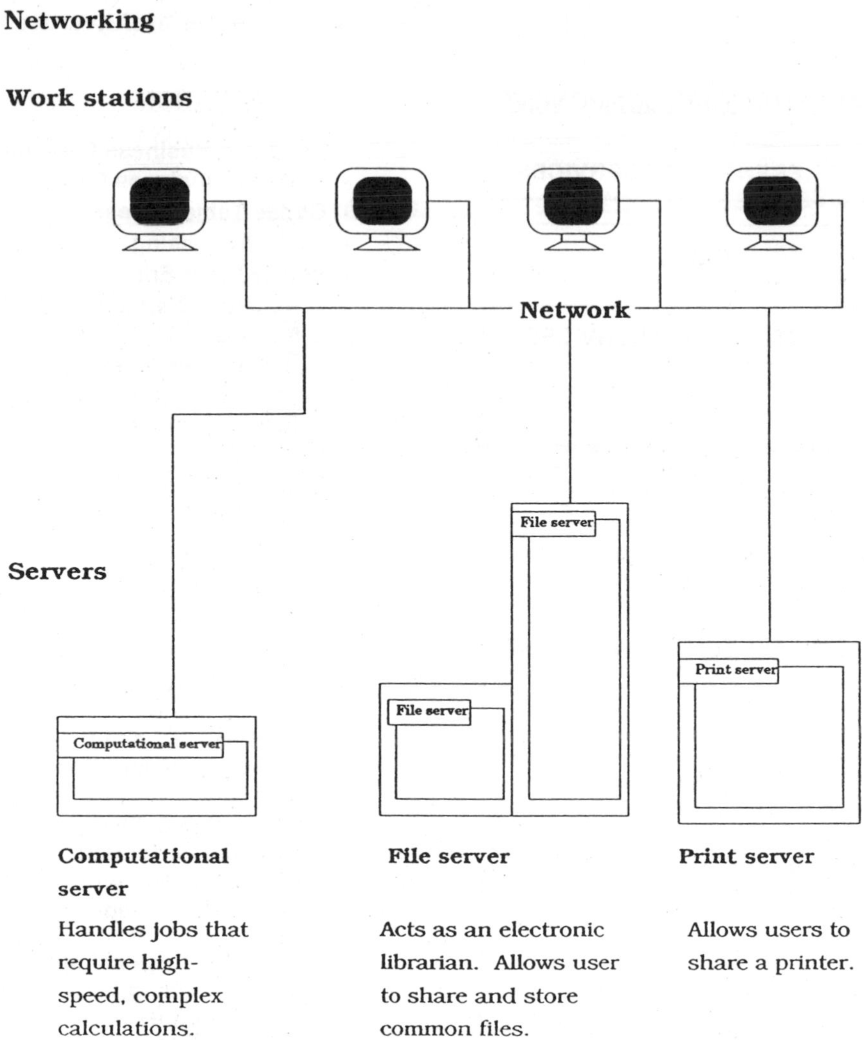

Fig. 9-12. In a typical network of desktop computers, some tasks, like printing, can now be handled by specialized machines called servers.

security, data administration, database record selection, database field aggregation, indexing and sorting various fields, as well as performing batch updates. Instead of doing everything on one processor, we are separating labor between client and server.

Let's consider the possible distribution of functions in a bank with client/server architecture (see FIG. 9-15). The microcomputer as a client could provide a graphical user interface. It could also calculate interest rate payments. With the help of the client microcomputer, the bankers could possibly draw up certain savings and loan plans. The microcomputer could be used for filling out loan applications. Rejection of some of the loan applications could take place right on the client microcomputer, if the applicant was an obvious loan risk.

- <u>PRINT SERVER</u>: Allows users to share a printer or printers. Documents to be printed are sent to a Print Server.

- <u>FACSIMILE SERVER</u>: Allows users to send or receive a facsimile transmission.

- <u>FILE SERVER</u>: Acts as an electronic librarian. Allows users to share and store common files.

- <u>COMPUTATIONAL SERVER</u>: Handles jobs that require high-speed, complex calculations (a number cruncher).

- <u>COMMUNICATIONS SERVER</u>: Connects one network to another.

- <u>APPLICATIONS SERVER</u>: Runs applications and retrieves information from data base(s).

Fig. 9-13. Types of servers.

Application Program (Front-End)	**Data Base Server** (Back-End)
• Forms Design	• Storage
• Presentation	• Security
• Application Logic	• Data Administration
• Data Manipulation	• Selections/Aggregation
• Query Tools	• Indexing/Sorting
• Menus/Utilities	• Batch Updates

Fig. 9-14. Client/server: the new division of labor.

Microcomputer	Server	Mainframe
	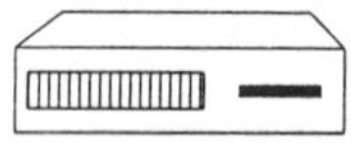	
■ Runs applications ■ Supports presentation services. ■ Calculates Interest rate payments. ■ Lets bankers draw up custom savings and loan plans. ■ Is used to fill out electronic forms such as loan applications.	■ Stores files programs and completed electronic forms. ■ Downloads blank electronic forms to the PC. ■ Supports the link to the mainframe. ■ Maintains interest rates. ■ Ships electronic forms to the laser printer.	■ Supplies customer account data to PCs as needed. ■ Downloads interest rate changes and software upgrades to the server. ■ Uploads completed electronic forms from the server.

Fig. 9-15. Possible distribution of functions in a bank with client/server architecture.

The "local" file server could possibly store files, programs and completed electronic forms. It could maintain interest rates. It could possibly play the role of a printer server.

The mainframe, as a "giant" database server, could provide data about the clients. It could maintain nationwide interest rates, and it could provide the clients with software upgrades.

Client tasks

The client has to work with user interfaces such as: Hewlett-Packard's New Wave, Microsoft's Windows, Sun Microsystem's Open Look, IBM's Presentation Manager, and NeXT Corporation's NeXTStep. It also has to format screen presentations and user actions in response, manage dialog between system and user, and determine the capability of the server task. The client also has to determine which server should receive a task.

The client needs some intelligence to determine which server should get the task. It has to make sure that the task is not sent to an inappropriate server. That could be the nearest server or a server determined by negotiations between the client system and the other systems in the network. If there are two servers, and one says I will give you this cheaper than the other one, the client has to be in a position to determine whether that's possible. It might be appropriate to locate the optimal server for performing the task. Instead of clients deciding about best-suited servers, it could be the superserver deciding about the appropriate server for a specific client task.

Implementing client/server architecture

A company should migrate to client/server architecture when it has a sophisticated microcomputer network and time-shared minicomputers and mainframes. If there's no need for networking, there's no need for investing in a client/server environment, because networking is a prerequisite for a client/server architecture.

Every installation wants to squeeze greater value out of existing hardware. Since there are hundreds or thousands of microcomputers in a number of organizations, management would like to develop some of the new applications on microcomputers. That's called *down-scaling*. To some extent it's a variation of the client/server environment. An organization wants to take certain applications from the mainframe and put them on smaller machines. In doing so, one of the major goals is increasing the price/performance ratio.

This is exactly the concept of cooperative processing. It's a division of tasks based on the best-suited platform for the job. There could be a division of labor between a host, probably a mainframe, and the microcomputer-based workstation. It's possible that some things that are done by the microcomputer-based workstations need to be brought up to the mainframe to communicate with other processors.

Benefits of client/server architecture

The client/server architecture should provide more power for less money by offloading applications from expensive processors to inexpensive processors. It should also allow more flexible and economical applications development on microcomputers.

Pitfalls of client/server architecture

Client/server architecture requires sophisticated data administration and security. It's a nascent technology and, as a result, it still has beta-version products and software bugs. Dealers and resellers don't have experience in implementing and troubleshooting the client/server environment. It's very hard to get assistance in case of problems.

The first generation of servers were IBM PC/AT class microcomputers as a work-group file server with a printer server. This was basically a LAN implementation.

Second-generation servers are Reduced Instruction Set Computer (RISC)-based, which are mostly Unix platform machines. They have much better performance and superior graphics capabilities, but basically they're providing functions similar to those provided by first-generation servers.

Third-generation servers are SQL servers. These are SQL engines running across the whole spectrum of systems from IBM PCs to mainframes, putting together many pieces to allow the servers to deliver a high level of service at the departmental or multidepartmental level. They're effectively an enterprise server or an open server.

Open server

An open server should be in an integrator's tool kit to provide connectivity, allowing users to build and customize their application-specific servers.

There should be a tool kit to provide integration between different types of data or services. Integration is between data stored in host databases such as DB2, Oracle, Rdb, RMS, VSAM, CA-DATACOM and CA-IDMS, just to name a few. Third-party applications, such as accounting applications and process controls, as well as public database services such as Dow Jones and electronic mail, should be made available.

Software definition of client/server

Distributing pieces of an application where they logically belong in the network sounds almost like cooperative processing. In order to implement it, a smart server is required. The smart server should model both the business and the data. That means, the business logic has to be put in the server in the form of business rules instead of putting the same logic in each application program. The logic is reusable, and it ultimately standardizes development while saving money.

Server architectures

Within each class of server (file, database, communications and others) three different architectures will be implemented:

1. Microcomputers or workstations as servers. Microcomputers and Unix workstations (RISC-based or CISC-based) will be used as low-end servers.
2. Mid-range/mainframes as servers. Organizations that already have a major investment in this type of hardware will use mid-range machines/mainframes as servers.
3. Network computers. These machines are specifically designed to serve workstations via a LAN. There will be two types of vendors supplying network computers. One type is the one that supports Unix workstations, and the other type is the one that supports microcomputers.

Server software and different tools

This will be developed by both MIS organizations and third-party vendors. There should be an extension to PC DOS-based databases. Existing single user PC DOS databases, like Paradox, DataEase and dBase will have access to data stored in DB2, Oracle, and other DBMSs. That could be the first step.

There should also be applications supporting access to data and the mailing of messages across the LAN from software such as spreadsheets, word processing and CAD/CAM. Front ends could leverage expert-system technology. This could be the next step in providing alternative interfaces, such as forms for office workers and sales-calls reporting. It should provide some form of EIS (Executive Information System).

The first activity performed is terminal emulation because there are millions of terminals installed. Communications facilities will manage the link to the host while the client portion controls all screen handling and keyboard mapping. This software will enable LAN users to access "old world" mainframe and minicomputer applications and data. Also needed are peer-to-peer applications links, which are the communications software servers that link mail, workflow and DDB systems on a peer-to-peer level.

Major networks

The major protocols used in client/server architecture networking are: Transmission Control Protocol/Internet Protocol (TCP/IP) in the Unix world, VAX-net in the DEC environment, and OS/2 LAN Manager and Novell's NetWare at the microcomputer level. Manufacturers of LANs are trying to get into client/server architecture implementations.

Key enabling technologies for a full-function client/server architecture

The major technologies used for a full-function client/server environment are:

- Distributed relational databases supporting synchronized multiuser updates.
- Application development tools supporting development of applications that are intended to work synchronously and dynamically, and perform on heterogeneous processor architectures.
- Object-oriented data structures.
- Network-communications processes that are topology insensitive.

Standards

The client/server architecture could be the wave of the future. But the organizations that have used IBM mainframes for decades will need tremendous adjustments to reap benefits from the "divide and conquer" strategy of client/server architecture.

Part IV

Evaluation and selection of DDBMS software

10

Choosing DDBMS software

A distributed database management system (DDBMS) has to be able to access data on various platforms, including mainframes, minicomputers, workstations and microcomputers. A DDBMS product is not going to be a mainframe-based product; it's going to be a "network-based" product that will enable organizations to develop future applications on cheaper cycles in the form of microcomputers and workstations. A DDBMS product is able to interconnect all platforms in an enterprise-wide manner. That means the product is going to be running with a client/server architecture and is going to access mainframe databases created over the past several years. Mainframe-based databases have evolved into life blood for most large organizations over the years. The databases represent customer records, product records, policy records, claims records, and money transaction records, just to name a few.

The DDBMS has to be able to communicate with all the other DBMSs installed. This almost sounds like a "big loan" to take care of all the "small loans!"

Typically, the selection of one software package involves the evaluation of other packages, somewhat along the lines of the domino principle. Selecting a DDBMS usually involves evaluating and selecting not only the DDBMS, but also a data dictionary/directory, a query package, a report generation language, a graphical user interface (GUI), networking hardware and networking software.

Too often, evaluators decide to buy the DDBMS for now and select a data dictionary/directory or GUI later. This is a dangerous act. Selecting a DDBMS or its associated satellite products without regard for the comprehensive list of future requirements reduces options for later evaluation and selection of other products.

Selection

To select a DDBMS, the following proven approach is recommended. It consists of five phases (see FIG. 10-1).

Phase 1. Need identification.
Phase 2. Elimination process.
Phase 3. Vendor evaluation.

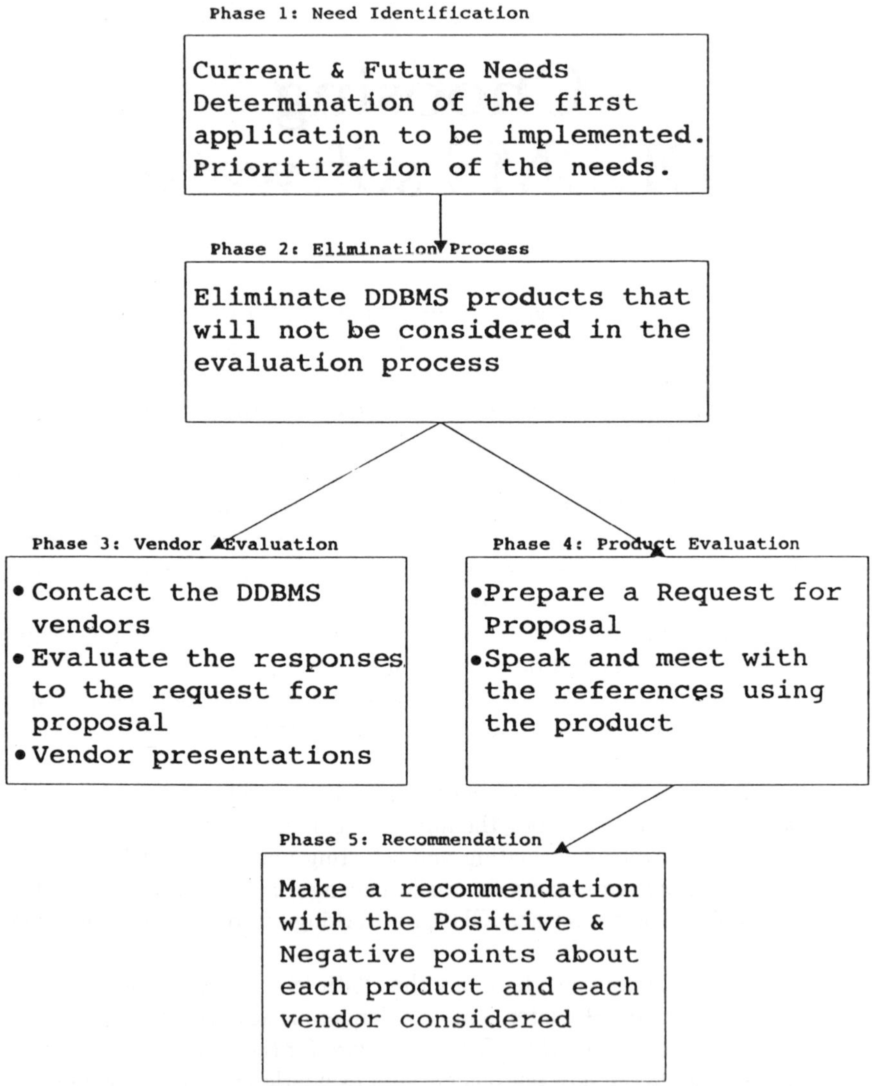

Fig. 10-1. Identifying, eliminating, evaluating, and recommending vendors and products.

Phase 4. Product evaluation.
Phase 5. Recommendation.

Need identification

The need identification phase is a crucial part of any major buying decision. Individual, departmental and corporate needs will be evaluated. Current requirements will be the driving factor for choosing the right product. The consideration of future requirements is also important, because if you outgrow the original product's capabilities, it will become much more expensive and time-consuming, perhaps virtually impossible, to convert to another product later on.

It's always ideal to find a product that addresses all of your current and future needs. But sometimes that too is impossible. It's important to prioritize the evaluation criteria so that no major compromise is made, let's say, on the first three very important criteria. Then the evaluation and selection process doesn't become a formidable task.

We also want to identify the first application that will be implemented using client/server technology. Which data will be accessed, located on what server platforms, and presented to what clients? The first application has to be a success. The application shouldn't be overwhelmingly large. It will then take years to finish the project. Some quick results within a six months' timeframe need to be shown.

One of the major activities here is acquiring management commitment for the evaluation, selection and implementation stages. Representatives from user management need to be a part of the evaluation process to ensure their continued support.

Needs analysis defines what the capabilities of the "right" DDBMS should be. Who defines the needs? For small projects it may be just an individual. But for larger projects or for projects that are implemented throughout the organization, it may involve a group of people, preferably a variety of people, some with a technical background, others with a user perspective. Wide representation and diverse viewpoints early in the decision process produce better decisions and fewer surprises later.

In today's environment, most of the installations need to support on-line transaction processing (OLTP), as well as a decision support system. Assessing the application development environment generates a set of questions related to application development tools. Investigating operating environments on various platforms enables you to think about the environments in which the software will run, as well as what is necessary to migrate the database and applications to the new environments.

Often, a corporation has selected a particular vendor or hardware architecture as its strategic direction. This means that further down the road, applications and databases may need to be installed on systems of a particular brand or type. Determination of the operating environments on various platforms assists in the next phase, the elimination process.

Elimination process

This phase will eliminate packages that should clearly be out of the race. There should be a reasonably small number of candidates. How small is reasonably small? Try to limit the number to three or four. The number should be kept this low to keep the evaluation cost to a minimum. With each additional candidate, the cost goes up. You have to collect and evaluate information in a number of categories. You will need to have meetings with vendor salespeople in order to validate that the product works on all platforms. It has to at least provide easy access to data on mainframes, clustered minicomputers, workstations and microcomputers.

How can the number be brought to three or four? Establish some baseline requirements (see FIG. 10-2) that might include the following:

- DDBMS should be compatible with the hardware to be supported.
- DDBMS should be compatible with the operating systems to be supported (e.g., PC DOS, PC DOS/Windows, OS/2, VMS, MVS, VM/CMS).
- DDBMS should support the implemented or planned LAN, MAN and WAN.
- DDBMS should support the SQL (Structured Query Language).
- DDBMS should have a screen painter, preferably the commonly accepted standard graphical user interface (GUI). In the case of IBM mainframe installations, consider support of common user access (CUA).
- DDBMS should have an easy to use report writer, ad-hoc query capability, prototyping facility and other common tools.
- DDBMS should support an integrated data dictionary/directory.

Vendor evaluation

This phase focuses on the evaluation of each vendor's background, services and financial stability. Database vendors must be able to provide various levels of technical support, both before and after purchase. In the client/server architecture and in downsizing implementations, the product pricing structure is important. Volume purchase discounts have to be considered, although this should not be the primary criterion. Most database decisions are not purchases of one or two units, since a number of people, each with their own copy of the product, will be sharing the database. When purchasing database products, the total volume purchase price is often more relevant than a unit price.

Find out if the vendor offers runtime versions of their products. Those versions are lower-cost subsets of the product, which allow users to run a previously created application, but not to build new ones. Figure 10-3 contains a list of questions that could be helpful in evaluating vendors.

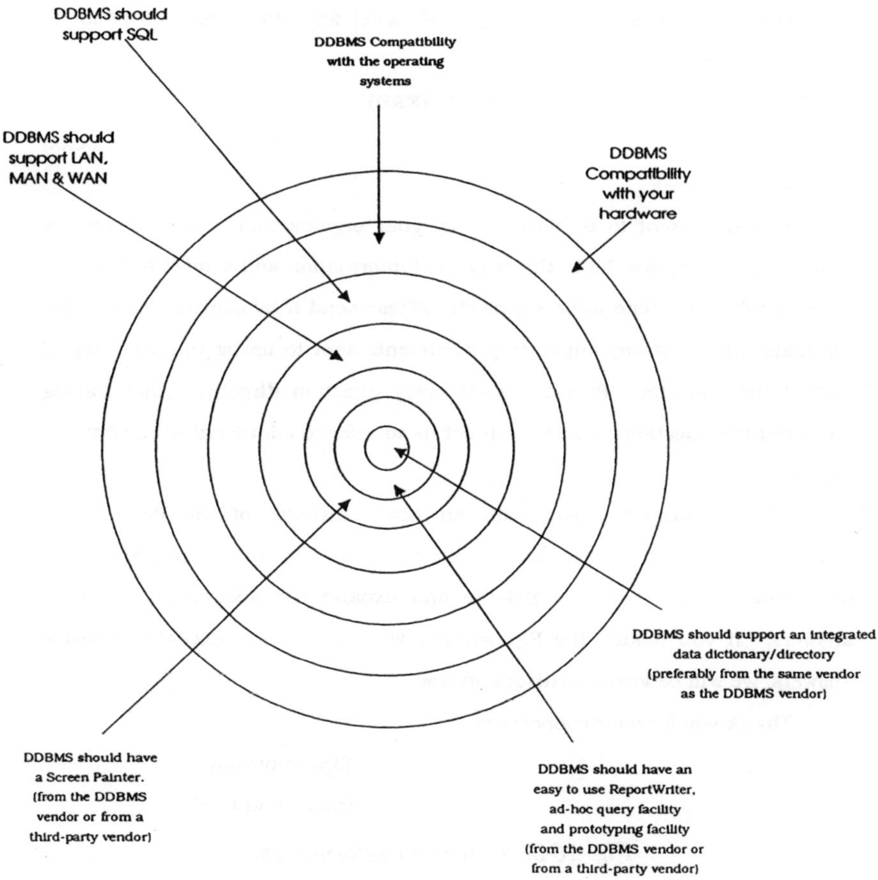

Fig. 10-2. The elimination process.

Product evaluation

There are several factors to investigate when performing a product evaluation.

Client/server architecture (See FIG. 10-4. Also refer to Chapter 9 for a detailed discussion.) Many conventional database products handle all database functions in one program. It's easier to implement the product, but the maintenance is complicated. Furthermore, they don't allow easy implementation of a distributed database across a network, and can often run only on systems with large memory capabilities.

A more recent database architecture is the client/server or requester/server approach. It's important that the DDBMS product supports this architecture.

The following is an example of a Request for Information (RFI) that is sent to vendors:

(LETTERHEAD)

(Date xx.xx.xx)

Dear (vendor name):

This document to be filled out by your organization is sent to you by courier service. Please fill in the requested information and send it to (address to be supplied) by (date to be supplied). Please send it by courier service. We will make this, and any supporting documents sent to us by you, an integral part of the contract. Please answer every question directly. After having answered the questions, you may direct us to refer to additional documents as a reference.

We are supplying you with an ASCII diskette of the Request for Information (RFI). We have used (name of wordprocessor) for preparing this document. Please use the diskette and expand the document with your answers. If you modify the RFI without written consent, except to provide answers, we will be forced to disqualify you.

Thank you for your cooperation.

Sincerely yours,

(name and title)

Fig. 10-3. Request for information.

REQUEST FOR INFORMATION CONTENTS

DDBMS Evaluation Schedule and Request For Information (RFI) Instructions

Fig. 10-3. Request for information (cont'd).

I. VENDOR/PRODUCT GENERAL INFORMATION

I.1 FINANCIAL BASE

Name of Product: ____________________

Name of Company: ____________________

Street Address: ____________________

City: __________ State: __________ Zip: __________

Technical Rep.: ____________________ Phone: ( ) __________

Sales Rep.: ____________________ Phone: ( ) __________

How long has your company been in business? ____________________

____

*Has ownership changed during the past five years? Yes ____ No ____

*Are you being sued? Yes ____ No ____

*Are you suing any other company? Yes ____ No ____

*Did somebody else develop this product for you? Yes ____ No ____

If you answered yes to any of the previous 4 questions, attach additional explanations.

When did you first sell this product for mainframes: __________

for minicomputers: __________
for workstations: __________
for microcomputers: __________

Please attach a list of 10 of your customers, their addresses, phone number and contacts.

Fig. 10-3. Request for information (cont'd).

Please complete the following:

YEAR	NUMBER OF INSTALLATIONS	GROSS SALES *
Current Year		
Current Year -1		
Current Year -2		
Current Year -3		
Current Year -4		
	TOTAL:	TOTAL:

Please attach a copy of your company's annual report for (put the year of interest)

Can we contact your bank? Yes ____ No _____

If no, please explain why.______________________________

If yes, please provide us with the following information:______________

Name of Bank Account Number(s): ______________________

Bank Address: ______________________________

City:__________________ State:__________ Zip: __________

Contact:__________________ Phone: ______________

What is your Dun and Bradstreet number?______________

____

What is your sales forecast for the next fiscal year?

____

***If you are a privately held corporation, we can sign a non-disclosure and confidentiality form so that you can release sales information.**

Fig. 10-3. Request for information (cont'd).

I.2 TECHNICAL SUPPORT

How many employees do you have now? ____________________

How many employees did you have last year? ____________________

How many employees are involved in product development/enhancements? ____________________

How many employees are involved in customer technical support? ____________________

How many employees are involved in customer training? ____________________

Do you have 24 hour hotline numbers for technical support? Yes ______ No ______

If Yes, please list them: (800) ___ _______ ( ) ___ _______

Do you have a multiple-site leasing agreement? Please attach information. Yes ______ No ______

Will you provide local support to us? Yes ______ No ______

Will we have to subscribe to an annual support service? Yes ______ No ______

If Yes, what is the cost of annual support? $ ____________________

What is the approximate number of new releases per year? ____________________

____

____

Will we automatically receive new releases? Yes ______ No ______

Will we periodically (every ______ months) receive maintenance fixes? ______

Please attach additional information about your past year's frequency of the fixes.

Fig. 10-3. Request for information (cont'd).

Do you provide consulting services? Please attach information about types of these services and consulting fees.	Yes _____ No _____
Do you have a user group?	Yes _____ No _____
If yes, does your user group assist you with priorities in your development effort?	Yes _____ No _____
How many times does your user group meet during a year?	__________
Can we contact a representative from your user group?	Yes _____ No _____
If yes, please give us contact and telephone number: User Group Contact: __________	( ) __________ Telephone #

Fig. 10-3. Request for information (cont'd).

I.3 CUSTOMER OPINION ABOUT PRODUCT

List 5 most outstanding features of your product reported by customers:

1. ______________________________

2. ______________________________

3. ______________________________

4. ______________________________

5. ______________________________

List 5 problem areas of your product reported by customers:

1. ______________________________

2. ______________________________

3. ______________________________

4. ______________________________

5. ______________________________

Please attach list of customers whose opinions you described here.

(Contacts and phone numbers.)

Fig. 10-3. Request for information (cont'd).

I.4 PRODUCT PRICES

What is the price of the complete package? (Including all optional modules.)

(List the hardware platforms you are evaluating to interconnect

with the DDBMS)

Fig. 10-3. Request for information (cont'd).

What discounts can you offer for a network of computers?

____

____

____

____

What discounts can you offer for multiple copies of IBM

or compatible PC version of your product?

____

____

____

____

Fig. 10-3. Request for information (cont'd).

II. AVAILABILITY AND ERROR RECOVERY

Please attach additional explanations for each of the following questions:

II.1 Is your DDBMS capable of supporting around the clock (24 hours a day, 7 days a week) online operation? Yes__No__

II.2 Is your DDBMS capable of supporting around the clock continued data base services with the data base subsets down for maintenance? Yes__No__

II.3 Does your DDBMS provide concurrent online reorganization utilities?

a. for performance tuning Yes__No__

b. for better disk space utilization? Yes__No__

c. for expansion of current hardware/ software configuration? Yes__No__

II.4 Does your DDBMS provide automatic recovery in the event of system failure? Yes__No__

II.5 Does your DDBMS allow isolation of the recovery procedures to the smallest system unit possible? (Incremental) Yes__No__

II.6 Does your DDBMS provide a data base snapshot type utility? Yes__No__

II.7 Does your DDBMS provide transaction control with the following capabilities:

- roll forward Yes__No__
- rollback Yes__No__

II.8 Does your DDBMS keep a journal of transactions during normal operation of the system? Yes__No__

II.9 When does the DDBMS write a record to the journal of transactions?

- before changes to the data base are made Yes__No__
- after changes to the data base are being successfully applied Yes__No__
- after a change was verified as being successfully applied Yes__No__

II.10 Does your DDBMS provide facilities for

Fig. 10-3. Request for information (cont'd).

the selective recovery of desired transactions? Yes__No___

II.11 Does your DDBMS support backup procedures, concurrent with the online operations, on the following levels:

- full data base Yes__No___
- file Yes__No___
- block Yes__No___
- record Yes__No___

III. DDBMS INSTALLATION AND ADMINISTRATION

PLEASE ATTACH ADDITIONAL EXPLANATIONS FOR EACH OF THE FOLLOWING QUESTIONS:

III.1 How long does it take to install the DDBMS?

III.2 What additional resources are needed during reorganization of the DDBMS file systems? (File space, tape drives, etc.)

III.3 What are the maximums allowed for block/buffer sizes? (List the operating systems of interest)

III.4 Does the DDBMS provide information about the following statistical parameters:

- CPU utilization Yes__No___
- main memory utilization Yes__No___
- storage utilization Yes__No___
- data base access Yes__No___
- efficiency of data base organization Yes__No___

III.5 Does the DDBMS provide information to allow chargeback accounting to multiple systems/applications that use the DDBMS? Yes__No___

III.6 PLEASE ATTACH INFORMATION ON PERFORMANCE COMPARISON BETWEEN YOUR ddbms AND OTHER VENDOR PRODUCTS. PLEASE DESCRIBE THE SPECIFICS OF ANY BENCHMARKS USED FOR EVALUATION PURPOSES.

IV. Data Integrity

IV.1 Does your DDBMS provide the integrity definition facilities? Yes__No___

IV.2 Are these facilities included in the Data Definition Language? Yes__No___

Fig. 10-3. Request for information (cont'd).

IV.3 Are the integrity definitions maintained in Data Dictionary? Yes__No__

IV.4 Is the referential integrity ensured? Yes__No__

IV.5 Is it possible to use these facilities from the following levels:

- SQL Yes__No__
- precompiler Yes__No__
- host programming language Yes__No__

IV.6 Do these facilities allow the definition and enforcement of integrity assertions at the following levels:

- file Yes__No__
- record Yes__No__
- subset of records Yes__No__
- field (data element) Yes__No__
- subset of fields Yes__No__
- relationship Yes__No__
- transaction Yes__No__

IV.7 Does the DDBMS provide exclusive locking at the following levels:

- file Yes__No__
- record Yes__No__
- field Yes__No__

IV.8 Does the DDBMS insure the integrity of concurrency controls? (Levels of locking) Yes__No__

IV.9 Does the DDBMS provide deadlock detection and resolution mechanism? Yes__No__

IV.10 Does the DDBMS insure the transaction processing integrity? (Integrity of logical transactions) Yes__No__

IV.11 Does the DDBMS perform all data checks through the data dictionary? Yes__No__

V. SECURITY AND PRIVACY OF DATA

V.I Does your DDBMS provide security definition facilities? Yes__No__

Fig. 10-3. Request for information (cont'd).

V.2 Are these facilities included in the Data Definition Language? Yes__No___

V.3 Are the security definitions maintained in Data Dictionary? Yes__No___

V.4 Is it possible to use these facilities from the following levels:

- SQL Yes__No___
- precompiler Yes__No___
- host programming language Yes__No___

INDICATE WHETHER YOUR DDBMS MODULES HAVE THE FOLLOWING SECURITY FEATURES:

V.5 Provide password protection on the data base level Yes__No___

V.6 Provide reports on security violations Yes__No___

V.7 Allow the assignment of restrictions on execution of application programs for:

- group of users Yes__No___
- group of terminals Yes__No___

V.8 Allow the definition of data access (find, read, add, update, delete) restrictions at the following levels:

- data base Yes__No___
- file Yes__No___
- record Yes__No___
- subset of records Yes__No___
- field Yes__No___
- subset of fields Yes__No___
- data element value Yes__No___
- relationship Yes__No___
- transaction Yes__No___
- group of authorized users Yes__No___

V.9 Provide data encryption capability (Encryption of actual data besides the password) Yes__No___

V.10 Provide external/logical views to insure the privacy of data Yes__No___

V.11 Administer all security checks through the data dictionary Yes__No___

Fig. 10-3. Request for information (cont'd).

VI. DATA DICTIONARY/DIRECTORY

VI.1 Does the DDBMS support cross reference capability for all data bases, views, reports, forms, processes, etc.? Yes_No__

VI.2 Does the DDBMS provide documentation for all data dictionary elements? Yes_No__

VI.3 Does the DDBMS support logical/physical views of data bases? (Mapping between logical/physical definitions) Yes_No__

VI.4 Does the DDBMS support integrated data dictionary standards control? Yes_No__

VI.5 Does the DDBMS support identification and elimination of redundant data elements? Yes_No__

VI.6 Does the DDBMS support batch and online inquiry/update of the dictionary? Yes_No__

VI.7 Is online inquiry/update of the data dictionary an interactive process? Yes_No__

VI.8 Does the DDBMS support any "extensibility" type features of a data dictionary? (Support of user defined segments in data dictionary?) Yes_No__

VI.9 Does the DDBMS provide facilities for security of the data dictionary (for updating and inquiry of data elements, views, etc.) Yes_No__

VI.10 Does the DDBMS support a user friendly report facility for the data dictionary? Yes_No__

VII. DATA TYPES

VII.1 Are all supported fundamental data types available on the following levels:

- SQL Yes_No__
- precompiler Yes_No__
- host programming language Yes_No__

VII.2 Does the DDBMS support the following DDBMS specific" field types:

Fig. 10-3. Request for information (cont'd).

- date Yes__No__
- time Yes__No__
- money Yes__No__
- text (raw data) Yes__No__
- keyword Yes__No__
- comment Yes__No__
- constant (character, decimal, hex, etc.) Yes__No__
- graphic (bit stream) Yes__No__

VII.3 Are all supported "DDBMS specific" field types available on the following levels:

- SQL Yes__No__
- precompiler Yes__No__
- host programming language Yes__No__

VIII. LOGICAL STRUCTURING

PLEASE ATTACH ADDITIONAL EXPLANATIONS FOR EACH OF THE FOLLOWING QUESTIONS

VIII.1 Does your DDBMS support the following relationships between record types:

- one-to-one Yes__No__
- one-to-many Yes__No__
- many-to-many Yes__No__

VIII.2 Does your DDBMS support the following relationship orders:

- fifo (first in, first out) Yes__No__
- lifo (last in, first out) Yes__No__
- sorted Yes__No__
- next/previous Yes__No__

IX. HOST PROGRAMMING LANGUAGE and PRECOMPILER

IX.1 Does your DDBMS provide the folloiwng utilities:

- host programming language interfaces (direct 3GL-like calls to DDBMS facilities Yes__No__
- precompiler interfaces (embedded SQL statements) Yes__No__

PLEASE LIST ALL SUPPORTED PROGRAMMING LANGUAGES.

IX.2 Do you provide interface with C programming

Fig. 10-3. Request for information (cont'd).

language? Yes__No___

- Which C? _________
- On which hardware platform? _________

IX.3 Are host language and precompiler applications portable between all listed above hardware and software environments? Yes__No___

X. SQL/4GL

X.1 Is your SQL/4GL an ANSI standard language? Please attach additional information for this question. Yes__No___

X.2 Which DDBMS products have compatible SQL/4GL like yours? (e.g., IBM's DB2, Oracle, etc.) _________

PLEASE ATTACH THE DETAILED LIST OF COMPATIBLE PRODUCTS.

X.3 Can all SQL/4GL utilities be shared by all users in a multi-user environment? Yes__No___

X.4 Are all application/development tools accessible from the SQL/4GL level? Yes__No___

PLEASE ATTACH ADDITIONAL INFORMATION FOR THIS QUESTION.

X.5 Does the SQL/4GL support both interactive online and batch operations? (It should be possible to use the same set of SQL/4GL statements for both interactive and batch access of the data bases). Yes__No___

PLEASE ATTACH ADDITIONAL INFORMATION FOR THIS QUESTION.

X.6 Do you have QBE-like facility in addition to SQL? (QBE - Query-By-Example) Yes__No___

X.7 Can the DDBMS users compile and save the SQL/4GL procedures in the data dictionary? Yes__No___

PLEASE ATTACH ADDITIONAL INFORMATION FOR THIS QUESTION.

X.8 Are all SQL/4GL procedures/functions administered? Yes__No___

X.9 Does the SQL/4GL allow its users to create

Fig. 10-3. Request for information (cont'd).

and maintain private data dictionaries? Yes_No__

X.10 Can the SQL/4GL automatically format data for input/entry and output files based on definition of the data contained in the data dictionary? Yes_No__

X.11 Does the SQL/4GL automatically optimize queries? Yes_No__

- Can your SQL/4GL automatically choose the appropriate data access strategy/method/path? Yes_No__
- Does the DDBMS provide the automatic navigation around the physical distribution of data for location and processing of the desired records? Yes_No__

X.12 Does the SQL/4GL allow queries by fields that are not indexed? Yes_No__

X.13 Does the SQL/4GL allow queries by joining data from multiple files? Yes_No__

X.14 Does the SQL/4GL support nested queries? Yes_No__

X.15 Can the SQL/4GL program output be redirected to the following:

- system/data base files Yes_No__
- online terminals Yes_No__
- printers attached to online terminals Yes_No__
- spooled printers Yes_No__

X.16 Does the SQL/4GL allow to pass arguments/parameters/variables between the following:

- different SQL/4GL programs Yes_No__
- SQL/4GL and precompiler programs Yes_No__
- SQL/4GL and host language programs Yes_No__
- SQL/4GL and independent shell scripts Yes_No__

X.17 Can the SQL/4GL generate documentation on code written by its users? Yes_No__

X.18 Are procedural constructs supported to allow complete programming within the SQL/4GL? Yes_No__

XI. HUMAN FACTORS

XI.1 Is your query language designed in such

Fig. 10-3. Request for information (cont'd).

a way that users can enter queries in terms of desired data without concern about internal DDBMS processing mechanism? Yes__No___

XI.2 Does the DDBMS allow users to specify actions and make requests for data in simple non-procedural phrase? Yes__No___

XI.3 Does your query language allow users to employ alternate forms of queries, corresponding to common alternatives in natural language? Yes__No___

XI.4 If query results in global data base retrieval, does the DDBMS provide user with the following options:

- **require user to confirm transaction** Yes__No___
- **offers user help options** Yes__No___
- **support user with tools to easily narrow query before processing** Yes__No___

XI.5 Does the DDBMS provide menu driven facilities for all integrated tools? Yes__No___

XI.6 Does the DDBMS support windows for query language dialogs? Yes__No___

XI.7 Does the DDBMS support windows for operating system commands and prompts? Yes__No___

PLEASE LIST THE GRAPHICAL USERS INTERFACES (GUI) IT SUPPORTS.

XI.8 Are query language commands organized in groups or layers for ease in learning and use? (i.e., commands for beginners, intermediate level and advanced commands) Yes__No___

XII. APPLICATION/DEVELOPMENT TOOLS

XII. 1 Report Writer/Generator

(If yes, indicate if your report facility has the following capabilities

- optional generation of report date and time Yes__No___
- optional generation of pagination Yes__No___
- default column headers Yes__No___
- user defined/selected column headers Yes__No___

Fig. 10-3. Request for information (cont'd).

- moving columns around Yes__No__
- default page headers Yes__No__
- user defined/selected page headers Yes__No__
- user defined/selected page footers Yes__No__
- conditional printing/formatting of fields Yes__No__
- printing of textual comments Yes__No__
- calculation of total, average, min, max, percent, count, etc. Yes__No__
- sorting records by multiple fields Yes__No__

XIII. DISTRIBUTION-RELATED FEATURES

PLEASE ATTACH ADDITIONAL EXPLANATIONS FOR EACH OF THE FOLLOWING QUESTIONS:

XIII.1 What is the overall architecture of the DDBMS? Yes__No__

- Does the DDBMS run on one (central) processor, and support access from other processors, OR Yes__No__
- Do components of the DDBMS run on all processors which have access to the DDBMS? Yes__No__
- Does the DDBMS distribution of individual files and/or data bases across multiple individual processors on the network? Yes__No__
- Does the DDBMS support downloading/uploading of subsets of data bases to individual processors? Yes__No__
- What other DDBMS can this DDBMS interoperate with? Yes__No__

XIII.2 Genral features of the DDBMS (Distribution-related considerations)

- What level of transparent data portability is provided? ______
- Is data transformation supported/required at either/both ends of a data transfer path? Yes__No__
- What level of performance and capacity will the overall DDBMS provide? ______
- How many interconnected processors (nodes) can be simultaneously supported by the DDBMS? ______
- How many nodes can be accessed simultaneously? ______
- How many data bases on different nodes can be accessed simultaneously? ______

Fig. 10-3. Request for information (cont'd).

- What level of error detection/correction/ recovery across the network is supported by the DDBMS? ________
- What level of data and/or transaction integrity across the network is supported by the DDBMS? ________
- What level of checkpoint/restart functionality across the network is supported by the DDBMS? ________
- What level of transaction concurrency control across the network is supported by the DDBMS? ________

PLEASE ATTACH ADDITIONAL EXPLANATIONS FOR EACH OF THE FOLLOWING QUESTIONS:

XIII.3 Physical network architecture

- What physical connectivity options are available? (e.g., all nodes on a LAN? All nodes connected via point-to-point links? Some combination?) ________
- Are both Local Area Networks and Wide Area Networks supported? Yes__No__
- Is node route-through supported? (e.g., can node A obtain data from node C by routing request through node B?) Yes__No__
- Can DDBMS components on MVS host processors be interconnected via channel-to-channel links? Yes__No__
- Can DDBMS components on UNIX processor be interconnected via a LAN, such as Etherent? Yes__No__
- Can DDBMS components on UNIX processors be connected to the MVS hosts
  - via a channel-attached device? Yes__No__
  - or only via serial lines? Yes__No__
- Can DDBMS components be interconnected across satellite links? Yes__No__
- Are all the required network hardware components standard products available from the vendors? not tailored? Yes__No__
- Is the required network hardware available off-the-shelf from third party vendors? Yes__No__
- Is any of the hardware required for the DDBMS proprietary? Yes__No__

Fig. 10-3. Request for information (cont'd).

XIII.4 Software network architecture

- What network software options are available? ________
- Is software architecture hierarchical or peer-to-peer? ________
- What network software components are required by the DDBMS?
  - VTAM under MVS Yes__No__
  - DECNET under Ultrix, etc. Yes__No__
- Is load balancing done across multiple paths between two nodes? Yes__No__
- How many interconnected processors can be simultaneously supported by the DDBMS network? ________
- What network protocols are required and/or supported by the DDBMS?
  - SNA or 3270 under MVS Yes__No__
  - TCP/IP under Ultrix Yes__No__
  - DECNET under Ultrix Yes__No__
  - Asynchronous Yes__No__
  - X.25 Yes__No__
  - Others Yes__No__
- What type of file transfer capabilities are provided or required by the DDBMS? ________
- What type of terminal emulation capabilities are provided or required by the DDBMS? ________
- What standards do the network software components adhere to? ________
- Does the DDBMS plan to migrate to ISO network protocols in the future? Yes__No__
- Are all of the network software components required for the DDBMS, standard products available from the vendors? not tailored? Yes__No__
- Is the required network software available off-the-shelf from third party vendors? Yes__No__
- Is any of the required network software proprietary? Yes__No__

XIII.5 Network-related performance characteristics.

- What level of performance and capacity must the underlying network provide? ________
- For serial lines, what line speeds are supported? ________
- What data transfer rates can be

Fig. 10-3. Request for information (cont'd).

achieved? ________

- Is there flow control on data transfers? Yes__No__
- Can the communication performance parameters be tuned? Yes__No__
- Are performance statistics kept on transmission time across each network link? Yes__No__
- Are traffic volume statistics kept for each network link? Yes__No__
- What are the network capacity needs for normal processing? ________

XIII.6 Network-related error handling and recovery.

- What are the network capacity needs for backup and recovery processing (assuming that is done through the network)? ________
- What does the system do when network capacity is exceeded? ________
- Can nodes isolated by network failure continue to operate? Yes__No__
- How do nodes recover when network communication is restored? ________
- If a network line goes down, can the DDBMS automatically begin using an alternate route? Yes__No__

XIV. DDBMS PHYSICAL PARAMETERS

XIV.1 What is the minimum size of main memory required by the DDBMS? (List the hardware platforms you are evaluating to interconnect with the DDBMS)

XIV.2 What is the minimum size of disk space required by the DDBMS? (List the hardware platforms you are evaluating to interconnect with the DDBMS)

XIV.3 What is the minimum block size supported by the DDBMS? (List the hardware platforms you are evaluating to interconnect with the DDBMS)

XIV.4 What is the maximum block size supported by the DDBMS? (List the hardware platforms you are evaluating to

Fig. 10-3. Request for information (cont'd).

interconnect with the DDBMS)

XIV.5 What is the minimum number of blocks per area?
(List the hardware platforms you are evaluating to interconnect with the DDBMS)

XIV.6 What is the maximum number of blocks per area?
(List the hardware platforms you are evaluating to interconnect with the DDBMS)

XIV.7 What is the maximum number of areas per data base?
(List the hardware platforms you are evaluating to interconnect with the DDBMS)

XIV.8 What is the maximum number of disk drives allowed per data base?
(List the hardware platforms you are evaluating to interconnect with the DDBMS)

XIV.9 What is the maximum number of disk drives that can be supported by the DDBMS?
(List the hardware platforms you are evaluating to interconnect with the DDBMS)

XIV.10 What is the maximum number of data bases that can be accessed by one user?
(List the hardware platforms you are evaluating to interconnect with the DDBMS)

XIV.11 What is the maximum number of concurrent users that can access one data base?
(List the hardware platforms you are evaluating to interconnect with the DDBMS)

Fig. 10-3. Request for information (cont'd).

XIV.12 **What is the maximum number of concurrent update processes allowed by the DDBMS?**
(List the hardware platforms you are evaluating to interconnect with the DDBMS)

XIV.13 **What is the maximum known data base size?**
(List the hardware platforms you are evaluating to interconnect with the DDBMS)

XIV.14 **What is the maximum known file size?**
(List the hardware platforms you are evaluating to interconnect with the DDBMS)

XIV.15 **Does your DDBMS support fixed length records?** **Yes__No___**

XIV.16 **Does your DDBMS support variable length records?** **Yes__No___**

XIV.17 **What is the maximum record size?**
(List the hardware platforms you are evaluating to interconnect with the DDBMS)

XIV.18 **What is the maximum field size?**
(List the hardware platforms you are evaluating to interconnect with the DDBMS)

XIV.19 **What is the maximum number of files allowed per data base?**
(List the hardware platforms you are evaluating to interconnect with the DDBMS)

Fig. 10-3. Request for information (cont'd).

XIV.20 **What is the maximum number of files allowed to be opened simultaneously by one user? (List the hardware platforms you are evaluating to interconnect with the DDBMS)**

XIV.21 **What is the maximum number of fields allowed per one file? (List the hardware platforms you are evaluating to interconnect with the DDBMS)**

XIV.22 **What is the maximum key size? (List the hardware platforms you are evaluating to interconnect with the DDBMS)**

XIV.23 **What is the maximum number of keys allowed per file? (List the hardware platforms you are evaluating to interconnect with the DDBMS)**

XIV.24 **Does your DDBMS support combination (composite) keys?**

Yes__No___

XIV.25 **What is the maximum number of fields allowed per one combination key? (List the hardware platforms you are evaluating to interconnect with the DDBMS)**

XIV.26 What is the maximum number of combination keys allowed per one file? (List the hardware platforms you are evaluating to interconnect with the DDBMS)

XIV.27 What is the maximum size of combination key? (List the hardware platforms you are evaluating to

Fig. 10-3. Request for information (cont'd).

interconnect with the DDBMS)

XIV.28 What is the maximum number of synonyms per field?
(List the hardware platforms you are evaluating to interconnect with the DDBMS)

XIV.29 Does your DDBMS support repeating fields within one record? Yes__No___

XIV.30 What is the maximum number of field replications allowed within one record? ___________

XIV.31 What is the maximum number of joins allowed per one read statement?
(List the hardware platforms you are evaluating to interconnect with the DDBMS)

XIV.32 What is the maximum number of data bases allowed per one report?
(List the hardware platforms you are evaluating to interconnect with the DDBMS)

XIV.33 What is the maximum number of files allowed per one report?
(List the hardware platforms you are evaluating to interconnect with the DDBMS)

XIV.34 What is the maximum number of joins allowed per one report?
(List the hardware platforms you are evaluating to interconnect with the DDBMS)

Fig. 10-3. Request for information (cont'd).

XIV.35 **What is the maximum number of fields allowed per one report?**
(List the hardware platforms you are evaluating to interconnect with the DDBMS)

XIV.36 **What is the maximum number of user variables allowed per one report?**
(List the hardware platforms you are evaluating to interconnect with the DDBMS)

XIV.37 **What is the maximum number of sorting keys allowed per one file?**
(List the hardware platforms you are evaluating to interconnect with the DDBMS)

XIV.38 **What is the maximum number of sorting fields allowed per one sort key?**
(List the hardware platforms you are evaluating to interconnect with the DDBMS)

XIV.39 **What is the maximum combined length of sort fields?**
(List the hardware platforms you are evaluating to interconnect with the DDBMS)

XIV.40 **What is the maximum number of data bases allowed per one form?**
(List the hardware platforms you are evaluating to interconnect with the DDBMS)

XIV.41 **What is the maximum number of files allowed per one form?**
(List the hardware platforms you are evaluating to interconnect with the DDBMS)

XIV.42 **What is the maximum number of fields allowed per one form?**
(List the hardware platforms you are evaluating to interconnect with the DDBMS)

XIV.43 **What is the maximum number of screens allowed per one form?**
(List the hardware platforms you are evaluating to interconnect with the DDBMS)

Fig. 10-3. Request for information (cont'd).

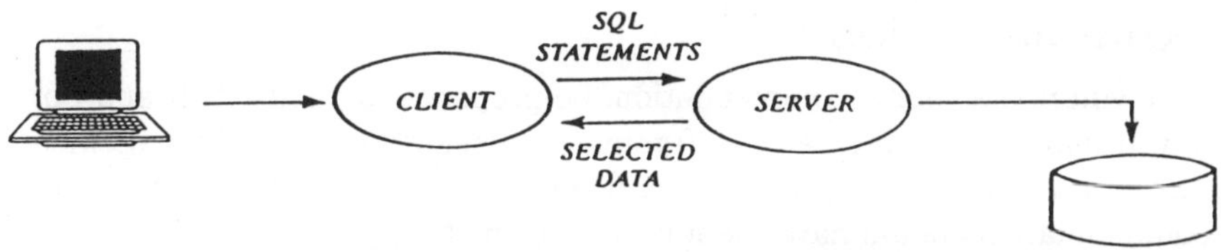

Fig. 10-4. Client/server architecture.

Downsizing (Refer to Chapter 7 for a detailed discussion.) Many users are interested in application portability across hardware and operating systems platforms. When an application is portable, it can be developed on one system and moved to other systems without having to recode. It's important to find out the operating systems and hardware on which the products run. The various hardware and operating system platforms should help to develop and run the applications using the best facilities of each platform.

SQL adherence The American National Standards Institute (ANSI) has adopted SQL as the standard database language. Some database products offer a subset of the ANSI standard; some offer extensions to the standard, while others offer a combination of subset and extensions. It's important to investigate the deviations from the standard.

Deviations may occur with data definition (create and modify tables, indexes, and views), data manipulation (select, insert, delete, etc.), or data control (database security). Adherence to the standard allows you to have the flexibility of moving from one platform to another, while extensions to the standard can provide additional flexibility and productivity.

Embedded SQL support provides a third-generation language (3GL) like C or COBOL for application implementation. The 3GL is used to code the device management and processing logic, while SQL statements are embedded in the 3GL for data manipulation.

SQL looks the same whether embedded or whether the statements are issued interactively. SQL queries can be validated before embedding them in the program. By using a database that uses SQL, you will increase the likelihood that you will be able to use cooperative processing solutions in the future.

Connectivity (Refer to Chapter 8, Networking.) Connectivity refers to the need to be able to connect the applications running on a PC to the database residing in a central computer, be it a mainframe or PC acting as a server. SQL is the language of that connectivity but connectivity is not a simple problem to solve.

Interfaces Another major advance in database implementation is the use of graphical user interfaces, also known as GUIs. They were invented at Xerox, but were popularized by Apple's Macintosh. GUIs provide you with pull-down menus, windows, dialog boxes, and a mouse to point, click and drag your way through an application.

Recommendation

Before you make your recommendation, be prepared to justify it. If appropriate, you may have to give a 20 – 30 minute presentation to top management. Make sure you make the presentation before the end of the budget year. The recommendation should have the following format:

I. Executive summary. Should not be more than two pages. Give the bottom line first, without getting into technical details.
   a. Products you are recommending. Is anyone from your competition using the product?
   b. Who is the vendor? What is the financial condition of the vendor?
   c. Why are you recommending that product?
   d. Which other products did you evaluate?
   e. Why aren't you recommending these products?
   f. What are the costs involved over the next five years?

II. Evaluation and brief description of products under consideration.
   a. Describe in brief the evaluation process with the seven-step approach.
   b. Provide the sample Request for Information (RFI) or Request for Proposal (RFP) and the Benchmark Specifications.
   c. Brief description (two paragraphs) for each of the DDBMSs evaluated and reasons for elimination. Also, give reasons for keeping a product in the race.
   d. Describe in more detail (four or five pages) the product recommended. Also describe in more detail the finalist that didn't make it (two or three pages).

III. Detailed Evaluation
   a. Elimination process description.
   b. Detailed description of the DDBMSs and the related products under consideration.
   c. Evaluation matrices for the vendors.

IV. Appendices
   a. Responses to RFIs and RFPs.
   b. Answers to Reference Phone Call questionnaires.
   c. Answers to Reference questionnaires at visits.
   d. Benchmark Evaluations, if any.

Appendix

Questions and answers

I've conducted a number of seminars on distributed databases, cooperative processing and networking over the past few years. Some of these questions were asked at the seminars, and some questions came up during my consulting engagements.

Expert systems

Question 1 What is an expert system? How do you develop an expert system? As expert systems evolve, will the job of a designer of cooperative processing and distributed databases get easier? Will expert systems optimize systems for the designer and the implementor, not only on an initial basis, but also track the applications that really need to be optimized? Would the expert systems accomplish this, advising where databases need to be stored so that the system is optimized even after a considerable change in the environment takes place?

Answer 1 Artificial intelligence is a field that consists of multiple subdisciplines, such as expert systems, natural languages, creation of vision, robotics.

An *expert system* should reflect expertise of humans. An expert system is a consolidation of software programs that could be used to complement or replace an expert person. An expert system is developed by using specialized software for that purpose. Basic components of an expert system are rules and corresponding actions. An expert system is supposed to take certain actions according to certain rules, exactly the way a human expert would do it.

Optimizing or optimization algorithm is one application of an expert system. The expert system for optimization will require a number of parameters to be provided by the designer or implementer, based on which the expert system would make certain decisions. Various parameters could be speed of transmission, volume of data stored in each database, communication line traffic, and preferred location of the required data if the data is replicated at multiple places. If the locations of the stored data are Chicago, New York, and Dallas, and if the person is calling from New York, then the expert system should first try the New York location.

It's conceivable that the expert system could keep track of the usage patterns of the databases, as well as of the applications, and come up with recommendations for optimization about the location of the databases, as well as of the applications' distribution.

Today's expert systems don't create their own code. The expert system doesn't make its own decisions. All parameters have to be provided to the expert system by humans. The expert system recommends certain choices, but the choices depend on what is provided to it. The expert system represents the expertise of the expert. If the person putting the information together for the expert system is not an expert, or is an expert but doesn't know how to communicate to the system, the expert system will not possess true "expertise." Today's technology doesn't create its own expertise. Its strength lies in storage and retrieval. Optimization algorithms consist of software modules, and the modules could be refined as the installation keeps on using them.

Data analysis and database design

Question 2 Which data characteristics should be looked at, and how can we analyze them if we want to implement distributed databases and cooperative processing?

Answer 2 There are four major components that should be looked at before considering data characteristics: business architecture, data architecture, network architecture (whether centralized or decentralized), and end-user computing architecture.

First and foremost there should be a business architecture. In order to develop a business architecture, the following analysis should be helpful.

Usually, an organization consists of multiple organizations or divisions. First of all, an organization needs to be looked at as different functional areas. Manufacturing is one of the very important functions of any organization. Manufacturing doesn't necessarily mean in the conventional sense of manufacturing. A product could be an intangible product too, such as an insurance policy. Banking has different products that the banks market such as savings, different types of cash management, and all the various money investment products. Manufacturing products, whether tangible or intangible, is one of the main functions of an organization.

Another function is marketing and sales. Products need to be planned for and then developed. The function that does planning and development in an organization is research and development. Then these products have to be distributed, and money needs to be collected for the sold products. The function that keeps track of money is accounting. In summary, manufacturing, planning, marketing, sales, research, development, distribution, collection, and accounting are the major functions that almost every organization has to perform.

In order to support these functions, an infrastructure is necessary. Each part of the infrastructure has some data that's most frequently used. We could make a statement, based on real-life experience, that 20% of the data is used 80% of the time.

Besides considering the data usage, the user groups need to be understood. Every organization has two, three or more user groups that are the most important user groups, without which the organization could not exist. In most organizations, sales is considered to be the number one activity. As a result, the sales department is considered to be the most important part of the organization. Next comes Research and Development (R&D) activity. In some companies, R&D is considered higher than sales, which is the long-term view. A database designer has to identify two or three user groups that are the most important user groups in the organization. Based on this analysis, database designers have to be able to put priorities on the groups of data. A priority list of two hundred items is far from prioritizing. Some people have a very hard time trying to distinguish the important from the unimportant. They come up with a list of two hundred things that are equally important. There can't be two hundred things that are equally important.

In summary, identify the functions along the vital five or six areas of the organization. Then identify two, three, or four major user groups that are very important to the enterprise. Then try to identify what data these user groups need, want, and did not have before. That's where big opportunity lies in a distributed database environment. That's where a bigger return on investment is going to be. If the users are getting data in two seconds instead of three seconds, of course, it's going to be important, but not as important in comparison to when they had to wait two days. For performing this function of identification, a person is going to need business expertise.

With all of this pertinent information, distribution of applications, which is cooperative processing, could be determined. The information will also equip the database designer to identify where and how the databases are to be distributed.

Question 3 What should be the best process for a systems development?

Answer 3 Once different types of data have been classified and functions to be implemented are identified, the process leading to tangible results should start.

The timeframe that needs to be considered for development is about six months. Within six months the project has to show some results. The days are over when an organization could spend four or five years coming up with a system. Many users have purchased microcomputers, and many of them know how to use dBase, RBase, Paradox, or some other micro-based DBMS. They know how to put together, in a few weeks timeframe, some database, even if it's not the fanciest. And they know within five days they could achieve something more than what most of the mainframe-based DBMS will deliver to them. Six months is the most a database team will get before a prototype or a pilot is developed, however small. A prototype does not mean a proposal on a piece of paper, but a prototype running on a computer—a prototype with some of the functions that the user has been looking for.

Study the organization from top to bottom and identify its most important functions. Let's assume you are in the retail industry. You have to identify which products are selling the most, today and maybe also tomorrow. Identify the change in the buying pattern, and then try to identify the sales demography and all of the things that you have to think about, bottom line, regarding the company. Thinking in terms of marketing and sales is one of the things that data processing people don't like to do. They think it's corrupt to think in terms of money. But when it comes to their own salary, that's a different story.

Distributed databases and cooperative processing is moving the functionality of centralized Management Information Systems (MIS) to locations of actual manufacturing distribution and sales, etc. The focus of system development has to move from developing gigantic centralized systems to developing smaller functions and location-oriented systems. Prototype development has to take that into consideration.

Another thing that many organizations have started to realize is that they develop software applications as if they're software vendors, and that the applications they have developed will be marketed one day. This orientation is due to the future possibility of the organization having to transfer the applications from one location to another location. In these days of mergers and acquisitions, the transferring of applications may take place much more frequently than in the past.

Question 4 Could you elaborate on one thing you said, that the high-level analysis should be done first before going far down vertically, and that a designer should certainly produce something in six months? However, you also said it should be something that you can touch and feel, and not just a piece of paper. Given that the designer is only doing a high-level analysis, what kind of transition could be made within a six-month period in actually building something?

Answer 4 In order to provide tangible results in a short amount of time, staffing these projects should be taken more seriously.

Assume that there are two "smart" people working on this project. One of the persons should have business as a major and technology as a minor. The other one should have technology as a major and business as a minor. At most, one or two weeks are spent defining the high-level view. The most important things can be identified very quickly. If these two people can't find the most important things, then they may not be the appropriate people for the job.

The next two weeks might be required to identify the most important users and their needs. The next step is identifying the most important classes of data. Those classes may consist of ten, fifteen, or twenty entity types. Entity types for an insurance company are types of policies, customers, policies sold, claims posted, etc.

A meeting should be held with top-level management. Getting a real commitment from top-level management is a challenging task. In order to get the commitment from them, at least one project has to be finished, and then there might be a better response from them later, because data processing doesn't have an excellent track record. "Under budget" and "on time" are two alien terms for most data processing people.

With the first few projects, use a microcomputer instead of going to the mainframe for providing tangible results. There are some software products that you can use to create only screens for the prototype. When a systems designer is speaking with the users, the designer has to find out what the users have been really wanting that they haven't received. By now, the designer is six or seven weeks into the project.

Consider some function where "important" users want to have access to data. Spend another two to three weeks putting those entities and relationships together. That's where a systems analyst has to get to a somewhat detailed level. Populate the dictionary on the hard disk on the microcomputer. Write some programs and prepare some screens. By this time four months are over. Keep one more month for testing and one more month for just in case. All of this time adds up to about six months.

Question 5 In our case, the phase that you're talking about we did two years ago. We're now sitting there with two thousand microprocessors and a number of mainframe databases with a lot of data. People want to have access to that data. They want it integrated with local data that's not on the mainframe. We're really trying to develop a distributed database, but part of the data is on the mainframe and part of it's on local microcomputers. What's the formula, during the analysis phase, that will help me figure out when I should dynamically get data, when I should download the data, and when I should keep the data locally? How do I know where I should have it?

Answer 5 Try to identify the usage pattern of data. Try to classify the data. Prepare two categories of data classes. One category should consist of four or five classes of data that are used mostly by mainframe-based applications, such as payroll, accounts receivable, accounts payable, etc. Identify the parts of the data that users would like to have on the microcomputers, such as inventories at various warehouses, shipping records from the warehouses, and time schedules kept by the workers at assembly plants, etc. Establish downloading mechanisms and timeframes. There are adequate facilities for downloading available in the market. Keep track of the complaints! Usually complaints indicate whether the distribution of data represents the actual needs versus the perceived needs. Analyze the complaints, identify patterns, and react accordingly.

Question 6 For developing software, how do you migrate it into a production stage? We would like to develop application software in one place and port it to another place.

Answer 6 There should be a test place. The software should be ported to other sites via a network. It has to be tested so that assurance is provided that the new software will not disrupt the existing production environment.

That means there's one place where testing is done and then there are different production-site platforms to which the test site is connected. Application software should be developed at the test site and then transferred to different production sites.

In a number of organizations, even if the production sites are not interconnected with a network, there are multiple data centers. Some data centers are assigned as production sites and some data centers are test sites. Instead of physically sending tapes to these different sites, you're going to transmit parts of the application software and data over the network. The main issue of multiple production sites with data is going to be how all of these sites are to be kept synchronized as far as the databases are concerned. If various test sites are developing different application systems, and they're using the same databases, how are all the sites going to keep the databases synchronized? These are mostly management issues that result in politics. The technology part is much easier to implement than the politics involved at various data centers. Since the field of cooperative processing is still new, there's no specific cooperative processing configuration management.

Question 7 How important is data modeling, and does any specific technique offer major advantages for designing distributed databases?

Answer 7 Data modeling is just as important in designing distributed databases as it is in designing relational databases because distributing databases is going to be much easier with relations as tables as compared to a hierarchy or a network.

A deadline has to be set for a data modeling project because there are too many companies spending not weeks, but months, in designing databases. They put too many people on the project and everybody starts arguing with everybody else regarding the design decisions. You have to set the timeframe, and you need a strong project leader. Data modeling is very crucial to designing distributed databases. Based on the design, it's easier to implement classes of most frequently used data and to partition accordingly. Entity relationships modeling could be used to design distributed databases.

Backup and recovery

Question 8 In our department we have guidelines regarding backups. But I see a few situations where we have lost data, and we couldn't recover it because no backups were taken.

Answer 8 Backup and recovery are two very sensitive issues with microcomputer users. There should be a training session, and in the training session there should be a little section where people will lose data. Put some magnets in the drawers or wherever they keep their diskettes. (This is done in order to create a real-life situation.) Make sure you have backups first. Most of the people don't believe in backing up until they lose data. No matter how often you tell them, it doesn't become real. After losing data once, they will back up the next few months. But then slowly they will fall into the same old mode. It's an ongoing process. Computer users have to keep on losing data from time to time in order to be thinking about backing up. There's a company that has two people who go from user group to user group to back up data. That's their job. Of course, these people don't stay too long on that job. The main point is that you have to make somebody responsible for backup.

Question 9 It seems to me that backup and security are two of the main concerns in a distributed database environment.

Answer 9 Yes, right after synchronization of data, backup and recovery are very important issues.

Distributed databases

Question 10 Should I use distributed database tools for databases when the size of databases reaches terabytes?

Answer 10 If the terabytes could be split in different ways and the database could still be put together, then a distributed database could be a desirable implementation. The main question that comes up regarding implementation is whether a mainframe or a database machine, such as Teradata's DBC/1012, should be used, or whether the data should be distributed on the network with the help of client/server architecture.

One of the applications with terabytes of data is collecting data about grocery purchases. An organization has been collecting huge volumes of data regarding purchases and is selling the collected data for performing trends analysis. The data is collected and used for retrieval only. Since data regarding every single purchase of each consumer good is collected for thousands, if not millions, of consumers, it reaches the size of terabytes in months. This is an ideal application for a distributed database environment with data collected at various supermarkets. Each supermarket could possibly be a node of the network.

Question 11 Do you see a need for a DDBMS in state and local governments in the near future, and if so, in what capacity?

Answer 11 In most government environments, database sizes reach terabytes very quickly. Some examples are the Department of Motor Vehicles, the Internal Revenue Service, and also the Federal Bureau of Investigation (FBI). In addition to the size of the databases, federal, state, and local governments have to look at the distributed database environment more seriously, because of the heterogeneous hardware and heterogeneous systems software environment.

Question 12 Please rate DDBMS software and suitability for online transaction processing (OLTP) for higher rates of transactions per second.

Answer 12 Let's assume that nothing else but the OLTP transactions are run standalone, even though that seems to be unrealistic! Assume that the database has a million database records. It could consist of multiple tables or it could be one table. Let's assume that a transaction requires four physical I/Os for one logical I/O. Let's further assume that a database record is two hundred bytes long.

A number of organizations are misled regarding the number of transactions per second they need to support. More than ninety percent of organizations require less than ten transactions a second. There's only one percent or maybe one-half a percent, such as airline systems, where you need to have up to two hundred transactions per second.

In that case, it's advisable to split one transaction into multiple transactions. Not one "giant" transaction is run, but multiple pieces are run. It's desirable to split a transaction into multiple transactions for performance improvement.

One major reason is the human factor. A person asking for some information doesn't have to wait for a long time at a stretch. Instead, that long time span is split into many small parts, and a person receives information in pieces. The second reason is if something goes wrong, not everything will be wasted because the requester already received some information. The third reason is based on queuing theory. Smaller jobs get done faster than one huge job. A DDBMS is more suitable than a centralized DBMS for handling online transaction processing if distributed unit of work, and preferably distributed request, is supported by the DDBMS.

Question 13 How is configuration management (CM) accomplished in a distributed database management system or in a cooperative processing environment?

Answer 13 Configuration management (CM) is configuring the placement of data sets and disks and selection of the channels that will support the transfer of data. First, access to already distributed data should be provided. The usage pattern should be established. Price performance needs to be determined in order to implement optimum configuration.

Question 14 How do we address access to distributed data from a large user community if we use microcomputers rather than centralized mainframes?

Answer 14 You already have distributed data if the only processors are microcomputers. In that environment, client/server architecture should be considered. It's also possible that multiple workstations are required as servers. Let's assume that most of your microcomputers are with Intel 80286-based processors. Those could be considered clients. The servers should be at least Intel 80386-based or higher. Client/server architecture could be implemented using local area networks. Please refer to Chapters 8 and 9 for further explanation.

Question 15 How do we maintain data for accuracy and currentness when distributed to multiple local platforms?

Answer 15 Even if the vendors have supplied various tools for implementing integrity, it's going to be the implementation and management that will enable the data to be accurate.

Each field has to be assigned to a specific node for the final authority of the contents. Each field should also have been assigned to a specific person or to a specific department that is the final authority for the contents. If the same field is repeatedly stored at multiple nodes, in a predetermined timeframe, the node that's the final authority for the contents of the field should send the latest contents to the nodes that are not the authorities. Keeping accurate and current distributed data on multiple local platforms is a painstaking job that is, unfortunately, not solved just by automated tools.

Question 16 Why aren't the vendors providing data management tools for their distributed database platforms?

Answer 16 It's a business decision on their part. The vendors would like to license as many copies as possible of the DDBMS engine or the main component. With it, they're going to get hold of the client base. If you sell many products to the same client, you have only one client. If you sell one product to many clients, you have many clients. On the bigger client base, the vendor can then grow with other tools. So it's more of a business decision on the DDBMS vendor's part. Also, the technology is moving so fast that the vendors don't really have time to develop supporting data management tools. The DDBMS vendors spend most of their time and resources trying to make the DDBMS engines as "bug free" as possible. They leave the field of supporting tools to the independent software vendors who develop the second tier software products for the DDBMS engines and, in many cases, build a consulting and services practice around them.

Question 17 What is the current state of the art of distributed access optimization algorithms?

Answer 17 They have a long way to go. They first have to manage one algorithm, and then go into distributed algorithms.

Question 18 For large databases—terabytes—do you recommend using a distributed database?

Answer 18 Whether or not to distribute the data is more a question of access than of size. Are particular portions of the database used more or exclusively by particular geographical locations? As we discussed previously, not all data is made equal. In most organizations, 20% of the data is used 80% of the time. And besides, the usage concentration on the particular data varies from locality to locality. If the much smaller percentage of data that's used by the localities is provided at those particular nodes, performance will be improved. Using distributed database technology is a very viable option to be considered by the organizations with large databases with terabytes of information.

Data dictionary/directory

Question 19 How can we use a data dictionary/directory effectively in a distributed database environment?

Answer 19 It's important to think about populating a data dictionary/directory and identifying who is using what and who can access what. Classifying data to be entered in a data dictionary/directory needs to be done first at a higher level. If it takes too long, the project will probably be either sidetracked or canceled, because management at higher levels wants to see results quickly. If the designers have designed the best model in the world on paper or on screen, they're still not getting any tangible results out of it. The designers have to have business understanding; some timeframe has to be established for finishing the tangible results of the project, and those deadlines have to be met. A number of useful reports could be prepared with the use of data dictionary. Frequency of usage, usage patterns, and mix of transactions are some examples. This information will enable a DDB designer to allocate the appropriate parts of the database to the appropriate nodes and thereby improve performance.

Mainframes, minicomputers and microcomputers

Question 20 Considering the growth in capabilities of microcomputers, how do you differentiate between micro, mini and mainframe computers?

Answer 20 There are three and one-half platforms of hardware. A mainframe is one platform; a minicomputer is one platform; a workstation is one-half of a platform; a microcomputer and workstation are each one-half of a platform. A workstation or microcomputer is considered only half of a platform because the differences between a microcomputer and a workstation are getting less and less. The main difference between all these computing environments is the price performance. The price includes not only the hardware equipment, but also the systems software and support requirements.

Question 21 What are some of the major pluses of mainframe DBMSs and microcomputer DBMSs?

Answer 21 Mainframe DBMSs are especially strong in the backup/recovery and security areas as compared to their microcomputer counterparts.

Specific user question

Question 22 We're running a financial department of the government. We have about three-hundred and fifty users. About one-hundred and ten thousand checks are written a year. We're getting some pressure from some of the people in our department to move that partially into a distributed environment. Right now we're using an Amdahl mainframe. I am not a technical person; I'm a financial officer, and I guess I'm a bit concerned about security. We're running Novell's local area network. I'm hoping to pick up a little information as to what we should be looking for and what other companies or organizations are doing with the more important systems they're running. Are they going with the distributed environment, or are they keeping it on the mainframe?

Answer 22 So far most of the organizations are keeping check processing on the mainframe. That function has been running on mainframes, and people who have control of it don't want to give it up. In their defense, we should also say that backup, recovery and security are much stronger on the mainframe. Besides, conversion is expensive, and there are not enough people to convert, maintain, and also do new development. The third reason is "pure inertia."

Unix

Question 23 Please describe some aspects of distributed database in the Unix environment.

Answer 23 The Tool Kit for application development in the Unix environment still needs to be improved as compared to IBM's MVS environment, as well as DEC's VMS environment. These tools are not sophisticated, especially the tools for the database administrator. Developers have not paid much attention to this area. The purpose of the tool kit is to increase productivity for development and provide ease of maintenance. Backup and recovery are two areas needing more improvement.

Glossary

active data dictionary/directory (DD/DS) A DD/DS is said to be active with respect to a program or a process if, and only if, that program is dependent on the DD/DS for its metadata (data explaining about data, similar to metalanguage).

after image A copy of a data base record or of a page after it has been modified or updated.

AI Artificial intelligence. The art that allows computers to mimic ordinary human intelligence and behavior.

AIX Advanced Interactive eXecutive. IBM's modification of Unix for the RS/6000, PS/2, and System/370—the AIX family definition. Basically an enhanced version of AT&T's Unix V. AIX is the version of Unix that's used together with Carnegie Mellon's "MACH" as the basis of Open Software Foundation's (OSF) Unix. (See OSF.)

alias A local name defined and used at a local site to access a table stored at a remote site.

ANSI American National Standards Institute. ANSI promotes standards for the American computer industry and coordinates American involvement in the International Standards Organization (ISO). (See ISO.)

API Application programming interface. The API in a product enables users to "attach" their own software with the product (e.g., VTAM API, DISOSS API, etc). Application programming interfaces are libraries and utilities for programmers that include procedures (code) for accessing the server and processing database queries. APIs are written for specific versions of a language. For example, for a program written in Microsoft C, an API provided by a server vendor for Microsoft C is necessary.

APPC Advanced program-to-program communications. An SNA facility (based on PU 2.1 and LU 6.2) for general-purpose interprogram communications. Very significant enhancement forming the foundation for IBM's future networking products. Often used synonymously with LU 6.2 (LU

6.2 is the architecture, and APPC is the programming to interface to it). IBM provides APPC applications for System/370, System/36, System/38, System/88, PC, RS/6000, AS/400, Display Writer, Scan Master, 3820 printer, etc.

AppleTalk AppleTalk is a proprietary protocol that's used to connect Apple computers and printers. AppleTalk is built into all Apple computer systems.

application software This allows the computer to do specific tasks, such as spreadsheets, word processing or graphics. Applications software can't work without an operating system.

APPN Advanced peer-to-peer networking. A software package providing mainframeless, peer-to-peer networking. IBM's answer to the minisuppliers' networking solutions. Initial releases were only for the System/36. AS/400 increases the limit on APPN networks from 150 nodes to several hundred thousand. However, the real missing component is a directory services feature to distribute information about connected equipment and routes. Despite limitations, APPN seems to be quite well thought of by AS/400 users. As an extension of SNA, APPN supports nonhost networking of small systems.

AS/400 Application System/400. IBM's mid-range processor aimed at the System/36/38 replacement and departmental/distributed machine market. Programs from the S/36 and S/38 machines can be transferred fairly readily to AS/400. The 48-bit addressing can be increased to 64-bit. Notable communications features include automatic transmission of messages to host NetView, NetView/DM for distribution and change management, ability to act as a 4 Mbps (mega bit per second) TRN file server (using integrated adaptor). Also supports X.21/.25 (see X.25), OSI (see Open Systems Interconnection), LU 6.2 (see LU 6.2), SNADS (see SNA Distributed Services), APPN (see APPN).

backward recovery A recovery technique that restores a database to an earlier state by applying before images. Also called rollback.

basic distribution Type of relational data distribution. Tables are uniquely distributed and stored at different sites; for example, the EMPL table at site 1, the DEPT table at site 2. The distribution of data is done at the table level.

baud rate A measure of the speed at which computers send data from one device to another, typically 300, 1,200 or 2,400, with the higher numbers representing faster transmissions. One baud is one bit of data per second.

before image A copy of a database before it has been updated or modified.

binding The process of linking an application program to its external schema or data description.

binding time The instant in time when the data description is "assigned to" or "bound to" the code. The data description was previously separated (i.e., defined independently). Binding time has a direct effect on the level of control because, once data descriptions are bound to a program, the program is no longer dependent on the DD/DS for its metadata. Thus, the longer the binding time can be delayed, the greater the level of control for the DD/DS. The longer the delay, the bigger the flexibility in changing the contents of the data. But, at the same time, the response time worsens.

bit Short for binary digit, the smallest unit of computer data. A bit can have only two states, on or off, which are commonly called one and zero. Digital computers, not analog computers, can deal only with data coded in this on/off fashion.

BSC Binary synchronous. A communications protocol evolved from the old async (start-stop) protocol. Originated by IBM in 1964. Synchronization of sending and receiving stations is established before the message is sent. Allows faster block-mode data transmission and fewer data errors than start-stop. Speed comes from the lower ratio of checking bits to data bits (i.e., it's not carrying as much overhead around as async). Widely used, but superseded within IBM's mainstream products by SDLC/SNA protocols (see SDLC and Systems Network Architecture (SNA)).

buffer A word that often implies buffer storage. It's storage used to compensate for a difference in rate of flow of data, or time of occurrence of events when transmitting data from one device to another. It is secondary storage used exclusively for assembly and transfer of data between internal and external storage. Buffers are used in terminals, peripheral devices, storage units and in the CPU.

byte Eight bits are in a byte, which is the amount of memory needed to store a single number or letter. A byte is the common unit of computer storage.

C A programming language. C originated within Unix, and has been very successful as a language for low-level programming of minis and micros. C is one of the languages within the CPI (see Common Programming Interface) of SAA (see Systems Application Architecture).

CAD Computer-aided design. Allows engineers and architects to design parts, products and building plans on a video screen rather than on paper.

catalog A directory of all data in a database. In a distributed database, the catalog will contain the locations of each database fragment.

CCITT Consultative Committee International Telephone and Telegraph. The CCITT works in conjunction with the IEEE (see Institute of Electrical and Electronics Engineers) to develop communications standards, in particular, the X series of standards (e.g., X.400, X.500).

CCS Common communications support. One of the pillars of SAA. Specifies the core communications functions and products for SAA-compatible systems. The basic elements of CCS are those of SNA—CCS introduced few new facilities or strategic directions. CCS includes both IBM and non-IBM elements—e.g., OSI was brought into CCS. A defined level of connectivity among all SAA participants. CCS defines objects for graphics and imaging, data streams, application services, session services, networking, and data link controls.

CD-ROM Compact disk read-only-media. A laser disk similar to a music CD, except that it holds billions of bytes of information, such as encyclopedias and catalogs. Information can't be written onto the disks, nor can the disks be altered.

chips or microchips Tiny electronic circuits etched in silicon, used in almost all electronic equipment. They process and store data.

CICS Customer Information Control System. General purpose teleprocessing monitor for terminal-oriented and intersystem transaction processing in MVS and VSE environments. Sits between user application programs, teleprocessing access method (e.g., VTAM), and database managers—i.e., CICS invokes user-written application programs in response to transactions entered at teleprocessing terminals. Provides similar functions to IMS/DC but is less secure and less resource hungry than IMS.

commit The process that allows database manager data, changed by one application or user, to be referenced by other applications or users. When a commit occurs, locks are freed so that other applications can reference the data that was just committed.

commit protocol An algorithm to ensure that a transaction is successfully completed, otherwise it's aborted. (See also two-phase Commit.)

common programming interface (CPI) Results in application portability across product lines in SAA networks.

common user access (CUA) One of the four pillars of SAA. Specifies the ways in which the user interface to systems is to be constructed. Includes standards for such things as the position of items on screens, the use of a mouse, meanings of terms, etc.

communications facilities A collection of processes and physical facilities that interconnect nodes.

communications network The collection of transmission facilities, network processors, and so on, that provides for data movement among terminals and information processors. (Also referred to as data communications network.)

concurrency control The DBMS function that prevents interference between transactions when several users are updating a database concurrently.

contention A condition on a communication channel or in a peripheral device when two or more stations try to transmit at the same time, or access to a resource is simultaneously required by two or more users. At the program level, it's the situation where two application programs attempt to access the same unit of data simultaneously.

cooperative processing The ability to distribute resources (e.g., programs, files and databases) across the network. Cooperative processing should allow transparent access across any system so that users don't have to know if the resource is local or remote.

coordinator The two-phase commit protocol defines one database management system as coordinator for the commit process. The coordinator is responsible for communicating with the other database management system involved in a unit of work. During a commit, the coordinator makes the commit or abort decision and coordinates the two-phase commit process.

CPI Common programming interface. One of the four pillars of SAA. Specifies the language conforming to the SAA. In theory, it will be possible for writing an application in one of the languages or application generators and then running it on any SAA architecture. CPI components include CSP, REXX, COBOL, C, FORTRAN, RPG and PL/I, among others. CPI results in application portability across product lines in SAA networks.

CPI-C Common programming interface for communications. A superset of IBM communications verbs containing bits of APPC/VM (see APPC), and SRPI (see server requester protocol interface). Provides a high-level interface to APPC, and consists of calls available in SAA high-level languages and other SAA subsystems. CPI-C comes in two versions—a "starter-set" and "advanced function." Available on VM, CICS, IMS, TSO and OS/2. Rapidly becoming an industry standard.

CPU Central processing unit. This is where the computer's "brains" reside. The CPU is the chip that stores and processes information. In a PC, the CPU and the microprocessor are the same.

CSP Cross system product. An application generator marketed by IBM. Runs on the mainframe, AS/400, and PS/2 and can be used to generate applications on mainframe, AS/400 and PS/2. Integrated support for DB2 and SQL/DS. (CSP has its own data dictionary that makes the problem of integrating it into a database environment cumbersome—if not extremely difficult.) CSP is IBM's strategic 4GL, and is included in SAA. It provides a consistent user interface across product lines participating in SAA networks.

data administration (DA) function The DA function has the overall responsibility for the enterprise's data resources and for the administration, control, and coordination of all data-related activities. DA has the responsibility of planning, managing, and defining the conceptual framework for the overall database environment.

database administration (DBA) function The enterprise's leading technical expert on database related activities. The DBA usually has technical responsibility for the day-to-day operations of all database related activities. These activities include definition, design, control, organization, documentation, protection, integrity, and efficiency of the database.

database management system (DBMS) An integrated set of computer programs that collectively provide all the capabilities required for centralized management, which are organization, access and control of a database that's shared by diverse users. This software will be the controlling program(s) to interface with the application program and the physical requirements of the data stored. The DBMS is responsible for the management, security, and control of the physical database structure. Examples are DB2, IMS, ADABAS, CA:IDMS, CA:DATACOM, dBase, etc.

Data Dictionary (DD) A data store of information about data. A central repository and directory of documentation about data. It provides a logically centralized repository of all definitive information about the relevant data in an enterprise, including characteristics, relationships, usage, and responsibility.

data dictionary/directory system (DD/DS) A system that's designed to comprehensively support the logical centralization of data about data (metadata). It's not only capable of storing metadata (data dictionary), but it's also capable of providing cross-reference information (directory) about the metadata. The dictionary provides information about what the data is and what it means (logical); the directory provides information about where data can be physically found and how it can be accessed. DD/DS is an automated facility that supports the data administration (DA) function.

DB2 Relational database management system for MVS environments. Its key strength is the SQL interface that's now a *de facto* industry standard. Strategic product for general information storage.

DCA Document content architecture. Set of rules (machine-independent data stream) about document formats, meanings of control characters, handling of nontest material, etc. Objective of DCA is to enable any DCA hardware or software to receive and interpret any DCA document in the same way. Key to IBM office automation plans, and well on the way to becoming an industry standard.

DDBMS Distributed DBMS (see distributed database management). A database system in which the physical data is distributed across different machines, but which presents a single database image to the user. Technically, it's extremely difficult, and no vendor has a complete solution. IBM made a start with distributed data management (DDM) capability. The DDM system is the favorite as the infrastructure for a full DDBMS from IBM in the future.

A DDBMS is a full-function database management system that provides end-users and application programs access to a distributed database as if it were stored at the local site.

DDM Distributed data management. CICS, PC or PS/2, System/36/38, and AS/400 function using LU 6.2 and APPC facilities to network processes on one machine with data on another. Thus, a PC user gets transparent access to data on another machine running the DDM software. Commit and recovery facilities are not adequate. The DDM product is part of a wider initiative to enable the exchange of data between disparate machines. DDM is the base architecture for IBM's distributed database. DDM is an SAA product, but the relationship between DDM and SQL (which is meant to be the only SAA data access mechanism) is unclear. IBM's strategic architecture for distributed transparent file access across dissimilar file systems.

deadlock A situation where two or more run units are competing for the same resources and none may proceed (contention), as each run unit is

waiting for one of the others to release a resource (such as a table, index, record, etc.) that another run unit has already claimed.

decision support system (DSS) A system that supports managerial decision making by providing information and modeling tools.

DIA Document interchange architecture. The set of standards and rules for sending documents around IBM computer systems—provides an "electronic envelope." Key to IBM office automation plans and rapidly becoming an industry standard.

Dialog Manager Application for creating CUA (see common user access) compliant systems on the OS/2. Dialog Manager sits on top of the Presentation Manager and provides a relatively easy-to-use environment for developing user interfaces. Because it offers only a subset of the Presentation Manager facilities, Dialog Manager enforces many CUA standards. Although the ISPF (a component of TSO) software for the 370, and EZ-VU II for the PC are analogous in function, there's no automatic conversion path to Dialog Manager from either.

Direct access storage device (DASD) Refers to the basic type of storage medium that allows information to be accessed by positioning the medium or accessing mechanism directly to the information required, thus permitting direct addressing of data locations. The time required for such access is independent of the location of the data most recently accessed. Synonymous with random access. File organizations can be sequential, direct or indexed sequential.

disks A hard disk is often permanently installed inside the hard-disk drive in the computer. It allows users to quickly store or retrieve data within their machines. Floppy disks come in two sizes: the older 5¼" disk and the newer, more powerful 3½" disk. Floppy disks allow users to store and move data from one computer to another. A disk drive is a storage device that allows users to load programs and data from a floppy disk to a computer's hard drive, and vice versa.

DISOSS Distributed office support system. Principal IBM mainframe system for office automation. Supports creation, storage, retrieval, transmission, and printing of documents, acting as a translator between incompatible products when documents arc distributed. DISOSS used to be IBM's OA (office automation) product par excellence, and was the first strategic implementation of DIA/DCA on a mainframe. Although it has been strategic for some time, DISOSS is becoming less important; much of the functionality is available through cheaper and simpler products and architectures: ECF (see enhanced connectivity facility), SNADS (see SNA distributed services), and some is now unnecessary as DIA/DCA compatibility becomes more widespread. However, DISOSS library services remain unique.

distributed catalog A distributed catalog is needed to achieve site autonomy. It means that the catalog at each site keeps and maintains information about objects in the local databases. It includes information on replicated and distributed tables stored at a given site and information on remote tables located at another site that can be accessed from the given site.

distributed data Distributed data concerns the distribution and access of flat files and relational databases. Data distribution across systems can be supported at various levels and implemented through various design choices.

distributed database A distributed environment is characterized by data of interest for the enterprise being located in different sites of a computer network. A distributed database environment is a collection of logically related data that's physically stored over different sites of a computer network. Each site of the network has autonomous processing capability and can perform local applications on a local database. A distributed database exists when a logically integrated database is distributed over several physically distinct, but linked, sites. So, in spite of data being located at different sites, each has similar properties that tie them together, and users may need to correlate data from different locations to satisfy their requirements. This property makes a distributed database different from a set of local databases that reside at different sites of a computer network. An important characteristic of a system supporting distributed databases is that the system itself, not the application, manages data at multiple locations. From the user's point of view, a set of distributed databases should look like a single database. The user should be able to think absolutely in terms of logical data objects and should not be concerned with where or how many times those objects might physically be stored. Integrity of databases distributed over multiple sites is controlled by the system without the application having to be aware of where the data is located. Support of this function in general implies that there has to be a database management system on each site involved in this type of distributed data. The software components that are typically necessary for accessing and managing distributed databases are: database management component (DB), data communications component (DC), data directory or catalog to represent information about the distribution of data in the network, distributed database component (D-DB). Among other services supported by a DDBMS are: database administration and control, transaction integrity, concurrency control and recovery of distributed transactions.

distributed database management (DDBMS) (See distributed databases.) A full-function database management system that provides end users and application programs access to a distributed database as if it were totally stored at the local site.

distributed data management (DDM) IBM's strategic architecture for distributed, transparent file access across dissimilar file systems.

distributed environment A set of related data processing systems in which each system has its own capacity to operate autonomously, but with some applications that execute at multiple sites. Some of the systems may be connected with teleprocessing links into a network in which each system is a node. The systems may operate on different hardware architectures or on different operational systems. A distributed environment means that, for whatever reasons, a company's or enterprise's important data is located in different sites of a computer network. In this context, site refers to each instance of a database management system (DBMS) that participates in a distributed environment. Two distinct database management systems on the same processor are two sites.

distributed files Some support for distributed files already exists. For instance, manually transferring files from one system to another has been supported since the early days of the computer industry, and most enterprises still do it regularly. There are also utilities, programs, and sets of programs that support moving files from one site to another. They usually address specific environments, and their processing capabilities vary. File distribution plays an important role in supporting distributed data processing.

distributed processing Distributed processing means that the location of the data determines where the application processing is done. The application function must be "moved" to the place where the data is located. To access data located at system 1, an application program at that location is needed. To access data at system 2, there must exist another program at that location. A logical process needing data that's located at different sites, therefore, has to be split into two processes with each process implemented by a separate application program. The data of one site may have to be moved to another site for processing the whole transaction at one site. This means that one of the basic characteristics of a transaction—atomic unit of execution—becomes more difficult to respect. Therefore, in this environment, the application may carry the responsibility for maintaining the data integrity within the logical transaction. Typically, distributed processing involves two or more computers linked together in a network. Application software, systems software, and hardware are used to allow the enterprise to manage data that's distributed among the multiple computer sites.

distributed request Less constrained type of distributed, relational data access. Within a single transaction or unit of work, each SQL statement can access objects stored at multiple distinct sites.

distributed table A table divided into several nonoverlapping portions, any of which can be located at a different site of a distributed database network. See also horizontal distribution and vertical distribution.

distributed table transparency A query accessing a (horizontally or vertically) distributed table. Doesn't have to know which rows or which columns are at which sites. Data across the multiple sites is accessed by an end-user as a single table. Sometimes it's called fragmentation transparency.

distributed unit of work Type of distributed relational data access.

Within a single transaction, or unit of work, objects that are the operands of SQL statements are allowed to span multiple store sites. However, all operands of a single SQL statement are constrained to exist at a single store site.

DTP Distributed transaction processing. A CICS facility that enables an application program to communicate with an application program running in another CICS system. The application programs are designed and coded explicitly to communicate with each other.

DXT Data extract program product. DXT is a tool for information portability, allowing administrators to manage movement of data from multiple sources into relational databases (including other relational databases).

dynamic SQL SQL statements that are prepared and executed within a program while the program is executing. In dynamic SQL, the SQL source is contained in host language variables rather than being coded into the application program. The SQL statement might change several times during the program's execution.

ECF Enhanced connectivity facilities. ECF is a set of programs for sharing resources between IBM personal computers connected to IBM S/370 host computers within MVS or VM. The functions available to the user by a requester/server program include: host data access, virtual disk, virtual file, virtual print, and file transfer.

EDI Electronic document/data interchange. Generic term for services supporting data transfer between systems, usually over a third party's network. EDI services are provided by many network vendors who also do the protocol, formatting, incompatibility resolution, etc.

EDIFACT EDI for administration commerce and trade. An international EDI standard developed by the ISO standards body. Supported by IBM in the expEDIte products.

end-user A person or group who uses data to meet organizational responsibilities but who typically has little or no experience with data processing technology but has a need for data processing.

enterprise Another term for an organization, be it a business, civic, nonprofit, school, or social operation that must maintain data for its operation.

Ethernet A LAN product, jointly promoted by Xerox, DEC and Intel. At one time was thought of as being the main candidate for a major international LAN standard despite the fact that IBM didn't back it with any enthusiasm. However, IBM now provides a high level of support for Ethernet, which makes things look a bit brighter. Ethernet is the base for the IEEE 802.3 LAN standard (although it doesn't actually conform fully), and is by far the most popular high-speed LAN product in the market.

expert system A system that captures the knowledge and experience of a human expert, in the form of facts and rules, so as to aid others in decision making.

extract The simplest way of distributing data. The user is involved in performing two steps: extracting of operational data into a portable file, and loading that file on another site into the receiving database management system. The data is usually used as read only.

EZ-VU PC product derived from the mainframe ISPF, and used to provide a dialog development environment.

Fiber Distributed Data Interface Standard (FDDI) An ANSI protocol for fiberoptic networks. It's based on a token-ring topology.

file server A computer that maintains a set of files in client/server architecture.

forward recovery A recovery technique that restores a database by reapplying all transactions to a before image of the database to bring the database information to its latest state before the interruption of the normal processing. Also called rollforward.

FTAM File transfer, access and management/manipulation. OSI-compatible protocol for distributed data management. A layer 7 application service element to be used for creating, accessing, and moving large structured files between heterogeneous systems. The FTAM standard considers all data to have a generalized "virtual filestore" structure consisting of named collections of hierarchically organized data. Included in SAA.

function shipping A CICS facility that enables an application program to access a resource owned by another CICS system. Both read and write access are permitted. The remote resource can be a file, an IMS database, a DB2 database, an Oracle database, etc.

gigaflop A common measurement of a supercomputer's speed. One gigaflop is a billion operations or calculations per second.

global deadlock In a distributed database, a deadlock (or deadly embrace) involving two or more sites.

global dictionary A dictionary that contains dictionary data that applies to all systems in the enterprise and is an authoritative source of information for other local dictionaries in the enterprise.

global transaction In a distributed database, a transaction that requires reference to data at one or more nonlocal sites to satisfy the request.

GOSIP Government open systems interconnection procurement/profile. Evolving U.S. and U.K. government standard for communications based on OSI and TOP. It will become the U.S. government's "sole mandatory, interoperable protocol suite."

GUI Graphical user interface. The user interface to the operating system with graphical icons. There are a number of GUIs—Motif, NeXTStep, New Wave, Open Look, Presentation Manager, Windows, X-Windows.

HDBV Host database view program. HDBV provides the PC user with transparent access to the facilities of VM or MVS systems. HDBV may also be used to access host data extracted by DXT.

HDLC High-level data link control. A set of ISO (International Standards Organization) standard link protocols. One variant is used by X.25; another is compatible with SDLC.

horizontal distribution (Also see vertical distribution and distributed table.) Splitting a table across different sites by rows. It allows rows of a single table to reside at different sites of a distributed database network.

icons Users manipulate data by moving stamp-sized pictures, or icons of files or folders on a screen, instead of working with lists of files and names. Icons are used as a way of commanding the computer, and can represent documents, applications programs and places to store data.

IEEE Institute of Electrical and Electronics Engineers. IEEE develops standards for LANs, including 802.3, and a standard for LANs that use the token-passing ring.

IMS/DC Teleprocessing monitor available under MVS to support applications using the IMS database system. There are signs that IMS/DC will be relegated to a minor role, and that CICS will become the only serious IBM offering in the teleprocessing monitor field.

IMS/ESA Composed of the IMS/ESA Transaction Manager, and the IMS/ESA Data Base Manager.

IPX Internetwork packet exchange. A communications protocol used in Novell NetWare. IPX is used in conjunction with the sequenced packet exchange protocol. IPX corresponds to the transport and network layers of the OSI model.

ISC Intersystems communication. A communication between systems in different hosts, with an SNA network. The ISC can be between two CICS systems, CICS and IMS/DC systems, two IMS/DC systems, and so on.

ISDN Integrated Services Digital Network. An international telecommunications standard that allows transmission of voice, video and data simultaneously.

ISO International Standards Organization. Body responsible for developing communications standards in conjunction with the CCITT (see CCITT). ISO developed the seven-layer OSI model for communications processing.

join A relational operation that allows retrieval of rows from two or more tables (or relations) based on matching values of specific columns.

kernel The set of programs in an operating system (mostly in the context of Unix) that implement low-level machine function.

LAN Local area network. Software that controls the traffic on networks of personal computers, or network operating systems, within an office, building or locality. It allows users to exchange and share data, and use the same peripherals, such as printers or databases.

LEN Low entry networking. LEN supports peer-to-peer, mainframeless networks with dynamic reconfiguration capabilities (although for small networks only). APPN on the System/36 is the first implementation of LEN.

like DDBMS environment A network of similar database management systems (for example DB2 to DB2), providing access to data residing at any of the locations that contain a participating instance of the database management system.

locality of processing A data distribution design objective that attempts to reduce remote access to data.

local site update Within a distributed unit of work, allows a process to perform SQL update statements referring to the local site. In addition, the process can perform select statements, referring to multiple sites. However, all operands of a single SQL statement are constrained to exist at a single store site.

local transaction In a distributed database, a transaction that requires reference only to data that's stored at the site where the transaction originated.

location The logical name of a site that participates in a distributed system. The location name is used for defining and accessing tables stored at a remote site.

location transparency If data location is "transparent," the DBMS knows where an object is currently stored, and there's no requirement for a user or an application to specify the data location in an SQL statement. If a table is moved to a different site, the name of the table doesn't change and, therefore, SQL statements that access the table don't have to be changed.

log A recording (journal) of all environmental changes relative to the database. It may include copies of all transactions, before/after images of updated records, time and date stamps, user and terminal ID, security breaches, and so on. It's used in conjunction with checkpoint data to recover a system's data sets.

logical An adjective describing the form of data organization, hardware, or system that's perceived by a program, programmer, or user; it may be different from the real (physical) form.

LU 6.2 Logical Unit Type 6.2. Peer-to-peer data stream *cum* network operating system for program-to-program communication (see APPC). LU 6.2 allows mid-range machines to talk to one another without the involvement of the mainframe. LU 6.2 also supports asynchronous (store-and-forward) networking. LU 6.2 is IBM's strategic device-independent process-to-process protocol, and acts as the session manager within SAA. Its marketing term is Advanced Program-to-Program Communications (APPC). As a subset of SNA, LU Type 6.2 is designed for more sophisticated capabilities fostered in SAA, which exploit intelligent workstations across distributed databases.

memory The computer's working storage area, which is constructed of RAM chips. (See RAM.) Memory determines the size and number of programs and information that can be stored in a computer.

menus Pop-up lists that allow users to select different functions of the computer. Menu-driven programs are easier to use than programs that require users to remember a string of commands.

metadata Data about data. The description of the data resources, its characteristics, location, usage, and so on. Metadata is used to identify, describe, and define user data. The data is organized in the form of entities, attributes, and relationships, and is generally stored in a data dictionary. Thus, the content of the DD/DS is metadata.

microcomputer Another name for a personal computer. The computer's CPU is contained in a single chip, or microprocessor. Minicomputers, mainframes and supercomputers are all successively more powerful, with each containing more powerful chips.

modem A device for transmitting and receiving computer data over telephone lines.

mouse A hand-held pointing device that allows users to move a cursor around the screen and select different functions from menus. Frequently used in lieu of a keyboard.

MSC Multiple systems coupling. An IMS/DC facility that allows two or more IMS systems to be interconnected in such a way that an end-user or program on one system can invoke a program on another system.

MSR (Multiple systems request) In a distributed unit of work, MSR allows a process to perform multiple SQL select statements referring to multiple sites. However, each select statement operand is constrained to exist at a single site. In a distributed request, MSR allows each SQL select statement in a process to access data from tables at multiple sites and return the results as a single unit of information.

MSU (Multiple systems unit) In a distributed unit of work, MSU allows SQL update and select statements referring to multiple sites. Each statement can access one site only. In a distributed request, MSU allows each update statement in a process to access multiple sites (for example an update to one site with subselect to other several sites, an update of a distributed table, and so on).

MVS Multiple Virtual Storage. IBM's standard operating system for large machines. MVS/SP, MVS/XA and MVS/ESA are incarnations of MVS.

MVS/ESA MVS enterprise system architecture. Capable of addressing up to 16 terabytes of data. Key strategic direction, and is the infrastructure for memory-based computing.

named pipes (Also see pipes.) Program-to-program protocol with Microsoft's LAN Manager. The named pipes API supports intra- and intermachine process-to-process communications.

NetBIOS Network basic input output system. Extension of the PC BIOS that traps calls to the BIOS and, where necessary, reroutes them to a LAN. Developed as the interface for the PC-Network program and on a number of non-IBM systems. Probably will be a long-term tactical solution for local networking; the long-term strategic solution will be APPC/LU 6.2. NetBIOS is a widely supported peer-to-peer protocol used by LAN vendors. Datagram peer-to-peer protocols are used when no connection between workstations exists; they're fast, but data delivery is neither tracked nor guaranteed by the operating system. Session peer-to-peer protocols are tracked, but communications are slower because of the overhead. NetBIOS can be used either as a datagram or session service.

NetView SNA network management product. Although it started as a rather half-hearted bundling of various network management products (including NCCF, NLDM, NPDA, VTAM node control application and NMPF), NetView is turning out to be an extremely important product. NetView will be the hub of future networks, and also act as the basis of future automated and remote operations. Key to its success is the incorporation of some expert systems techniques to manage large complex networks.

NetView/PC Multitasking personal computer subsystem (software plus adaptor) running on the AT or XT under PC/DOS. Connects and sends information upstream to and from TRN, voice networks and/or non-SNA systems. In effect, it's a gateway to pass network management between two disparate networks (typically an SNA network and an OSI network). Part of SAA.

network A computer network consists of a collection of circuits, data switching elements, and computing systems. The switching devices in the network are called communication processors. A network provides a configuration for computer systems and communication facilities within which data can be stored and accessed and DBMSs can operate.

NFS Network file system. Set of Unix/AIX protocols for data sharing across a LAN.

NIA Network interface adaptor. IBM protocol converter allowing SDLC products to attach through an X.25 network to an SNA host system.

node Technically, a point in the network where data is switched. A node in a network consists of a computer processing facility, an operating system for executing user processes, and maybe a DBMS.

operating system (OS) Key software programs that control or define the basic operations and functions of a personal computer. For example, DOS or OS/2. Users need an operating system before they can begin working with an applications program.

OS/2 Extended Edition (EE) Compared to OS/2 Standard Edition, OS/2 EE has a database manager, communications manager and presentation manager. OS/2 EE communications manager supports, for instance, IBM and Digital terminal emulations, LU 6.2, PU 2.1, X.25 wide area networking, SDLC, and token-ring LAN connectivity.

OSF Open Software Foundation. A consortium of vendors (including IBM, DEC, H-P) has developed a version of Unix as an alternative to the official AT&T version. IBM's AIX together with Carnegie Mellon's "MACH" is the basis of OSF Unix.

OSF/1 The first release of the Open Software Foundation's Unix-based operating system.

OSI Open Systems Interconnection. Set of international standard protocols and services for communications systems, partially overlapping in function but incompatible with SNA, and still under development. Main gaps at present are in the areas of network management and virtual terminal. IBM affirms its commitment to OSI and has included OSI as part of SAA. A seven-layer model for communications developed by the ISO. Working from software to hardware, the OSI model contains the following seven layers: application, presentation, session, transport, network, data link, and physical. Each layer is responsible for a different communications function. Here's a simplified view:

application The application layer manages communications for LAN-wide applications such as E-mail.

presentation The presentation layer is responsible for making sure the sender and receiver understand each other.

session The session layer establishes and ends conversations between machines. Logging on to a network is an example of a session-layer activity.

transport The transport layer is responsible for reliable transmission of data packets.

network The network layer determines the path a packet takes on the network.

data link The data link layer is responsible for getting the packet out onto the cable. Network interface cards are associated with the data link layer.

physical The physical layer transmits information across the cable.

participant The two-phase commit protocol defines one or more database management systems as participants of the commit process. The participant is responsible to communicate to the coordinator database management system the success or failure of its involvement in a unit of work. At commit each participant awaits the coordinator's commit or abort decision and implements it.

partitioning A method of distributing data in a network whereby only a subset of the entire database is located at a user's node.

peer-to-peer An unconstrained network topology that gives computers the flexibility to function as a primary or secondary processor in relation to other network nodes. It has decentralized control, and no mainframe is required.

physical An adjective, contrasted with logical, that refers to the form in which data or systems exist in reality. Data is often converted by software from the physical form to a form in which a user or programmer perceives it.

pipes (Also see named pipes.) Vehicles for passing data from one application to another. If the data is to be passed from one application to another on the same machine, e.g., in the multitasking mode, "anonymous" pipes can be used. In the multiuser mode, when data needs to move from one user to another, "named pipes" are used.

POSIX Portable operating system interface standard. Operating system

(Unix) interface standard. Set to become the procurement reference standard with the aim of ensuring source-level application code portability. Selected as part of the basis of the OSF standard.

precompilation A processing of programs containing SQL statements that takes place before compilation. SQL statements are replaced with statements that will be recognized by the host language compiler. Output from this precompilation includes source code that can be submitted to the compiler.

Presentation Manager Software that creates the user interface to OS/2 Extended Edition. Enables users to create an interface conforming to the SAA's (see Systems Application Architecture) CUA (see common user access). Presentation Manager most likely will be used by software developers rather than users, who will prefer to use Dialog Manager. Analogous in function to ISPF of TSO on the mainframe.

PROFS PRofessional OFfice System. Office system aimed at the professional, technical, managerial user. Provides text management, diary, messaging, etc. Most parts of PROFS are highly regarded by users. Runs on 370 machines under VM.

program preparation The process of producing an executable program. When using a database manager, this process includes precompilation, compilation, and sometimes bind.

projection Relational operator that provides a subset of columns of a table.

PU Physical Unit Type 2.1. Its marketing term is Low Entry Networking (LEN). Limited to adjacent node connectivity, PU Type 2.1 allows either node to assume the role of primary or secondary processor.

PUx Physical Unit type within SNA (also known as Node Type or NT). The software in an SNA node controlling the node's communications hardware. In general, the higher the "x," the greater the intelligence in the PU. For practical purposes, we can say that PU1s are dumb controllers/terminals, PU2s are intelligent cluster controllers/terminals, PU4s are communications controllers, and PU5s are mainframes. Synonymous with "node type" within SNA. The type 2.1 node is currently the most interesting version since it allows local user ports to communicate without going through a host node's SCP services. The type 2.1 node plus LU 6.2 bring democracy to autocratic, host-dominated SNA via VTAM.

RAM (random access memory) This is the computer's work area, where programs and data are temporarily stored when in use.

remote access Remote access defines an environment in which data is copied from another source and made available to a receiving "local" site. The data received is then processed on the local site. The data is moved to the location where the processing takes place. The data at the remote site is usually maintained by a database management system. To obtain data, a user at the "local" site sends a request to the database management system at the remote site. To provide remote access, a program at the local site (requester) has to communicate with a program at the remote site (server) to process the request for data. Consequently, the requester, through the application or some other means, has to know where the data is located. The application usually has to take care of data integrity. This kind of environment is often restricted to read only access. So, there's no integrity control by the remote database management system for these kinds of requests. Typically they're initiated by programs on intelligent workstations or query products running on the host. IBM's products HDBV and ECF support this type of environment. Remote access is the ability to move the data from a remote site, where it's located, to a local site where the processing takes place.

remote relational access support (RRAS) A SQL/DS facility that allows end-users or application programs in the VM environment to access SQL/DS databases on either locally or remotely connected VM systems.

remote request An application program sends one single SQL statement to a remote site, and the optimization and access are done at this remote site. Typically, the site that sends out the request at which the application executes does not contain a local relational database management system.

remote unit of work Type of distributed relational data access. An interface implemented on a local system allows SQL requests to be submitted (at the remote system) to a host where a database management system resides. A database management system doesn't need to exist on the local system, and the user or application at the local site doesn't need to know where the data is located or use special procedures to move the request and the results between systems. Results are returned to the user or application at the local site. For example, a remote unit of work on a personal system might allow SQL requests to be made at the personal system and executed on an MVS host running DB2. The results would be returned to the personal system.

R* IBM's operational, experimental, distributed database management system prototype that supports SQL.

remote update The ability for users to update data in relational tables at remote sites. Concurrency control, recovery, and deadlock detection are handled by the database management systems at the multiple remote sites.

replication A method for keeping copies of a table at multiple sites synchronized. A local, read-only copy of tables is given to users (so response time is not subject to communications delay) and, when the source table is updated, the update is dynamically propagated to the other sites where the replicated tables are kept.

replication transparency A query accessing a table doesn't have to know which replicated table will be accessed by the system and where it's physically stored.

repository Generic term for the generalized data dictionary database system that acts as a central store for information about systems. The repository uses DB2 as its own database.

requester A program that sends a request to another site through a server requester programming interface. Contrasts with server.

rollback The process of restoring data changed by SQL statements to the state of its previous commit point. All locks are freed.

router An ECF program that interprets requests for services and directs them to the specified server.

SAA Systems Application Architecture. This is designed to provide consistent interfaces across the products that conform to it. Although it was originally promoted by IBM as a way of achieving software portability, the real function of SAA is to provide an infrastructure for distributed and cooperative processing. The four pillars of SAA are CPI (common programming interface), CUA (common user access), CCS (common communications support), and common applications. SAA is a set of software interfaces, conventions and protocols. It serves as the framework for developing consistent applications across the future offering of the three major IBM computing environments: S/390, AS/400 and PS/2. The goals of SAA are the consistent look and feel of applications, consistent application environment, and consistent communications for cooperative processing.

SAA-compliant Products that can interwork with SAA applications are SAA-compliant. SAA-compliant products include, among others, IMS/DB, CICS, VSE.

SAA-conformant Products whose internals are built according to SAA specifications are SAA-conformant. SAA-conformant products include, among others, DB2, SQL, CSP, COBOL, C, RPG/400, FORTRAN.

SAA Dialog Manager Standardizes development of interactive applications. The Dialog Manager "navigates" through applications, controlling interaction with the user and communicating with users through the Presentation Manager.

SAA Office IBM's office applications written around the SAA standards.

SAA Presentation Manager The SAA external interface to workstations. It supports keyboards and a mouse. It's a major component of OS/2 Extended Edition.

SAA Query Manager A high-level interface to SAA database services for invoking interactive programs and queries.

SDLC Synchronous Data Link Control. IBM data communications protocol, used in SNA and covering the physical and link control levels. SDLC is, to a large extent, compatible with the HDLC international standard. SDLC has largely replaced BSC and async (start-stop) protocols.

Security Prevention of access to or use of data or programs without authorization. As used in this text, the safety of data from unauthorized use, theft, or purposeful destruction.

SELECT Relational operator that provides a subset of rows of a table.

server A program that responds to a request from another site through a server requester programming interface. Contrasts with requester.

single site update In a distributed unit of work, a single site update allows a process to perform SQL update statements referring to a remote site. The process can update only one site and perform select statements referring to multiple sites. However, all operands of a single SQL statement are constrained to exist at a single store site.

site An instance of a relational database management system that participates in a distributed system network.

site autonomy The ability to administer different database sites independently and to have single nodes in the distributed system operating when connections to other nodes have failed.

SNA Systems Network Architecture. IBM's data communications architecture defining levels of protocols for communications between terminals and applications, and between programs.

SNADS SNA Distributed Services. SNADS provides a general, de-synchronized (delayed delivery) data distribution facility for SNA LU 6.2 systems. Originally developed for document exchange, but being extended to cover data, image and voice. Key to networking support for office systems. Not a separate product as such—consists of software residing in SNA nodes.

snapshot A snapshot is a named, derived table that's stored for read-only data access. Creating a snapshot is similar to executing an SQL query. The definition of the snapshot and the time of its creation are stored in the system catalog. The snapshot is "refreshed," or recreated, according to the interval specified in the snapshot's definition.

SNI System Network Interconnection. SNA software in NCP and VTAM enabling dissimilar SNA networks to exchange information. Similar functionality is available from independent vendors (Netlink and Netmaster).

SPAG Standards Promotion and Applications Group. Predominate European organization that helps specify OSI standards and carries out OSI conformance testing.

SPX Sequenced Packet Exchange. A Novell NetWare communications protocol that works in conjunction with the Internetwork Packet Exchange. SPX corresponds to the session layer of the OSI model.

SPX/IPX These are the sessions and datagram service protocols used by Novell.

SQL Structured Query Language. IBM and ANSI standard for access to relational databases. Relational data language using English-like, keyword-oriented facilities for data definition, query, data manipulation, and data control. SQL is supported by SQL/DS in VM and VSE environments, DB2 in MVS environment, and on the AS/400. A nonprocedural (or rather a less-procedural as compared to COBOL or FORTRAN), set-oriented language for the relational data model. SQL is the language defined by SAA for access to data. SQL can be used within application programs or interactively to define relational data, access relational data, and control access to relational database resources.

SQL API SQL Application Programming Interface. An interface that allows SQL request to access databases. The SQL API is the database interface in SAA for access to both nondistributed and distributed databases.

SQL/DS Structured Query Language/Data System. Relational database system for VM and VSE environments. It has referential integrity, performance and RAS enhancements. SQL/DS and DB2 present a similar external view to the user, although there are significant differences in areas like space management, logging and recovery.

SRPI Server Requester Protocol (sometimes "Programming") Interface. IBM architecture supporting interactive access between workstations and servers. It surprised some developers by being non-LU 6.2 (probably because of inadequacies in VTAM and the PC); instead, SRPI is a 3270 LU 2 data stream protocol. Implemented in ECF, for which SRPI provides the API.

static SQL SQL statements that are embedded within a program, and are prepared during the program preparation process before the program is executed. After being prepared, the statement itself doesn't change (although values of host variables specified by the statement might change).

SunOS Sun Microsystems, Inc.'s Unix-based operating system.

surge protector A device that protects the delicate circuitry of a computer from electrical power surges and spikes, which can damage a computer.

SVID System V interface definition. The specification for AT&T's System V operating system.

synchronization The process of ensuring that the component parts of a distributed database are logically consistent.

System V AT&T's Unix operating system.

TCP/IP Transmission Control Protocol/Internet Protocol. Set of protocols for network and transport layers of a packet-switched data network. Developed in the U.S. for the Department of Defense, Darpanet system, and has become a *de facto* standard used by many vendors particularly on top of Ethernet. Worth keeping an eye on if you're planning a mixed system (especially if it involves Unix). TCP/IP is not part of SAA, although IBM has stated that it plans to enhance CPI-C to include a TCP/IP interface. TCP/IP is the peer-to-peer protocol standard supported by the U.S. Department of Defense and is widely used in the minicomputer world. TCP provides session service, IP, the datagram service.

teleprocessing monitor A software module that provides a shared interface between application programs and remote communications devices.

token ring Generic term for a type of network, of which IBM's October '85-announced product is an example. The most interesting thing about it is its "openness"; the specifications are publicly available to encourage third-party vendors to help establish it as a standard.

transaction A sequence of steps that constitute some well-defined business activity. A transaction may specify a query, or it may result in the creation, deletion, or modification of database records.

two-phase commit A protocol that's used to ensure uniform transaction commit or abort between two or more participants (transaction manager and distributed database management system). The protocol consists of two phases: the first to reach a common decision and the second to implement this decision. One participant is defined as coordinator and manages the execution of the two-phase commit protocol.

Ultrix Digital Equipment Corporation's Unix-based operating system.

union A relational operation that combines the results of two or more select statements. Union is often used to merge lists of values obtained from several database manager tables.

unit of work A sequence of SQL commands that the database manager treats as a single entity. The database manager ensures the consistency of data by verifying that either all the data changes made during a unit of work are performed, or none of them is performed.

Unix A hardware-independent operating system for minicomputers, developed and owned by AT&T. Original development was done for use on minicomputers.

unlike DDBMS environment A network of dissimilar database management systems providing access to data residing at any of the locations that contain a participating database management system. (For example, a distributed relational database management system on an MVS system and a distributed relational database management system on a VM system accessing data at each other's site.)

vertical distribution Splitting a table across different sites by columns. It allows columns of a single table to reside at different sites of a distributed database network.

VM Virtual machine. Mainframe operating system that can act as a supervisor, enabling users to run multiple operating systems on a single machine. There are two main components of VM—the supervisor, which provides the resources to the virtual machines, and CMS, which provides conversational and timesharing facilities. For years VM was largely incompatible with SNA, but is becoming increasingly integrated into the SNA world.

VSE Virtual Storage Extended. IBM's principal operating system for medium-size mainframes. IBM now calls VSE "A strategic transaction processing environment for mid-range 370."

VTAM Virtual telecommunication access method. The main SNA subsystem resident in the mainframe. VTAM manages session establishment and data flow between terminals and application programs, or between application programs.

X.25 CCITT international (non-IBM) standard for attachment to packet-switched networks. SNA host node access to X.25 networks is available using the NPSI facility in the FEP. IBM support has in general been more verbal than real, but inclusion of X.25 in SAA gives a new lease on life to X.25 within the IBM world.

X.400 Series of draft international standards for message-handling systems. X.400 allows dissimilar E-mail systems to communicate. E-mail services including MCI Mail and CompuServe have accepted it as a standard.

X.500 X.500 is a directory services protocol that was drafted by the CCITT and ISO. It provides a global distributed directory for connected LANs.

X-Open A group of vendors, originally all European, but now with some Japanese and U.S. members (including IBM) that's setting up standards (particularly for Unix). Unlike Unix International and OSF, X/Open tries not to be partisan in the Unix battle.

XPG3 Portability Guide III. Specifications for a common application environment (CAE) produced by X/Open Co., Ltd., an international consortium of vendors.

X-Windows Developed originally at MIT (as part of the DEC/IBM/MIT Project Athena) but picked up by the wider Unix community. Has been an influence on the Motif GUI being developed by the OSF. IBM is involved in the evolution of X-Windows through the MIT X Consortium, which provides a forum for discussion of the standard.

References

Altman, Rosse. April 20, 1990. Are you ready for cooperative processing? *Information Center,* Weingarten Publications.

Bochenski, Barbara. December 17, 1990. Client/server products: every which way but easy. Product spotlight. *Computerworld.*

Fox, Jackie. November, 1990. Unraveling the LAN Mystery. *PC Today.*

Hancock, Bill. September 24, 1990. What's a Server, anyway? *Digital Review.*

Knowles, Anne. December 10, 1990. DEC's networks. *Communications Week.*

Korzeniowski, Paul. October 15, 1990. Users Revise LU 6.2 plans. Study: IBM protocol a lesser priority.

Melymuka, Kathleen. Honey, I shrunk the mainframe! *CIO* Volume 2 (No. 12).

Miller, Thomas C. January, 1991. Cooperative processing with PCs. *Enterprise Systems Journal,* Pages 64-68.

Reinsch, R. 1988. Distributed database for SAA. *IBM Systems Journal,* Volume 27 (No. 3).

Index

D

E

F

G